INVENTING ATLANTIC CANADA:
REGIONALISM AND THE MARITIME REACTION TO
NEWFOUNDLAND'S ENTRY INTO CANADIAN
CONFEDERATION

When Newfoundland entered the Canadian Confederation in 1949, it was hoped it would promote greater unity with the Maritime provinces, as Term 29 of the Newfoundland Act explicitly linked the region's economic and political fortunes. On the surface, the union seemed like an unprecedented opportunity to resurrect the regional spirit of the Maritime Rights movement of the 1920s, which advocated a cooperative approach to addressing regional underdevelopment. However, Newfoundland's arrival did little at first to bring about a comprehensive Atlantic Canadian regionalism.

Inventing Atlantic Canada is the first book to analyse the reaction of the Maritime provinces to Newfoundland's entry into Confederation. Drawing on editorials, government documents, and political papers, Corey Slumkoski examines how each Maritime province used the addition of a new provincial cousin to fight underdevelopment. Slumkoski also details the rise of regional cooperation characterized by the Atlantic Revolution of the mid-1950s, when Maritime leaders began to realize that by acting in isolation their situations would only worsen.

COREY SLUMKOSKI researches and teaches Canadian and Atlantic Canadian history.

COREY SLUMKOSKI

Inventing Atlantic Canada

Regionalism and the Maritime
Reaction to Newfoundland's Entry
into Canadian Confederation

UNIVERSITY OF TORONTO PRESS
Toronto   Buffalo   London

© University of Toronto Press Incorporated 2011
Toronto Buffalo London
www.utppublishing.com
Printed in Canada

ISBN 978-1-4426-4288-1 (cloth)
ISBN 978-1-4426-1158-0 (paper)

Printed on acid-free, 100% post-consumer recycled paper with vegetable-based inks.

Library and Archives Canada Cataloguing in Publication

Slumkoski, Corey James Arthur, 1972–
Inventing Atlantic Canada : regionalism and the Maritime reaction to
Newfoundland's entry into Canadian confederation / Corey Slumkoski.

Includes bibliographical references and index.
ISBN 978-1-4426-4288-1 (bound). – ISBN 978-1-4426-1158-0 (pbk.)

1. Regionalism – Political aspects – Maritime Provinces – History – 20th
century.   2. Regionalism – Economic aspects – Maritime Provinces –
History – 20th century.   3. Newfoundland and Labrador – History – 1949–.
4. Maritime Provinces – Politics and government – 1945–.   5. Maritime
Provinces – History – 1945–.   6. Atlantic Provinces – History.   I. Title.

FC2034.S58 2011   971.5'04   C2010-907323-1

This book has been published with the help of a grant from the Canadian
Federation for the Humanities and Social Sciences, through the Aid to
Scholarly Publications Program, using funds provided by the Social
Sciences and Humanities Research Council of Canada.

University of Toronto Press acknowledges the financial assistance to its
publishing program of the Canada Council for the Arts and the Ontario
Arts Council.

 Canada Council   Conseil des Arts   ONTARIO ARTS COUNCIL
for the Arts   du Canada   CONSEIL DES ARTS DE L'ONTARIO

University of Toronto Press acknowledges the financial support of the
Government of Canada through the Canada Book Fund for its publishing
activities.

For Murthu ...

Contents

Acknowledgments

Although this book has taken a number of years to complete, it seems like this is the most difficult bit to write. In large part this is because over the years it took to complete this book I've become indebted to so many people who have contributed to my understanding of history and of the Atlantic region.

This study began as a dissertation at the University of New Brunswick under the supervision of Margaret Conrad, who not only taught me how to write history but to be a historian as well. The rest of my committee – David Frank, Gail Campbell, Don Wright, and external examiner Jim Kenny – were also invaluable in helping mould my ideas concerning Newfoundland's entry into Canadian Confederation. It was completed while I was teaching at Mount Saint Vincent University, where my colleagues were without fail supportive and encouraging.

Atlantic Canada is often held up as a bastion of friendliness. This certainly describes the Atlantic Canadian scholarly community, which has to be one of the kindest and most supportive ones around. A number of scholars generously offered me their time and expertise. In particular, Hal Fredericks allowed me access to his personal copy of Senator A. Neil McLean's unpublished *Letters of a Business Man to a Student of Economics*, Stephen Henderson pointed me to some important leads in the Angus L. Macdonald Papers, Ed MacDonald helped me understand the personalities of Prince Edward Island politics, and Jim Hiller not only answered my queries about 1940s Newfoundland but also directed me toward granting agencies that helped fund my research. These agencies, the J.R. Smallwood Foundation for Newfoundland and Labrador Studies and the Institute for Social and Economic Research at Memorial University, provided research grants which allowed me to bridge the Cabot Strait and better incorporate Newfoundland into this story. In addition, UNB's School of Graduate Studies and Canada Research Chair in Atlantic Canada Studies provided funding that was necessary to complete this study.

The University of Toronto Press has been a dream to work with. Len Husband has been the ideal editor, guiding a first-time author through the often confusing world of publishing with interest, care, and kindness. The two anonymous reviewers selected by the University of Toronto Press offered insightful comments. Their suggestions have improved the final product and resulted in a stronger book. Likewise, Wayne Herrington and Doug Richmond have deftly guided this book through the production stages, while copy editor Matthew Kudelka cleaned up the text and helped me to avoid a number of embarrassing errors.

Librarians and archivists at a number of repositories have assisted me in countless ways. I would like to express my gratitude to the staffs at the Harriet Irving Library at the University of New Brunswick, Angus L. Macdonald Library at St Francis Xavier University, Library and Archives Canada, Provincial Archives of New Brunswick, Prince Edward Island Public Archives and Records Office, Nova Scotia Archives and Records Management, Provincial Archives of Newfoundland and Labrador, University of New Brunswick Archives, Acadia University Archives, Dalhousie University Archives, and Memorial University Archives and Manuscripts Division. My sincerest thanks as well to Sheldon MacDonald of the St Francis Xavier University Digital Lab for helping me digitize the cover images.

The support and encouragement of family was also very much appreciated. My mother and father were always there for me – financially and emotionally – and I look forward to their comments on the finished product. My brother Casey and sister-in-law Kelly were always willing to put me up (and put up with me) while researching in Ottawa. My adopted family in the Maritimes are also very much appreciated. Special thanks to Miriam and Chris for buying a new house so I wouldn't have to sleep on their couch, and to Dorothy, who from my first visit to Debec made me feel like part of the family.

I remember sitting in the library at Carleton University, looking at various university calendars, trying to decide where to go for graduate work. Little did I know that choosing to attend UNB would be a life-altering decision. Entering my first class in Fredericton I was a nervous newcomer, far from home, who took an empty seat next to the friendliest face in the room. Four years later we were married. My sincerest thanks to Martha Walls, my wife and best friend, who has patiently read every page of this book – in all its various manifestations – offering perceptive criticisms and kind encouragement every step of the way. Thanks Mart, for everything.

INVENTING ATLANTIC CANADA:
REGIONALISM AND THE MARITIME REACTION TO
NEWFOUNDLAND'S ENTRY INTO CANADIAN
CONFEDERATION

Introduction

Growing up in small-town Ontario, I was only dimly aware of the 'Maritimes' and 'Atlantic Canada,' and what little I knew of these terms and these regions reflected well-worn stereotypes. For me, the Maritimes and Atlantic Canada were synonymous with each other: both referred to the poorer provinces clustered along Canada's eastern seaboard – places that received wealthy tourists during the warm summer months and that sent their youth 'down the road' in search of employment in the industrial cities of Central Canada. It was only later, while taking classes on Atlantic Canadian history at university, that the differences in meaning between the two terms and the two regions became more readily apparent. The Maritimes, which refers to the provincial trio of Nova Scotia, New Brunswick, and Prince Edward Island, was the older of the two terms, with roots stretching back to the earliest days of colonization. Atlantic Canada was a much more recent invention. That term, which encompasses the Maritimes and Newfoundland and Labrador, came into widespread use only during the 1950s, following Newfoundland's entry into Canadian Confederation in 1949.[1]

This book is a study of Maritime and Atlantic Canadian regionalism – its presence and its absence – through the lens afforded by the Maritime Provinces' reaction to Newfoundland's entry into Canadian Confederation.[2] When Newfoundland became Canada's tenth province at the stroke of midnight on 31 March 1949, the region of 'Atlantic Canada' formally came into existence through Term 29 of the Newfoundland Act, which tied Newfoundland's economic destiny to that of the Maritimes. With union Newfoundland would impose new taxes and increase existing ones to help fund the improved social services that Confederation was bringing. For the first eight years after Confederation, Ottawa would supply Newfoundland with a transitional grant to assist it in providing social services to an acceptable standard without overly burdening its population with these new and increased taxes. Term 29 mandated that at the end of this eight-year transitional period, a Royal Commission would be appointed to ascertain what, if any, future grants the new province would receive. As this clause of the legislation that brought Newfoundland into Confederation specified,

> In view of the difficulty of predicting with sufficient accuracy the financial consequences to Newfoundland of becoming a province of Canada, the Government of Canada will appoint a Royal Commission within eight years from the date of Union to review the financial position of the Province of Newfoundland and Labrador and to recommend the form and scale of additional financial assistance, if any, that may be required by the Government of the Province of Newfoundland and Labrador to enable it to continue public services at the levels and standards reached subsequent to the date of Union, without resorting to taxation more burdensome, having regard to capacity to pay, than that obtaining generally in the region comprising the Maritime Provinces of Nova Scotia, New Brunswick, and Prince Edward Island.[3]

With these words, Ottawa revealed that even during the negotiations to bring about union, it saw Newfoundland as an extension of the Maritime Provinces; it was the Maritime provincial average – not the Canadian one – that would be the new province's benchmark for economic and social development. It is moot whether Ottawa intended to create a new region, for the outcome is clear: when Newfoundland was linked to the Maritime Provinces through Term 29, the political entity 'Atlantic Canada' was born.

In a somewhat ironic turn of events, federal fears of Maritime intransigence regarding Newfoundland's financial terms of union contributed to Term 29's linking of the two jurisdictions. Ottawa was well aware that after Newfoundland joined Confederation, its social services would have to be improved; and that this would be difficult, given Newfoundland's generally poor population and limited tax base. Likewise, the federal government feared that if the standard of living in Newfoundland was raised to above that in the Maritimes through federal subsidization, or if Newfoundland was seen to be receiving substantially more in grant payments than were the Maritimes, a wave of outrage would emanate from the east. As Prime Minister William Lyon Mackenzie King confessed to his diary, the Maritimes '[may be] resentful at giving better terms to a bankrupt colony than we would to our own provinces.'[4] Instead of treating Newfoundland's Confederation as an opportunity to raise economic prospects and social services in the newly minted Atlantic region to national levels, the federal government was content simply to try to raise services in Newfoundland to the standard of its three Maritime cousins through similar levels of taxation supplemented by a federal subsidy. The hope here was that Maritime opposition to the merger would be muted, as Newfoundland's financial position would be no better than that of the three Maritime Provinces. While this move was no doubt borne of financial and political considerations – after all, to raise the region to the national average would be very expensive and would likely prompt calls from the Prairies for similar subsidized economic and social development – the result was that Ottawa's fear of Maritime opposition to Newfoundland's terms of Confederation contributed to the Maritime Provinces being used as Newfoundland's developmental benchmark.

This linking of the Maritimes and Newfoundland through Term 29 also reflected a tendency among federal policy makers to see the two regions as one. Newfoundland was situated less than 100 kilometres off the Cape Breton coast, and its economy was similarly based on fisheries, forestry, and trade; as a consequence, many Ottawa politicos viewed it as a natural extension of the Maritime Provinces. As Prime Minister Louis St Laurent explained to the House of Commons on 7 February 1949, 'the section of the Canadian economy generally described as the maritimes was felt to be the one which would be most nearly comparable to the situation which would be apt to develop in Newfoundland.'[5] In responding to the prime minister, CCF Leader M.J. Coldwell took the argument one step further; not only was the Newfoundland economy similar in orientation to that of the Maritimes, but it was also similar in its condition of underdevelopment. As a remedy for this, Coldwell proposed that more industry and investment be located in the region. Moreover, the CCF leader welcomed Newfoundland into Confederation because of the added economic and political clout it would give to the Maritime Provinces. As he suggested, 'we should consider Newfoundland and Labrador as part of the whole maritime region, which incidentally is a region that cries aloud for a new deal.'[6] The inclination of Ottawa mandarins and politicians to view Newfoundland and the Maritimes regionally was evident in the negotiations over Newfoundland's terms of union. For example, an 8 November 1948 Department of Transport memo specified that 'the Island of Newfoundland will be considered as within the Maritime Region for the purposes of the Maritime Freight Rates Act,' while the Newfoundland Railway would 'be deemed an extension of the Canadian National Railways service in and through the Maritime Provinces for the purposes of determining freight, passenger and express rates.'[7] As federal Minister of Reconstruction and Supply Robert Winters made clear in an address to the Saint John Board of Trade shortly after Confederation, the 'union makes the *greater Maritime region* a more influential segment of Canadian Federation, economically and politically.'[8]

Despite Winters's optimism, Newfoundland's entry into Confederation did little to alter the region's economic or political position within Canada. As this book reveals, a dearth of Maritime regionalism during the late 1940s resulted in an incoherent regional response to the union. Consequently, that region's reaction to Newfoundland's entry was significant in its absence; not until the middle of the next decade would a Maritime and Atlantic Canadian regionalism (re)emerge as a political strategy, as illustrated by the creation of regionally based institutions such as the Atlantic Provinces Economic Council (APEC) and the Atlantic Premiers Conferences (APCs). The rise of these regional bodies during the 1950s can be traced, in part, to Newfoundland's entry into Confederation and Term 29. Since this clause grouped the four Atlantic Provinces together as an economically distressed region, it only made sense for the provinces to use the same regional framework and to collaborate in their attempts to foster meaningful economic development. Through Term 29, then, the federal government did as much to create 'Atlantic Canada' as a political category as any of the responses of the Maritime provincial governments – responses rooted in provincial, not regional, interests – to Newfoundland's entry into Confederation.

Maritime Public Opinion of Newfoundland's Confederation

The Maritime Provinces seemingly had the most to gain or lose with the inclusion of a new eastern province, yet their reaction to the merger has received little academic scrutiny.[9] When it has been addressed, scholars have tacitly accepted Prime Minister King's perspective that

'[Nova Scotia Premier Angus L.] Macdonald, as well as [New Brunswick Premier John] McNair, might prove very difficult in agreeing to the terms [of union] being suggested' without question.[10] Yet it is not at all certain that King read the matter correctly. To some degree the Maritime Provinces viewed Newfoundland's Confederation as inevitable, for they had little input into the union process, which was being dictated from Ottawa and St John's. But at the same time, they viewed the merger with optimism, believing that the addition of a fourth 'Maritime' province might help alleviate regional underdevelopment. Indeed, the responses of Maritimers as revealed in this study were not those of insular and petty politicians wracked with jealousy regarding Newfoundland's relatively generous financial terms of union – responses that Prime Minister King feared. Instead, they were the actions of skilled political players who tried, albeit with limited success, to make the union pay dividends for themselves, for their constituents, and for their provinces.

Prime Minister King's pessimistic view of the Maritime reaction to Newfoundland's entry into Confederation likely stemmed from Gallup polls conducted on 31 July 1946 and 21 June 1947 that painted the Maritimes as the stronghold of opposition to the merger. In the 1946 survey, 24 per cent of Maritime respondents indicated that they were against offering Newfoundland admission into Canadian Confederation; in 1947 that percentage remained essentially unchanged at 23 per cent. In comparison, only 13 per cent of those on the Prairies were opposed to union.[11] As historian Peter Neary has observed with regard to Canadian public opinion about Newfoundland's Confederation, 'the further Canadians got from Newfoundland the better it looked.'[12]

Yet to focus on the 23 per cent of Maritimers supposedly against Confederation is to obscure the fact that 40 per cent were in favour and 37 per cent undecided. A historian might look at the same survey and ask why 77 per cent of Maritime Canadians were *not* opposed to the union. What reasons did they have for supporting Newfoundland's entry into Confederation? These questions cannot readily be answered for the region as a whole. The Gallup poll grouped the Maritime Provinces together in its survey, yet support for Newfoundland's union undoubtedly varied across, and within, provincial boundaries. The region was not a bloc of like-minded individuals. Each province had its own reasons for supporting (or opposing) Newfoundland's entry; each would use the union to give weight to calls

Table 1
1947 Gallup Poll: 'Do you think Canada should invite Newfoundland to become the tenth province or not?'

	Yes %	No %	Undecided %
National	49	16	35
Maritimes	40	23	37
Quebec	38	18	44
Ontario	54	15	31
Prairies	55	13	32
British Columbia	55	14	31

Source: *Documents on Relations between Canada and Newfoundland, vol. 2, 1940–1949, Confederation.* Vol. 2, Pt I, ed. Paul Bridle (Ottawa: 1984), 575–6.

for provincial development schemes; and each had its own class, geographic, occupational, and political divisions that influenced how the merger was viewed.

A more useful survey of Maritime opinion about Newfoundland's entry into Confederation, conducted by the Canadian Institute of Public Opinion (CIPO), was published on 24 March 1949 in the *Saint John Telegraph-Journal*. According to the CIPO survey, nearly 60 per cent of adult Maritimers believed that Newfoundland's entry into Confederation would make the Maritimes 'better off,' compared to 10 per cent who thought the union would prove detrimental. Also, urban and rural opinion on the merger differed 'very little,' and business interests were more likely than labour interests to believe that the union would be beneficial.

Some of the those who viewed the merger unfavourably feared that Newfoundland would be a drain on Canada's economy; that union would promote increased competition in the fishery between the Maritimes and the new province; and that after Confederation, unemployed Newfoundlanders might migrate to the Maritimes and compete for jobs.[13]

Unfortunately, this CIPO survey was the only source I uncovered that detailed Maritimers' opinions of Newfoundland's entry into Confederation. As a result, this book necessarily focuses on what more accessible and vocal political and economic elites in the three Maritime Provinces thought of the merger. To gauge their opinions I have drawn on newspaper accounts, board of trade papers, government documents, and politicians' papers. Some newspapers – especially those in

Table 2
Canadian Institute of Public Opinion Poll: 'In the long run, do you think the Maritime Provinces will be better off or worse off by having Newfoundland in Confederation?'

Maritimes will be better off	57%
Maritimes will be worse off	10%
It will make no difference	19%
Undecided	14%

Source: *Saint John Telegraph-Journal*, 24 March 1949.

Sydney, Halifax, and Charlottetown – were particularly informative; editors such as H.P. Duchemin of the *Sydney Post-Record*, W.H. Dennis of the *Halifax Herald*, and James R. Burnett of the *Charlottetown Guardian* were interested in the impact that Newfoundland's entry would have on their cities and provinces. In contrast, the editors of the *Fredericton Daily Gleaner* and the *Saint John Telegraph-Journal* appeared uninterested in Newfoundland's entry, and letters to the editor in these papers on the subject were either not forthcoming or not published. Indeed, most New Brunswick dailies seemed content to simply run Canadian Press stories that merely informed the reader of the merger's political process – a trend that held true in both English and French newspapers. It is interesting that some smaller New Brunswick newspapers, such as Blacks Harbour's *The Fundy Fisherman* and the *Sackville Tribune-Post*, carried the torch for Newfoundland's entry, and in such cases I examine their reasons for doing so. While Newfoundland factored into board of trade discussions in Saint John, Charlottetown, and Halifax, the papers of the Sydney Board of Trade, which had strong connections to Newfoundland since North Sydney was the focal point of mainland trade to the island, have unfortunately disappeared. Similarly, government reports and political papers reveal little evidence of interest in Newfoundland's entry into Confederation. New Brunswick Premier John McNair's papers are almost devoid of references to Newfoundland, and the issue appears only briefly in Nova Scotia Premier Angus L. Macdonald's papers. Newfoundland is well represented in the papers of Prince Edward Island Premier J. Walter Jones, but the loss of his papers after 1947 has blunted efforts to carry the story to 1949. Notwithstanding the shortcomings of the various sources when examined individually, examined *in toto* they provide a window on the Maritime response to Newfoundland's entry into Confederation and the formative stages of the modern region of Atlantic Canada.

A New Region?

In Canada, the term 'region' has often been linked to formal political divisions or groupings, such as to provinces or groups of provinces, with the Maritime Provinces and the Prairies being two prominent examples of this trend.[14] This seems to be the framework the federal government had in mind with Term 29, for this clause of the Newfoundland Act brought the geopolitical region of Atlantic Canada into existence the moment Newfoundland entered Confederation. Yet regionalisms and regional identities are more difficult to construct than geopolitical regions, and many factors lead to their emergence beyond simple intent, political boundaries, and/or proximity. As Margaret Conrad and James Hiller have pointed out, 'while the Atlantic "region" can be easily found on a map, "regionalism" implies a political stance, a consciousness of shared outlook that can be summoned up when other structures – familial, communal, provincial, national, global – fail.'[15] Thus while an Atlantic region could itself be easily created, an Atlantic Canadian regionalism would prove far more elusive. Indeed, an Atlantic regionalism would not emerge until the Atlantic Revolution of the mid-1950s, and even then the bonds proved tenuous. This delay illustrates how the invention of 'Atlantic Canada' through the tying of Newfoundland's economic development to the Maritime standard was fraught with difficulties.

The formation of regional identity, beyond the mere conveniences of favourable physical geography, has been the subject of considerable scholarly inquiry. Janine Brody's *The Political Economy of Canadian Regionalism*, for example, illustrates how Canada's federal policies tended to organize the nation's political economy along a metropole–hinterland spectrum, with wealth being increasingly concentrated in the central provinces.[16] As a result, the peripheral provinces, such as the Maritimes, tended to be exploited by Central Canadian capital. This could have led to the formation of a regional identity; as geographer Randy William Widdis has suggested, a region can be 'predicated on the idea that geographical borders, by symbolically differentiating "here" from "there," delineate belonging.'[17] Though historian Colin Howell has cautioned against using this underdevelopment paradigm as the sole one to account for regional identity – against 'mixing victimization and regional patriotism to create a more genuine Maritime consciousness' – it is clear that policies detrimental to the periphery contributed to the rise of regional movements, such as the Maritime Rights crusade of the 1920s.[18] Exploitation and underdevelopment remain important markers of Atlantic Canadian regionalism, yet they are not the only ones.

Recent studies of Canadian regionalism have begun to examine the notions of culture, communication, place, and imagination in the construction of region. Scholars such as Gerald Friesen have shown how concepts of region are fluid – how they change over time as new communicative forms and processes arise.[19] Building on Benedict Anderson's important point that all identities are imagined, these works contend that specific imagined geographical and cultural images are associated with specific regions, even if the imagined does not necessarily correspond to the regional reality.[20] As Andrew Nurse has cautioned, 'the commonly understood regions of Canada correspond at best poorly to the parameters of Canadian physical geography.'[21] Thus, what is assumed or imagined about a region's physical geography is more important to the construction of regionalism than the physical geography itself. In other words, the imaginary is more important than the reality since regions are mental constructs invented through the shared imagining of what constitutes the region.

. Therein lay the problem. Though the Maritime Provinces and Newfoundland shared some common experiences – underdevelopment, staples-based economies, and a commitment to ocean-going trade – their populations did not (and still do not) conceive of a common identity or imagine themselves as partners in a broader region. Newfoundlanders remained rooted to their island, while Maritime identity was associated largely with the individual Maritime Provinces or tied to ethnic and racial heritage, such as with the Acadians, Mi'kmaq, and Africadians.[22]

Consequently, little was done following Confederation to link Newfoundland and the Maritimes as a cultural region or to foster cultural ties between the two jurisdictions. For example, when the final terms of union were being worked out in 1948, Ottawa decided against grouping Newfoundland's Canadian Broadcasting Corporation radio services as part of the Maritime region; and following Confederation, Newfoundland retained provincial control over education and other local and municipal concerns.[23] The result, Raymond Blake argues, was that the integration of Newfoundland into the Canadian mosaic 'became mostly a bureaucratic and administrative affair [with] few radical changes to have a negative impact on people's daily routine.'[24] Thus it fell to Term 29 to bind the new region economically and politically – to link the Maritimes and Newfoundland – which is why Newfoundland did not become a 'Maritime Province' on entering Confederation. That term was already in widespread use, and its meaning was clear. Instead, by joining Confederation, Newfoundland inspired new terms and political designations – 'Atlantic Provinces' and 'Atlantic Canada' – which emerged in the mid-1950s and 1960s to describe the collective of Nova Scotia, New Brunswick, Prince Edward Island, and Newfoundland.[25]

The invention of Atlantic Canada during the late 1940s and early 1950s was further complicated because Maritime regionalism was itself fragmented during those critical years. Maritime regionalism as a political posture has a tendency to ebb and flow; during the late 1940s, when Newfoundland was contemplating entering Canadian Confederation, it was at its nadir.[26] This is evident in the actions taken by each Maritime province in preparation for Newfoundland's entry into Confederation. In Nova Scotia, politicians and newspaper editors incorporated Newfoundland's Confederation into arguments for such things as the building of a link between Cape Breton and the mainland, the expansion of the Sydney steel industry, and the modification of the Maritime Freight Rates Act. Even Nova Scotia Premier Angus L. Macdonald, who was personally wary of Newfoundland's entry, tried to use the merger to secure annual dominion–provincial conferences – a pet project of his. In New Brunswick, Liberal senator and fishing magnate A. Neil McLean was a staunch advocate of union who secured from Newfoundland support for the expansion of his herring plant in Newfoundland's Bay of Islands, while provincial politicians tried to use Confederation to justify a proposed canal across the Isthmus of Chignecto. Prince Edward Island Premier Walter Jones saw increased agricultural trade with Newfoundland as key to PEI's economic future; he actively courted the Newfoundland market and lobbied for increased federal subsidization for the PEI–Newfoundland steamship route. Even a movement for regional union that arose during the late 1940s – a movement that was willing to embrace Newfoundland – fell victim to interprovincial squabbling and disintegrated amidst concerns that the Maritime Provinces could accomplish more independently than they could together.

In this context, then, there existed a distance – both geographical and ideological – between Newfoundland and the Maritime Provinces, one that is revealed by the fact that most historians of Atlantic Canada have tended to treat the two jurisdictions in isolation; attempts to write a genuine regional synthesis have been few and far between.[27] That W. Stewart MacNutt was the first historian to treat the four Atlantic colonies as one region, that he did not do so until 1965, and then only at the request of the editors of a national project, is indicative of this trend.[28] As historian James Hiller explains, 'there is a strong sense that while the Maritimes may indeed constitute an historical region, Newfoundland does not "fit."'[29] This isolation of Newfoundland from the Maritimes in the region's historiography stems not just from its geographic distance from the mainland, but from its having for many years followed a separate political trajectory. When Newfoundland rejected the idea of Canadian Confederation in 1869, the colony inadvertently banished itself from the narratives of future Canadian historians. This, Hiller contends, needed not be so: 'That Newfoundland chose a different political path does not override its essential family relationship with the Maritime Provinces.'[30] But if Hiller is correct that Newfoundland and the Maritime Provinces do indeed constitute a family, then Newfoundland's connection to the Maritimes has been more akin to that of a distant cousin than a sibling. And even this family metaphor is perhaps overstated. As an *Antigonish Casket* editorial welcoming Newfoundland into Confederation made clear, 'some folks will tell you that you are joining the family. That is not quite true, Newfoundland. There is a close relationship in this group, all right, but we don't get along quite well enough to be called a family.'[31]

While perhaps not a 'family,' the success of Term 29 in defining Atlantic Canada, and the commonalities of experience between the Maritime Provinces and Newfoundland, suggest that the two can be grouped and studied as a single region for the post-1949 period. Indeed, historian David Alexander encouraged scholars to follow his lead and 'bridge the Cabot Strait' to reveal the connections between Newfoundland and the Maritimes – connections such as underdevelopment and a shared marginalization.[32] Yet while the Maritime Provinces and Newfoundland both experienced underdevelopment, this did not lead to a shared sense of regionalism. As historian Ian McKay noted in an address to the 1998 Atlantic Canada Workshop,

Atlantic Canada can be a region but lack regionalism. In this talk, McKay noted the 'sheer difficulty of articulating "region" as the object of social-scientific or historical discourse'; he contended that '"region" as a concept and "Atlantic Canada" as an application of that concept, were weakly articulated [in the region's historiography], and they were easy subjects for "deconstruction" even before the term had been invented.'[33]

This study seeks not to deconstruct Atlantic Canada, but instead to examine its invention through the prism of the Maritime region's reaction to Newfoundland's entry into Confederation. It reveals that the processes of underdevelopment inhibited a Maritime regionalism during the 1940s, which in turn shaped the regional reaction to Newfoundland's Confederation. The negotiations relating to the entry of a new 'Maritime' province into Confederation offered a unique chance to advance a comprehensive and cooperative approach to addressing regional underdevelopment; however, Maritime politicians – conditioned by years of acting in isolation in their efforts to secure federal assistance – tended to look out for their own interests by acting provincially, not regionally, when it came to courting development programs and determining public policy. As this study shows, underdevelopment undermines economies and can actually impede regional collaboration and contribute to an anaemic public policy.

Maritime Regionalism and Underdevelopment

Underdevelopment is a long-running trope in the Maritime Provinces' history, and one that coloured the regional reaction to Newfoundland's entry into Confederation.[34] With roots stretching back to years before the Confederation of British North America in 1867, regional underdevelopment contributed to the tendency of the Maritimes to act provincially, not regionally, in their dealings with the federal government during the 1930s and 1940s. By the time Newfoundland was contemplating entering Canadian Confederation, underdevelopment had conditioned the Maritime Provinces to act independently in their dealings with Ottawa in efforts to look after their own provincial interests. Regional development programs, and regional collaboration, were of secondary importance.

As early as the late 1870s, the Maritime Provinces began to see their interests as less important to the federal government than the interests of the larger Central Canadian provinces. For example, the 1879

National Policy – designed to construct an economic nationalism within Canada by means of railway construction, immigration, and tariff protection of industry – had a deleterious effect on the Maritimes. Maritimers were being compelled to purchase goods in a protected home market while selling their output in a market that was 'virtually unprotected'; moreover, the National Policy's protective tariff seemed to undermine the region's traditional shipping and shipbuilding industries.[35] Though the region initially adapted quite well to the protective economic climate afforded by the National Policy, over time the region's fragile secondary industries collapsed and newly arrived settlers bypassed the region on their way to Central and Western Canada.[36] By the 1920s the effect of the National Policy on the Maritimes was clear. Between 1874 and 1921 Maritime representation in the House of Commons fell from 43 seats to 31, even while the number of seats in the House increased from 206 to 235.[37] As the Maritime component of the House of Commons fell from 21 per cent to 13 per cent in approximately fifty years, the region's political clout was substantially reduced and regional politicians found it increasingly difficult to protect the interests of their constituents.

By 1921, when the Board of Railway Commissioners raised Maritime railway freight rates to the Ontario level – a 40 per cent spike that precluded Maritime business interests from competing effectively in the lucrative Central Canadian market – many in the region had seen enough.[38] This rate hike contributed to the emergence of a non-partisan regionalist movement that demanded federal recognition of certain 'Maritime Rights.' Maritime politicians of all stripes came together to lobby the federal government for policies that would allow the region to participate more effectively in the nation's economic growth. After alternately punishing Conservative leader Arthur Meighen and Liberal leader Mackenzie King in consecutive elections, the region obtained some concessions from Ottawa, the greatest of which was the appointment of a Royal Commission to investigate the Maritime grievances.[39]

In 1926, the Royal Commission on Maritime Claims – commonly referred to as the Duncan Commission, after its chair Sir Andrew Duncan – began its investigation. Duncan's report concluded that, while there were certain structural causes to Maritime underdevelopment – the decline of the 'wood, wind, and sail' economy, for example – the region had also been hamstrung by unfavourable federal policies. Duncan's recommendations resulted in the introduction of the Mar itime Freight Rates Act of 1927, which granted the region a 20 per cent reduction on railway freight rates. Still, the actions of the federal government in addressing Maritime grievances were insufficient, and the Maritime Freight Rates Act, while beneficial, was designed more to quell Maritime unrest than to redress the fundamental problem of underdevelopment. As historian E.R. Forbes has pointed out, the Duncan Commission 'devised a program for Maritime economic rehabilitation, only to have the federal government turn it into a program for political pacification.'[40] The limited actions taken by the King government following the Duncan Commission resulted in growing disillusionment among Maritimers with Ottawa and with regional collaboration as a remedy for regional problems.[41] By 1929, with the election of Liberal Premier A.C. Saunders in Prince Edward Island, the regional front had broken down amidst interparty squabbling. Saunders began to question the merits of the regionalist approach, as he believed that he could gain more for his province by independently lobbying the Liberal government in Ottawa than by tying his fortunes to the Conservative premiers of New Brunswick and Nova Scotia. The ensuing decades would see further fracturing of the regional alliance as the experience of Depression and war encouraged the Maritime Provinces to deal with Ottawa on an individual basis.

The onset of the Great Depression in the 1930s exacerbated the Maritime economic situation as provinces and municipalities struggled to cope with responsibilities they could no longer afford. Maritime per capita income remained well below the national average; so, too, did the region's relief payments, while unemployment rates were higher.[42] Overall, the experience of the Great Depression in the region was on par with that on the drought-ravished Prairies. So dire was the situation across Canada that the federal government was compelled to take action, but unfortunately for the Maritimes the solution it proposed failed to take into account the region's precarious financial position. Ottawa initiated a series of one-third matching grants, whereby the federal, provincial, and municipal governments would each bear one-third of the cost of administering relief. This system was only as strong as the weakest link in the chain, and more affluent municipalities in Central Canada were more fully able to participate in the scheme than those in the cash-strapped Maritimes. This meant that, paradoxically, those areas that were most immune to the Depression were the areas that could receive the most relief from it, whereas those areas most in need of help were entitled to smaller payments.[43] Moreover, since the system was geared toward the provinces, not the region, it helped consolidate and entrench provincial cleavages within the Maritimes as each province lobbied the federal government individually for its share of relief allocations.

By December 1937 the financial situation had deteriorated to such an extent that the National Employment Commission called for the federal government to assume full responsibility for unemployment relief. Yet Prime Minister King, always the fiscal conservative, was reluctant to take action. Instead he appointed a Royal Commission to investigate the problem of federal–provincial relations.[44] For two years the Royal Commission on Dominion–Provincial Relations – the Rowell-Sirois Commission – commissioned studies and conducted public hearings across the country. When, in 1940, the commission issued its report – a revolutionary document calling for a complete reworking of the structure of federal–provincial fiscal relations – the moment for action had temporarily passed. Canada was by then embroiled in the Second World War and – as Ontario Premier Mitchell Hepburn suggested during the Dominion–Provincial Conference called to discuss the report – wartime was not the time to discuss a peacetime document.[45] Nor was a national crisis the time to advance regional concerns. Canada was faced with the spectre of a protracted conflict in Europe; thus, the broader recommendations of the Rowell-Sirois Report were quickly set aside.

The war accelerated Maritime underdevelopment as Ottawa's wartime policies, far from alleviating regional inequities, helped consolidate them.[46] During the war the federal government, reluctant to invest in the Maritimes, allocated wartime contracts primarily to Central and Western Canada. Powerful Minister of Munitions and Supply C.D. Howe, whose task it was to distribute wartime contracts, resorted to the lack of Maritime infrastructure – roads and hydroelectric facilities – and the region's proximity to the Atlantic seaboard, and therefore to German attack, to justify policies that led to the centralization of Canadian industry.[47] Though the Maritime provincial governments did benefit to some extent from the war – the conflict relieved them of much of their social spending and provided the economic spinoff of full employment – Ottawa's unwillingness to grant contracts to the Maritimes and the internecine competition among the Maritime Provinces for what limited funds were available meant that the region emerged from the conflict fragmented and in an even weaker position relative to the rest of Canada than it had been in during the Depression.[48]

The tendency of the Maritime Provinces to act independently of one another continued after the war. This was the era of Keynesian economics and the expansion of both the federal and provincial states – necessary precursors to the postwar reconstruction plans developed in isolation by each of the provinces. Thus New Brunswick Premier John McNair turned his attention to the development of provincial infrastructure and, in an effort to answer Ottawa's implicit criticism of the region, allocated much of his reconstruction budget to the building of roads and hydroelectric facilities. Meanwhile, Prince Edward Island Premier Walter Jones focused his reconstruction efforts on revitalizing the export trade, and Nova Scotia Premier Angus L. Macdonald investigated the modernization of the provincial fishery.[49] Implicit in these reconstruction plans was the recognition that a more interventionist state was necessary. This may have influenced Maritime support for Newfoundland's Confederation, in that the new province would require much federal support in order to meet the standard established by Term 29.

The postwar fragmentation of the Maritime region is illustrated by the events of the 1945–6 Dominion–Provincial Conference. Over three conference sessions a broad system of social welfare was proposed in exchange for the provinces' surrendering the right to levy certain taxes. This provoked the hostility of Ontario Premier George Drew, who was reluctant to cede his province's lucrative tax fields to Ottawa. Prime Minister King used Drew's objections to adjourn the meetings *sine die*, and in June 1946 J.L. Ilsley's budget speech announced the federal government's intention to negotiate ad hoc tax rental agreements with the provinces.[50] New Brunswick Premier McNair was quick to enter into an agreement with Ottawa, but he soon saw the error of his hasty actions. When provinces that had delayed entering tax rental agreements with Ottawa, such as Nova Scotia, received better terms as enticements for their cooperation, New Brunswickers called for a renegotiation of their deal, and McNair was eventually granted terms on par with Nova Scotia. All of this points to the lack of regional cooperation that prevailed in the Maritimes in the years immediately preceding Newfoundland's Confederation.[51] Indeed, not until the 1950s, after Newfoundland had entered Confederation, did the Maritime Provinces begin to act regionally in their efforts to alleviate underdevelopment. A change in political will (carefully cultivated by the Maritime Provinces Board of Trade) and an increasing acceptance of government intervention in the economy led to the gradual re-emergence of regional collaboration to foster economic development – collaboration that became known as the Atlantic Revolution.[52]

It should not surprise us that a sense of Maritime regional purpose could be absent during the late 1940s only to emerge full bloom less than a decade later. If regionalism, as Conrad and Hiller contend, is a political tactic that emerges when other options have failed, then regionalism can at times lie dormant, only to be revitalized at a later date.[53] This is precisely what happened in the Maritimes between the late 1920s and the early 1950s. When the Maritime Rights movement of the 1920s met limited success, the regional front broke down. During the harsh days of depression and war, regionalism was trumped by larger concerns, and federal policies toward the Maritimes helped consolidate narrow, provincially based development strategies. In the early postwar era, as Newfoundland contemplated joining Confederation, there was a lack of regional cooperation in the Maritimes since each province believed it could secure greater federal assistance by going it alone than by tying its fortunes to the regional whole. Yet the entry of Newfoundland into Confederation, and Term 29's linking of the new province to the Maritimes, gradually prompted the re-emergence of regional cooperation. By the mid-1950s it had become painfully clear to the Maritime provincial governments that acting in isolation was an ineffective strategy for improving the region's economy, and a renewed sense of regionalism came to the forefront in the form of the Atlantic Revolution, which helped bind the newly invented region of Atlantic Canada.

1 Newfoundland–Maritime Connections from Colonization to Confederation

When Newfoundland entered Canadian Confederation in 1949, the Canadian Broadcasting Corporation (CBC) held a 'welcoming broadcast,' which featured 'a specially arranged fantasia of Newfoundland folk music which had its origin among the fishermen, loggers, miners and farmers of the region.' This broadcast, to be directed by J. Frank Willis, former Halifax supervisor of feature broadcasts for the CBC, also had a political purpose. It was designed to 'point up the similarities in the traditions of Newfoundland, Nova Scotia, New Brunswick, [and] Prince Edward Island ... symbolising the new province's natural ties with Canada's older eastern provinces.'[1] In doing so, the CBC was recognizing that such connections needed to be explained to Maritimers – that the natural ties between Newfoundland and the Maritimes were perhaps not so natural after all.

The CBC's broadcast, which was meant to link Newfoundland with the Maritimes, stemmed in part from the separate yet symbiotic relationship that had developed between Newfoundland and the Maritimes – the part of Canada to which the new province would be explicitly linked through Term 29 – from the period of initial colonization in the seventeenth century until the 1949 merger. By the time Newfoundland began to seriously contemplate joining Canada in the 1940s, the tenor of Maritime–Newfoundland relations was well established: political negotiations with Newfoundland largely bypassed the Maritime power centres, first in favour of London and then, following Confederation in 1867, in favour of Ottawa. As a result, most of the Maritimes' dealings with Newfoundland revolved around individual initiatives: Maritime elites invested in Newfoundland industry; Maritime farmers supplied hungry Newfoundlanders with foodstuffs;

surplus Newfoundland labour filled vacant jobs on the mainland; and ambitious Newfoundland students attended Maritime colleges and universities. Because of the lack of formal political involvement between Newfoundland and the Maritimes, the region known as Atlantic Canada would be built on tenuous bedrock after Newfoundland's Confederation in 1949.

Colonial Connections

Throughout the seventeenth century, France and England jockeyed for control of what would become known as Atlantic Canada, and each had an interest in and a claim to Newfoundland and the mainland. France attempted to establish permanent settlement on the mainland, at St Croix Island in 1604 and then at Port Royal in 1605; meanwhile, England developed a semi-permanent migratory fishing base on Newfoundland. The island was also important to the French fishing fleet, whose crews erected fish flakes on shore to dry their catch. For more than a century, France and England fought over Newfoundland's lucrative fishery, each claiming the island as its own. The often bloody struggle featured raid and counter-raid, especially during times of declared war between France and England.[2] European claims to Newfoundland were clarified somewhat with the 1713 Treaty of Utrecht, under which France relinquished all rights of settlement to Newfoundland in return for the gulf islands of Ile St Jean (now Prince Edward Island) and Ile Royale (now Cape Breton Island). Following the treaty's signing, French fishing and trading families in Newfoundland were moved to the ice-free harbour that would, by 1720, host the fortress of Louisbourg.

At the time of Halifax's founding in 1749, the Maritimes and Newfoundland were sparsely settled by Europeans. A key difference between the two jurisdictions related to settlers' places of origin. Before 1749 there were three European enclaves in what would eventually become Atlantic Canada. The majority of settlers were French: about 8,000 were clustered around the Bay of Fundy; another 6,000 fisherfolk and French military personnel were settled at Ile Royal, most of them near the French fortress of Louisbourg. In contrast, Newfoundland was populated by roughly 6,000 souls from either Ireland or the West Country of England, who engaged in the fishery and over-wintered in the craggy coastal outports.[3]

Demographic differences between Newfoundland and the Maritimes were heightened after 1749, when the British began concerted

efforts at settlement. In 1755, the Acadians were expelled from Nova
Scotia by Governor Charles Lawrence. Within a decade, more than
7,000 New England settlers – the 'Planters' – had been recruited to take
over the Acadians' vacated farmlands.[4] The Planters did not settle in
Newfoundland; even so, their arrival influenced the development of
Maritime–Newfoundland relations.[5] The Planters maintained ties with
New England and developed communities that reflected their roots in
the Thirteen Colonies. They brought their religious convictions with
them; they continued to correspond with New England friends and
family; and their towns in Nova Scotia mimicked the New England
style of township governance.[6] All of this strengthened religious,
familial, cultural, and economic ties between Nova Scotia and New
England.[7] So strong were economic ties to New England that New
Englanders, who controlled much of the northern colony's commerce,
attempted to curtail the economic development of Nova Scotia, fearing
a nearby rival. This meant that few trading relationships were established between Nova Scotia and potential Newfoundland or
Caribbean markets.[8] Thus the Planter influx further separated Nova
Scotia from Newfoundland; not only did it continue the pattern of dif-
fering origins of Newfoundlanders and Maritimers, but it also pulled
Nova Scotia closer toward New England's sphere of influence. All the
while, Newfoundland remained primarily a fishing hinterland for
Britain.

By the time the American Revolution erupted between the Thirteen
Colonies and Great Britain in 1775, the influence of transplanted New
Englanders had begun to wane, even though they still accounted for
about half of Nova Scotia's population.[9] Nova Scotia was not a signatory
to the Declaration of Independence and declined to participate in the
conflict; even so, the war had a profound impact on the colony.[10] At
war's end, the sudden influx into Nova Scotia of as many as 35,000 Loyalists – those who supported the British Crown during the conflict –
ushered in many changes, foremost among these the creation of New
Brunswick as a colony in 1784. After the war, Britain's mercantile regulations barred American merchants and traders from the Maritime and
British West Indies markets; this effectively granted Maritimers a
monopoly on the lucrative Caribbean trade. Unfortunately, this system
worked better in theory than in practice. Maritime entrepreneurs were
unable to meet even their own domestic needs during the 1780s, and
widespread American smuggling of goods in Maritime and Caribbean
waters undermined the system and the promised Maritime monopoly.[11]

In contrast, the American Revolution had very little impact on Newfoundland. American Loyalists flooded Nova Scotia and New Brunswick, but few went to Newfoundland, and American independence did little to change the island's relationship with the southern colonies. By the terms of the 1783 Treaty of Paris that ended the revolution, American fishermen retained access to Newfoundland's waters and permission to come ashore to dry their catch. Before the war the Thirteen Colonies had been major suppliers of foodstuffs and provisions to Newfoundland; this continued unabated after the conflict. The very different treatment afforded Newfoundland and the Maritimes stemmed from the fact that, though Newfoundland had a substantial year-round population, to Britain it remained primarily a fishing base.[12] As an outpost earmarked for neither British settlement nor government institutions, Newfoundland was less important to London than the Maritimes and was therefore not bound by the same strictures as the mainland British North American colonies.[13]

Indicative of this subservient position to the Maritimes was Newfoundland's ecclesiastical connection with the mainland. In 1787, shortly after the Loyalist influx, Charles Inglis was named Anglican Bishop of Nova Scotia with dominion over all British North American possessions, including Newfoundland. In practice, though, the bond was extremely weak: Inglis never set foot on Newfoundland. In 1839 even this tie between Newfoundland and the mainland was broken when Newfoundland became part of the new bishopric of Newfoundland and Bermuda.[14]

Agricultural Connections

The dearth of concrete political or religious ties between Newfoundland and the Maritimes did not impede some Maritimers from establishing commercial relations with the fishing colony. One area that proved especially profitable was agriculture. Since Newfoundland had little agricultural potential, its population relied on imported foodstuffs and provisions. Geographer C. Grant Head has calculated that in the 1780s it would have taken more than 20,000 fertile acres of land to supply Newfoundland's bread and flour requirements alone.[15] With only 6,000 acres reserved for agriculture, the great majority of the island's foodstuffs had to be imported, and for this many Newfoundlanders looked to the Maritimes.

Not until the end of the eighteenth century did Maritime agricultural output reach levels that allowed for modest exports. By the early 1800s Prince Edward Island–Newfoundland agricultural ties were strong enough that European visitors to North America took notice. During his travels through British North America in 1803–4, Lord Selkirk observed that most of the cash earned by Prince Edward Islanders came from exporting cattle to Newfoundland.[16] Indeed, the exchange of agricultural and other primary products became one of the threads that bound Newfoundland to Nova Scotia, New Brunswick, and Prince Edward Island during the nineteenth century. This network was of particular importance to PEI – something made clear in a 15 March 1819 edition of the *Prince Edward Island Gazette*, which stated: 'Newfoundland is entirely supplied by this Island with live cattle, fowls, corn, potatoes, and even garden stuff.'[17] But it was not just PEI produce that was crossing the Cabot Strait. Nova Scotia–grown foodstuffs made the voyage as well, with the Cape Breton community of Middle River particularly well situated to take advantage of the Newfoundland market. Located less than 500 miles from St John's – a distance manageable even by small vessels – Middle River was by the late 1840s exporting the bulk of its agricultural production to Newfoundland.[18] Though studies of New Brunswick's agricultural connections with Newfoundland have yet to be undertaken, New Brunswick was a net importer of agricultural goods, as it had a huge demand for foodstuffs for the forestry, shipbuilding, and shipping trades.[19] As a result, New Brunswick likely had limited agricultural links to Newfoundland.

By the 1860s, Prince Edward Island was the most important of the three Maritime provinces to the Newfoundland market for agricultural goods. Indeed, between 1858 and 1872 the trade warranted Prince Edward Island's keeping of detailed information on imports from and exports to Newfoundland.[20] In 1857, PEI shipped 10,319 pounds' worth of goods to Newfoundland. The next year the value of goods exported from PEI to Newfoundland rose to 15,853 pounds. This amounted to over 10 per cent of the small island's total exports – what would prove the high-water mark in terms of the value of the Newfoundland trade. By 1870, though the value of trade from PEI to Newfoundland remained relatively constant at 15,612 pounds, it amounted to a mere 3.6 per cent of PEI's total exports of 430,840 pounds. Still, Newfoundland remained a steady and reliable market for PEI.

Table 3
Prince Edward Island–Newfoundland trade, 1857–70

Year	Imports (value in £)	Exports (value in £)
1857	1,005	10,319
1858	1,307	15,853
1859	4,888	15,057
1860	4,082	18,421
1861	3,539	14,060
1862	2,275	10,815
1863	1,865	11,241
1864	3,038	11,059
1865	3,111	14,767
1866	4,708	9,472
1867	4,345	14,740
1868	3,213	13,637
1869	2,058	13,933
1870	2,746	15,612

Source: Compiled from *Journal of the House of Assembly of Prince Edward Island*
(Charlottetown: King's Printer, 1858–71).

Industrial Connections

The Maritimes and Newfoundland were also connected through the
fishing, shipbuilding, mining, and forestry industries. However,
though they were linked industrially, some important differences
began to appear between the two areas during the late eighteenth and
early nineteenth centuries. The Maritimes and Newfoundland were
tied to the same British mercantile system until its demise in the 1840s,
but while Newfoundland remained largely dependent on the cod
fishery during this period, the Maritimes began to diversify economically. As a result, with the exception of the fishery, many of these
industrial ties reveal either Newfoundland consumers purchasing
Maritime goods or Maritime entrepreneurs investing in Newfoundland staples.

The fishery linked Newfoundland to the mainland colonies. Established as a fishing outpost of the British Empire, Newfoundland was
originally tied via the codfish to world markets to a much greater
extent than was Nova Scotia – a fact best revealed by the two colonies'
involvement in the international fishery during the late 1780s. While

Table 4
Dry and wet fish shipped from the Maritimes and Newfoundland, 1787

Colony	Dried fish (quintals)	Wet fish (barrels)
Newfoundland	732,216	3,865
Cape Breton	36,736	1,021
PEI	186	10
Nova Scotia	44,729	13,363
New Brunswick	2,017	3,703

Source: Irving's Report on the American Fisheries, A2, vol. 8, 89, MG 23, LAC, as cited in Neil MacKinnon, *This Unfriendly Soil: The Loyalist Experience in Nova Scotia, 1783–1791* (Montreal and Kingston: McGill–Queen's University Press, 1986), 216n19.

Nova Scotia exported more barrels of wet fish, Newfoundland's dominance of the dried fish trade was striking. In 1787 Newfoundland shipped 732,216 quintals of dried fish, more than sixteen times the 44,729 that Nova Scotia exported.[21] Most of Newfoundland's dried fish found its way to European, Caribbean, and South American markets.[22]

By the nineteenth century there was more direct competition between the Nova Scotia and Newfoundland fisheries, with Nova Scotians participating in the Newfoundland herring fishery, especially around St George's Bay, and actively trading along the Labrador coast. At an 1852 public meeting in St Mary's, Newfoundland, local fishermen expressed concerns about Canadian encroachment on Newfoundland's fishing territory. Around the same time, Labrador's herring fishermen were occasionally clashing with their Nova Scotian counterparts over methods of fishing.[23] Newfoundland's 1862 decision to impose duties on all goods brought to Labrador raised an outcry from Nova Scotia fishermen, who had long been trading with Labradorians, and even prompted a protest from the Nova Scotia legislature.[24] Throughout the nineteenth century, Newfoundlanders remained disgruntled with certain Nova Scotia fishing policies and practices, most notably Nova Scotia's competition for the West Indies saltfish market.[25]

Newfoundland was also an important consumer of Maritime industrial output. During the late eighteenth and early nineteenth centuries, for example, Newfoundland buyers gave breath to the nascent Prince Edward Island lumber and shipbuilding trades, since the proximity of the two islands guaranteed PEI shipbuilders who sold to Newfoundland a quick return on their investment. The industry prospered in two ways: the shipbuilders could sell their vessels to Newfoundland; they could also send them across the Cabot Strait filled with Island produce. Indeed, Newfoundland became the primary market for PEI-built vessels, with Newfoundlanders purchasing half the sixty ships built in PEI between 1800 and 1810.[26]

As well, the mining industry bound Newfoundland to the Maritimes, with Bell Island, a rock outcrop rising from Newfoundland's Conception Bay, being the primary supplier of iron ore for the Cape Breton steel industry between 1895 and 1966. Though the mineral potential of Bell Island was known as early as 1610,[27] not until 1895 did exploitation of this valuable resource began in earnest, undertaken by Nova Scotia interests. That year, the Nova Scotia Steel and Coal Company began to develop the mining capacity of Bell Island in order to supply the steel mills of Cape Breton. But though foreign capital such as that provided by the Nova Scotia Steel and Coal Company was welcomed in Newfoundland, the threat of foreign workers taking potential jobs was not, and the fear of Nova Scotia workers taking Bell Island jobs provoked a 'general uproar' in the mining community.[28]

Maritime entrepreneurs were also heavily involved in Newfoundland forestry. In the late nineteenth century, as Maritime tree stands began to be depleted, Maritime lumbermen turned to the rich forests of Newfoundland. A Halifax-based merchant constructed a sawmill at Corner Brook in the mid-1860s, which attracted workers from as far away as Sheet Harbour and Stewiacke, Nova Scotia, with that province receiving a large proportion of the sawmill's output.[29] However, the sawmill boom was relatively short-lived. Once the larger trees necessary for sawmilling had been harvested, Newfoundland was left with forests of stunted black spruce and balsam fir, trees that lent themselves to the emerging wood pulp industry.[30] Nova Scotian Harry Crowe, who arrived in Newfoundland in 1902, became one of the major players in that burgeoning Newfoundland industry. After a series of negotiations with the Newfoundland government and the Reid Newfoundland Company, Crowe helped consolidate Newfoundland's east coast wood pulp industry. Two companies were established in the Exploits River and Bay of Islands areas: Newfoundland Timber Estates Ltd., of which Crowe was a vice-president, and the New Land Lumber and Pulp Co. Ltd., with Crowe as sole proprietor. In this manner a Nova Scotian ensured that 'no matter where pulp and paper manufacturing started up [on the eastern side of Newfoundland], they would profit from the development.'[31]

Increasing Personal Connections

Personal connections between Newfoundland and the Maritimes strengthened markedly between the 1860s and the Second World War. This was in part because of a similarity of experiences between the two jurisdictions. During this period both saw the commercialization of their primary industries and undertook efforts to industrialize. The most obvious sign of the growing integration of Newfoundland and the Maritimes in this period is found in demographic trends: Newfoundlanders were making their way to the Maritimes – particularly to Cape Breton and Halifax – to find work.

The Maritimes of the 1840s and the 1850s was 'relatively prosperous,' but this would gradually change during the 1860s.[32] That decade saw the end of the American Civil War and abrogation (in 1866) of the Reciprocity Treaty of 1854, which reduced American demand for Maritime primary exports such as lumber, fish, agricultural products, and coal. Moreover, Maritime farmers found themselves increasingly competing with Central Canadian interests, which compelled them to 'adapt to the production of specialties such as apples, dairy goods, and fur.'[33] As a result, between 1860 and 1900, Maritimers, facing 'persistent depression and economic dislocation,' left their region in unprecedented numbers.[34] At the same time, the Maritimes was becoming increasingly urbanized. This was not, however, simply a pattern of rural to urban migration; indeed, some urban areas, such as Saint John and Lunenburg, actually experienced population declines.[35] Maritime out-migration during this period reflected what T.W. Acheson has termed a 'two generation pattern of emigration.'[36] The first generation moved to a growing town or city in order to find better work; their children then left the region for exactly the same reason. Thus, at a time when many Maritime towns were industrializing, the region as a whole was experiencing net out-migration. In this climate, Newfoundlanders themselves were on the move in search of employment, across the Cabot Strait and into the Maritimes.[37]

Newfoundlanders were not lured solely by the pull of Maritime jobs; they were also being pushed by their own economic problems. Indeed, that they were moving to the Maritimes during these tough

times in search of employment underscores the difficulties Newfoundlanders faced at home. Between 1880 and 1900, Newfoundland's
saltfish-based economy experienced a crisis when the price of a quintal
of salt cod plummeted approximately 32 per cent, while production
volumes dropped 20 per cent. All told, gross industry earnings in the
saltfishery fell 36 per cent. These economic hits affected the male
labour force engaged in the saltcod fishery, which fell from a historic
peak of 60,000 in 1884 to under 37,000 in 1891.[38] While some of this lost
labour was absorbed into other Newfoundland industries, such as the
railway and lumber industries, many of the unemployed journeyed
across the Cabot Strait to take up jobs in Nova Scotia. The most immediate beneficiary of Newfoundland labour was the Cape Breton coal
and steel industry.[39] Newfoundlanders coming to Cape Breton were
recruited to Sydney by agents of the Dominion Iron and Steel
Company and the Dominion Coal Company to take jobs in the mills
and mines, which in many cases were being abandoned by Nova
Scotian workers, who felt the work was too dangerous.[40] Newfoundland labourers apparently had no such reservations, and would enter
the industrial workforce at the bottom of the unskilled labour market
in order to acquire the skills that would allow them to move up in the
segmented Cape Breton labour market.

Owing to its proximity to Newfoundland, Nova Scotia was the most
popular Canadian destination for Newfoundland emigrants. Between
1851 and 1901, more than 18,000 Newfoundlanders took up residence
in Nova Scotia. By 1860–1, roughly 1,700 Newfoundlanders made their
home in Canada, with almost 1,000 having settled in Nova Scotia.[41] By
1881, the number had grown to 2,058 Newfoundlanders living in Nova
Scotia. By 1901, the total had increased threefold to 6,414, of whom
3,671 (about 57 per cent) lived in Cape Breton.[42]

Perhaps because so many Newfoundlanders lived in Nova Scotia,
Newfoundland was one of the most generous jurisdictions in offering
assistance following the Halifax Explosion. Four days after the 6 December 1917 collision of the French munitions ship *Mont Blanc* and the Nor-
wegian steamer *Imo* – a tragedy that saw approximately 2,000 killed and
9,000 injured – the Newfoundland cabinet voted to send $50,000 in aid.[43]
Moreover, Newfoundland was unique among foreign countries in that
it sent missions to Halifax to rescue and assist any Newfoundlanders
affected by the explosion. Historian Malcolm MacLeod presents Newfoundland's financial and personal assistance to Halifax as proof that

Newfoundland and Nova Scotia shared a regional identity during the First World War.[44] While Newfoundland no doubt shared many connections with the mainland province, these contributions were more the result of Newfoundland's generosity and proximity than the product of any overriding sense of regionalism or common identity.[45]

Educational connections between Newfoundland and the Maritimes were also strengthened following the First World War. Since Newfoundland did not have a university of its own until 1949, Newfoundlanders desirous of a university degree were compelled to travel abroad. Between 1860 and 1899, Britain was their destination of choice, with almost half of all Newfoundlanders seeking higher education continuing their studies there, and only one-quarter coming to Canada. This changed after the war, as Newfoundlanders increasingly chose Canada, and in particular Nova Scotia, for higher education. Between 1919 and 1949, 62 per cent of university-bound Newfoundlanders studied in Canada, with almost half of these students enrolling at Maritime institutions.[46] Of particular attraction to Newfoundland students was Halifax's Dalhousie University, which housed professional faculties of law, dentistry, and medicine. By 1940, for example, 25 of the 55 Newfoundlanders attending Dalhousie University were studying in these faculties.[47]

Newfoundlanders chose Nova Scotia for work or study in part because of generous Canadian immigration policies. Until 1910, Newfoundlanders were treated practically the same as Canadians by immigration officials. This policy changed with the passage of the 1910 Immigration Act, when Ottawa assumed a more regulatory approach to Newfoundland immigration.[48] This did not mean that Ottawa consistently applied the more stringent regulations contained in the 1910 act. Indeed, historian Peter Neary contends that Newfoundlanders still had preferential status after the act's passage. In times of economic hardship, however, such as during the Great Depression of the 1930s, Ottawa used the act to limit the number of Newfoundlanders entering Canada.[49] Throughout the 1930s, Newfoundland fishers found it difficult to enter Canada unless there was a dramatic labour shortage – an exclusionist policy endorsed by Nova Scotia's fishers, who were increasingly concerned about the number of Newfoundlanders in their industry.[50] Not until the Second World War would strict Canadian policy toward Newfoundlanders ease; at that time, Canada relaxed its immigration policy toward Newfoundland in an effort to alleviate an acute shortage of wartime labour.[51]

Second World War Connections

Relations between Canada and Newfoundland changed profoundly with the outbreak of the Second World War. On 8 September 1939, Canadian Prime Minister William Lyon Mackenzie King pledged that Canada would undertake the protection of Newfoundland during the conflict. This vow brought the two nations closer together; it also helped pave the way for Newfoundland's entry into Confederation a decade later.

In the Maritimes, young men rushed to enlist in the war, with a full 47.5 per cent of the eligible male population volunteering. Zeal for the war effort was similar in Newfoundland, where more than 11,000 Newfoundlanders joined the British or Canadian armed forces.[52] The widespread enlistment of young men in both the Maritimes and Newfoundland, and the guaranteed employment promised by the armed services, helped alleviate the economic deprivations that had strangled the Maritimes and Newfoundland during the previous decade. Further relief would come to Newfoundland in the form of Canadian and American wartime construction.

Canada did not want to leave the entrance to the St Lawrence River wide open to possible attack, and recognized early in the war that it would have to include Newfoundland in its wartime defence planning. By June 1940, Canadian troops were stationed at Gander; by year's end, military bases at Botwood and Gander were under Canadian control. The Canadian military presence at these locations was accompanied by a flurry of military construction. In 1941 the Canadians began to build an air base at Torbay, which was soon joined by the Avalon naval base. By 1943, 3,600 Canadian troops were stationed at Avalon, making it Canada's second-largest naval installation. And Canadian military construction was not confined to the island – in 1941 the Goose Bay airbase in Labrador was added to the list. In all, the Canadian military investment in Newfoundland during the war amounted to $65,000,000.[53]

The growing importance of Newfoundland in Canadian policy circles during the Second World War is also illustrated by the establishment of the Canadian High Commission in St John's in 1941, with Nova Scotia's Charles Burchell as Canada's first High Commissioner to the island. Burchell had long served in the Canadian civil service, most recently as Canada's first High Commissioner to Australia. However, Burchell's experience was not the sole criterion for his appointment; he was recommended for the Newfoundland position in part because he was a Maritimer from Nova Scotia, which speaks to the tendency in Ottawa to view the Maritimes and Newfoundland as a region.[54]

The appointment of a Canadian High Commissioner to Newfoundland was also a response to a growing American interest in Newfoundland. Early in the conflict, Britain found it difficult to prosecute the war effort owing to a lack of military hardware. In September 1940 the British and the Americans negotiated the Leased Bases Agreement: in exchange for supplying Britain with fifty aging destroyers, the United States would be entitled to lease base sites in Newfoundland, Bermuda, and the Caribbean for ninety-nine years. The Americans quickly took advantage of the agreement and began building military installations – Fort Pepperell army base near St John's, Fort McAndrew army base at Argentia, a US navy base at Argentia, and the Harmon Field air base at Stephenville – that surpassed in size and in scope those of the Canadians.[55] In addition, the Americans leased part of St John's harbour and stationed troops at the Canadian bases of Gander and Goose Bay. At the height of Canadian and American military involvement in Newfoundland during the Second World War, more than 10,000 American and 6,000 Canadian soldiers were stationed on the island.[56]

The importance of Canadian and American military involvement in Newfoundland cannot be overstated. Not only did it serve as a window for Newfoundlanders to the 'North American' way of life, but the 16,000 foreign soldiers stationed on the island also bolstered the economy by spending their wages in Newfoundland. Also, nearly 20,000 Newfoundland civilians found employment on the foreign bases at the peak of base construction, and even after the building boom ended more than 5,000 Newfoundlanders continued to work on the bases.[57]

Some far-sighted Newfoundland officials, recognizing that the wartime boom would likely be temporary, anticipated that problems could arise once the war ended. Before the war, 28 per cent of Newfoundland's workforce had been unemployed. The construction of military bases, the widespread enlistment that accompanied the conflict, and a wartime boom in the Newfoundland fishery had lowered unemployment rates by 1942, but it was anticipated that the prosperity would be fleeting. Thus, Newfoundland's newly created Department of Labour strived to gain improved access to the Canadian labour market for Newfoundland workers.[58]

Table 5
Newfoundland men employed on military bases, 1942–5

Date	Canadian Forces	U.S. Army	U.S. Navy	Total
June 1942	6,943	6,930	3,472	17,345
September 1942	6,728	9,524	3,500	19,752
December 1942	3,829	6,866	2,600	13,295
December 1943	4,131	3,519	1,150	8,800
March 1944	3,929	2,565	982	7,476
October 1944	–	3,208	1,050	–
August 1945	–	3,724	1,612	–

Source: Parsons, Labour Relations Officer (Acting) to Commissioner for Justice and Defence, 29 September 1945, File 19, 'US Effect of Agreements on Colonies,' box 365, GN 13/1/B, PANL, as cited in Steven High, 'Working for Uncle Sam: The "Comings" and "Goings" of Newfoundland Base Construction Labour, 1940–1945,' *Acadiensis* 32, no. 2 (Spring 2003): 88.

In 1943 a shortage of labour in Canada prompted Canadian companies to lobby their federal government for permission to import Newfoundland workers. The Nova Scotia provincial government played an active role in luring Newfoundland labourers. Premier A.S. MacMillan tried in November 1943 to recruit workers on behalf of the Mersey Paper Company, but he was still subject to a federal government that controlled immigration.[59] As a result, not all Canadian recruitment efforts succeeded; they were stymied by selectively enforced immigration requirements in both Ottawa and St John's and by the boom conditions that continued on the island.[60] Even so, the number of Newfoundlanders crossing the Cabot Strait during the war rose markedly, to a high of 4,500 in 1945.[61] Not until Newfoundland's entry into Confederation in 1949 would Newfoundlanders again receive the unfettered access to the mainland that they had enjoyed prior to the 1910 Immigration Act.

Political Connections

When Newfoundland rejected Confederation with Canada in the late 1860s, political connections between Newfoundland and the Maritimes waned. The Maritimes became subordinate provinces to a federal union empowered to conduct foreign relations. As a result, political relations were focused on Ottawa and St John's, bypassing Maritime capitals. Nevertheless, the Maritimes and Newfoundland followed parallel political trajectories.

A useful starting point for a survey of Canada–Newfoundland political connections is the 1864 Charlottetown Conference. Originally convened to discuss Maritime Union, the outcome of the Charlottetown Conference was an agreement to meet again a few weeks later in Quebec City to discuss a broader British North American union. At Quebec, seventy-two resolutions were hammered out that would form the basis of the British North America Act and Canadian Confederation. Tellingly, no Newfoundland delegates were present at Charlottetown. This exclusion was less a cause of Newfoundland's decision to reject Confederation than a reflection of the differing orientations of Newfoundland and the mainland colonies. With an economy still geared to shipping and the fish trade, Newfoundlanders saw little appeal in the subsequent Quebec Resolutions. Only 5 per cent of island trade was with the British North American colonies, and the talk of building an Intercolonial Railway designed to entice the Maritimes into union only pushed Newfoundland away, as Newfoundlanders were little interested in funding infrastructure they would never use or benefit from.[62] Talk of union persisted, however, and two years after the passage of the British North America Act, Newfoundland politicians fought an election on the issue. Even when offered more generous terms, Newfoundland's anti-confederates led by Charles Fox Bennett trounced the pro-confederates led by Frederick Carter in the 1869 election by a two-to-one margin.[63]

In the 1890s, relations between Canada and Newfoundland became so strained that Confederation was seemingly put finally to rest. In 1890, Newfoundland's colonial secretary and future prime minister, Robert Bond, negotiated an agreement with American Secretary of State James Blaine for reciprocal trade and American fishing rights in Newfoundland waters.[64] This agreement made Ottawa nervous. The Canadians, who as recently as 1888 had tried to secure reciprocity with the United States, viewed Newfoundland's success with barely concealed jealousy. Moreover, the Canadians feared that the agreement might lead to a Newfoundland movement for annexation to the United States, thereby ending any hope of its entry into Confederation.[65] Armed with these concerns, the Canadian government successfully lobbied the British Parliament to withhold the necessary ratification of the Bond–Blaine agreement. Canada's thwarting of this treaty prompted a short-lived tariff war between the two British territories, with Newfoundland levying a protective tariff on Canadian flour and Canada countering with a charge on Newfoundland fish – a levy that pleased Maritime fishers.[66]

This tenuous state of affairs was still in effect in December 1894, when Newfoundland's banks collapsed. Still reeling financially from the St John's fire that had levelled parts of the city in 1892, the colony's economy was devastated by the bank crash. One of the banks that closed its doors – the Union Bank – was also the Newfoundland government's financial agent.[67] As a result, the crash endangered Newfoundland's public credit and the government was unable to pay a January interest payment without outside assistance. After a series of failed negotiations with Britain, Newfoundland, prompted by the severity of its financial situation, reluctantly approached Canada.[68] Any prospect of Newfoundland joining Canada in the 1890s was dashed, however, by the hardline negotiations of Canadian Prime Minister Mackenzie Bowell and by Newfoundland Prime Minister Robert Bond's success in securing from the city of London a loan that temporarily alleviated the island's financial troubles.[69]

The bank collapse of 1894 weakened political connections between Newfoundland and Canada; but it also strengthened economic ties between the two as Canadian banks rushed to fill the void, with the Bank of Montreal even taking over from the Union Bank as the government's financier. Canadian banknotes accompanied the arrival of Canadian banks, and this sudden influx of foreign currency compelled the Newfoundland government to make Canadian and Newfoundland notes equal and convertible. This, historian Malcolm MacLeod contends, meant that Canadian currency essentially replaced that of Newfoundland, though not until 1931 did Canadian bills under $5.00 formally become legal tender.[70]

This would not be the last time Newfoundland experienced profound financial troubles. The island was particularly vulnerable to economic downturns, for the construction of a paper mill at Corner Brook, the building of the Newfoundland Railway, and the development of mines at Buchans were the only substantial additions to Newfoundland industry prior to the outbreak of the Great Depression.[71] As a result, Newfoundland was hard hit by the Depression, when rising debt payments and sinking revenues again put the dominion in danger of default. This time there was no Robert Bond to secure a welcomed last-minute loan. Rather, London and Ottawa agreed to assist

Newfoundland in meeting its financial obligations provided that the colony agreed to a committee to investigate the causes of Newfoundland's economic woes and to make recommendations on their remedy. The resulting Amulree Commission blamed the island's financial troubles on the Newfoundland government and recommended that Britain assume responsibility for Newfoundland's debt payments. In return, Newfoundland would temporarily suspend responsible government for an appointed Commission of Government.[72] Despite a lack of public support for the idea, a Commission of Government governed Newfoundland from February 1934 until the island entered Confederation on 31 March 1949.

The boom of the Second World War, coupled with a resurgence in the fishery, meant that by war's end Newfoundland was in excellent financial shape and that the reasons to suspend responsible government no longer existed. Newfoundlanders would now have to decide the future shape of their government. In 1948, they went to the polls to vote in a referendum in which they were presented with three options: (1) A continuation of the Commission of Government; (2) A return to responsible government as it had existed in 1934; or (3) Confederation with Canada. In the event that none of the options gained a clear majority, the lowest polling choice would be eliminated and a run-off referendum held between the two remaining options. In the first referendum, held on 3 June 1948, responsible government received 44.6 per cent of the vote, Confederation 41.1 per cent, and the Commission of Government 14.3 per cent. Since none had gained a clear majority, a second referendum was held a month and a half later, on 22 July. In that contest, Confederation emerged the victor by 4.6 per cent. With that, Newfoundland's political fate was decided, and within a year it was a Canadian province.

Conclusion

When Newfoundland entered Confederation on 31 March 1949, it had been growing closer to Canada for more than two hundred years, a trend amplified during the late nineteenth and early twentieth centuries and reaching its height in the 1940s. Since most political dealings between Newfoundland and the mainland occurred between St John's and Ottawa, Maritime provincial governments – whose provinces and constituents seemingly had the most to gain or to lose with Newfoundland's entry into Confederation – had little direct experience dealing with the old colony. As a result, they showed little interest in the forthcoming union. Despite Term 29's explicit linking of Newfoundland and the Maritime Provinces, these two jurisdictions, shaped by histories of political separateness, had no lofty illusions about being part of an Atlantic region. Not until after Newfoundland had been welcomed into the family of Canadian provinces would any sort of broader regional collaboration come to the forefront. In the years following the Second World War, when Newfoundland's entry into Confederation was being negotiated, Maritime–Newfoundland relations continued to be conducted in much the same fashion as they had been during the preceding centuries – as private and personal transactions based in large measure on immediate financial or political concerns. As the following three chapters reveal, despite couching their ambitions in the language of regionalism, each Maritime province attempted to use Newfoundland's entry into Confederation to further its own provincial development programs.

2 A Province Divided:
Nova Scotia and Newfoundland's Entry
into Confederation

For the students of Halifax's Mount Saint Vincent College, the union of Newfoundland and Canada was cause for celebration. Long a destination for female Newfoundland Roman Catholics seeking higher education, the college staged a pageant to welcome its Newfoundland students as Canadians shortly after Newfoundland's entry into Confederation. As the *Antigonish Casket* described it:

> The infant country was depicted through its long struggle for independence, with Great Britain, Canada and the United States always ready to hold out an invited hand. The hard choice being made, the new province was welcomed by Mother Canada who called in the nine provinces to extend individual welcomes, bring their gifts, and witness the crowning of Newfoundland as a tenth province.[1]

Despite the warm welcome given by Mount Saint Vincent's collegians, and despite the symbolism of their production, not all Nova Scotians were pleased that Newfoundland had become a tenth province.[2] This chapter examines the responses of Nova Scotians as represented in their newspapers and by political and business leaders to Newfoundland's entry into Confederation. It shows that support for the union was strongest in Cape Breton, where it was believed that Newfoundland's entry could improve a troubled local economy, and that endorsement of Confederation waned as one approached the provincial capital, where some people feared that the terms of union would harm the province's shipping and fishing industries. The muted response in Halifax was echoed by provincial Premier Angus L. Macdonald, who was wary of expressing an opinion on the merger owing to concerns about its financial implications. Still, Macdonald's misgivings did not prevent him from attempting to use Newfoundland's entry into Confederation to buttress his calls for greater provincial rights.

Newspaper Opinion in Sydney and Halifax

As the Second World War ended and Newfoundland's future became a topic of debate, newspapers in Sydney and Halifax addressed the Confederation issue. H.P. Duchemin, editor of Cape Breton's daily newspaper, the *Sydney Post-Record*, was at first pessimistic about the possibility of Newfoundland actually joining Confederation. In December 1945 he acknowledged that 'political union with Canada would undoubtedly help the Newfoundlanders' as they would benefit from Canada's social welfare net and from Canadian capital necessary to develop Newfoundland's natural resources, but he concluded that 'for a time at least, Newfoundland would be rather a liability than an asset.'[3] Nor were Newfoundlanders perceived as likely candidates to become Canadians. As a 26 June 1946 editorial in the *Post-Record* on 'The Newfoundland Conundrum' made clear, 'like the Greeks of old, Newfoundlanders have always been dead against the relinquishment of their local autonomy, or the surrender of any part of it to the Central Government or any national organization or confederacy of states.'[4]

The pessimistic view of the *Sydney Post-Record* regarding Newfoundland's entry persisted into the fall of 1946, even though that summer had seen three new ships acquired to serve the growing Cape Breton–Newfoundland freight and tourist trades.[5] As late as September 1946 the paper maintained that the possibility of Newfoundland joining with Canada was remote.[6] Its view changed, however, on 12 October 1946, when the paper printed the results of an informal poll conducted by the *St John's Sunday Herald* of Newfoundlanders' preference for their constitutional future. Of the more than 10,000 respondents, the largest proportion – 3,734 voters – favoured a government consisting of a commission of elected Newfoundlanders. Finishing an unexpected second, with 2,018 votes, was Confederation with Canada.[7] Said the *Sydney Post-Record*, 'quite ... surprising is the substantial vote recorded for Confederation with Canada, heretofore regarded as anathema to an overwhelming majority of the people.' The results of this poll led Duchemin to suspect that Newfoundlanders would favour either a Commission of Government or Confederation, and that, were the National Convention to put either of these options before the electorate, 'public opinion could be swung strongly behind either of them.'[8] Still, the newspaper remained sceptical of Newfoundland's Confederation. A 5 July 1947 editorial in the *Sydney Post-Record* looked askance at the potential union, suggesting that it had little to offer Canada and that 'this Dominion has enough troubles of its own already without taking on what might prove an added liability.'[9] Within a month the *Post-Record* was tempering its view; that August, Duchemin – perhaps suspecting that a union proposal would soon be announced – suggested that terms of union could easily be reached between Canada and Newfoundland provided each side was committed to Confederation.[10]

Editorializing about Newfoundland reached a crescendo when the terms of a proposed union were announced in the fall of 1947. Cape Bretoners viewed them as 'generous.'[11] As an editorial in the *Sydney Post-Record* suggested, the proffered terms were 'more generous, not to say prodigal, than those enjoyed by any of the nine Provinces now constituting the Dominion.' In particular, the editorial was concerned with the fact that, while the population of Nova Scotia was twice that of Newfoundland, Nova Scotia would receive only half the subsidies offered the potential new province.[12] Despite this concern, the editorial favoured Newfoundland's entry:

> No one should under-estimate the importance of having Newfoundland become a tenth Canadian Province. Its entry into the Canadian Confederation would have more than sentimental value. Newfoundland's natural resources, particularly those of mining and lumbering, and fishing, are vast and valuable, and are capable of yielding enormous returns for decades to come.[13]

Newfoundland's natural resources would soon prove a prominent factor in the Cape Breton newspaper's support for the union.

Though generally less vocal than the Sydney paper about Confederation, Halifax newspapers also approved of the idea of union. In that city, much of the support for union stemmed from a sense of imperial loyalty rooted in events occurring halfway around the world. In August 1947, India achieved independence, which the *Halifax Herald* implied was sufficient grounds for the generous terms offered Newfoundland. As the *Herald's* news editor Ralph Vaughan made clear:

Were the times and circumstances what they used to be as affecting the British Family, there would be a disposition on Canada's part to do some closer bargaining. But with portions of the Empire falling away into independence, there is need today for demonstrations of British unity wherever they may be possible – and the Canadian Government has had this need in mind in offering to Newfoundland terms of a generous character.[14]

Thus the independence of India made the *Herald* 'glad to see Newfoundland a province of Canada.'[15] Though that newspaper was pleased that Newfoundland would become a Canadian province, in practice some of the provisions for Newfoundland's entry became quite contentious.

Support in Cape Breton: The Canso Crossing

In Nova Scotia, Cape Breton emerged as the strongest pocket of support for Newfoundland's Confederation. This should not be surprising, given that Cape Breton, located just 100 kilometres from Newfoundland's southwestern tip, was the focal point for Newfoundland–Canada trade and immigration. In 1949, for example, almost 22,000 passengers passed through North Sydney on their way to or from Newfoundland.[16] That same year, North Sydney shipped 56,795 tons of freight to Newfoundland and received 5,940 tons of freight, most of it fish.[17] So important was the Newfoundland trade to Cape Breton that in 1949, Sydney's Board of Trade set up a 'Newfoundland Relations Committee.'[18] What is more, the 'largest concentration' of Newfoundlanders in Canada could be found in Nova Scotia, with many of them calling Cape Breton home.[19]

The presence of Newfoundlanders in Cape Breton did not automatically mean that they would endorse Newfoundland's Confederation with Canada. A 22 July 1948 editorial by Helen Champion in the *Halifax Herald* noted that letters to the editors of the St John's papers from expatriate Newfoundlanders living in Canada were split equally between those who supported and those who opposed Confederation.[20] Whether this accurately reflected expatriate sentiment on the union or was simply a reflection of the various pro- and anti-Confederation newspapers selecting for publication letters that supported their stance is impossible to determine.[21] However, if a concentration of expatriate Newfoundlanders living in Cape Breton does not alone explain that island's endorsement of Newfoundland's Confederation, the anticipated material benefits that would accrue with union surely helped tip the balance of opinion. Cape Bretoners used Newfoundland's entry to justify important industrial development projects. One such project was a fixed link across the Strait of Canso.[22]

The idea of linking Cape Breton Island to the Nova Scotia mainland was not new in 1949. Some sort of connection had been actively sought since the early 1800s. At first, Cape Bretoners seemed content with a ferry connection between the two jurisdictions. In the 1880s, some began to lobby for the construction of a bridge across the strait, but these calls went unheeded. Demand for a fixed crossing flared again in the 1930s; unfortunately, the timing was poor as the economic difficulties of the Great Depression made remote the chances that a link would be built.[23] The Second World War reversed the nation's economic fortunes; as the conflict wound down, the federal and provincial governments began to focus on desirable infrastructure projects as they pondered postwar reconstruction. In its 1944 survey of Nova Scotia's postwar prospects, the MacGregor Dawson Commission on Provincial Development and Rehabilitation endorsed the idea of a link across the strait.[24]

At first, the entry of Newfoundland into Confederation factored little into 1940s calls for a Canso Strait crossing. For example, a 5 June 1946 'Memorandum in the matter of The Proposed Bridge or Causeway at the Strait of Canso' prepared by Rand H. Matheson, Transportation Manager of the Transportation Commission of the Maritime Board of Trade, contains no mention of Newfoundland. Indeed, Matheson's memorandum was ambivalent about the construction of a fixed crossing, for he did not think that a bridge or causeway across the strait would aid in getting Cape Breton goods to Central Canada, though he noted that 'the causeway would cost no more in the long run than the car ferry.' Yet Matheson recognized that there were other reasons to endorse the crossing; he acknowledged that 'the project is of importance in the aid of national defence and as an undertaking to provide employment during the transitional period in the Cape Breton area.'[25]

Supporters of the Canso crossing argued their case more vigorously in 1949, when Canadian and American commitments to the construction of the St Lawrence Seaway became apparent.[26] Noting Ottawa's support for this megaproject, Nova Scotians argued for the building of the Canso crossing along distinctly regional lines. H.P. Duchemin, editor of the *Sydney Post-Record*, made clear that he was 'glad to see Canada prosper and expand economically in any and every direction,' but he expressed frustration at the lack of a corresponding Maritime project 'that will give them [the Maritimes] equality of economic opportunity with rest of the Dominion.' For the editor of the Sydney newspaper, a fixed link at Canso would be such a project. 'Is it too much to ask,' wrote the editor, 'that ... the bridging of the Strait of Canso be undertaken also without further avoidable delay? This means as much to the Maritimes as the St Lawrence seaway can ever mean to the Central Provinces.'[27]

The pro–Canso crossing attitude of the *Sydney Post-Record* was adopted by some Maritime MPs. For example, Conservative Cumberland MP Percy Black argued that 'there has been much talk about the Canso bridge or causeway and the Chignecto canal project but nothing had been done about them, although many bridges and canals had been built in Central Canada.'[28] Black's outrage at the inequitable division of infrastructure projects between the Maritimes and Central Canada paled in comparison to that of fellow Conservative and Colchester-Hants MP Frank Stanfield. Speaking of the St Lawrence Seaway project in 1949, Stanfield, a self-confessed 'good maritimer,' suggested that the massive amount of money expended on the seaway would bring very small return to Maritimers. This perceived lack of regional fairness led Stanfield to state that he 'could not vote for that [St Lawrence Seaway] project if we in the maritime provinces did not get something in return to offset the expenditure of money; and in that connection I suggest the bridge across the strait of Canso.'[29] For Stanfield, the coming of Newfoundland into Confederation added weight to calls for a Canso crossing. As he explained, 'now that Newfoundland has been brought into Confederation the question of a bridge across the strait of Canso has become a matter of great importance. The people of Newfoundland have to get to and from that island, and that is going to be our responsibility; which makes the bridging of the strait of Canso very necessary indeed.'[30] And Stanfield was not the only Nova Scotian to use Newfoundland's pending Confederation as justification for the construction of a Canso crossing. As early as 16 July 1947, when a Nova Scotia delegation travelled to Ottawa to lobby the federal government for a fixed link across the strait, Newfoundland's entry was used to justify a crossing.[31]

Mention of Newfoundland in demands for the crossing increased markedly after Newfoundlanders cast their ballots in favour of union

in 1948. Representative of this trend was the Canso Crossing Association (CCA), a Sydney group formed in May 1948 to coordinate the
activities of a number of associations seeking to convince the provincial and federal governments to build a crossing. In January 1949, a
CCA brochure explained why a fixed link was necessary. One of the
CCA arguments revolved around the 'Advent of Newfoundland.' The
association contended that the signing of the terms of union between
Newfoundland and Canada the previous December had made the
development of a better crossing imperative, since 'much is expected
from the opening up of new avenues of inter-provincial trade' between
Newfoundland and Nova Scotia.[32] An undated CCA memo carries the
argument one step further, suggesting that a crossing would improve
Cape Breton's trade with all parts of the country and therefore should
be a matter of national priority:

> A new and important element has been introduced into the matter of the
> Canso crossing by the imminent admission of Newfoundland into the
> Confederation. It broadens the scope of the subject, beyond that of a
> merely local issue: the project becomes stamped as an urgent need, on a
> national scale, inasmuch as the prospects are for greatly increased trade
> and traffic both ways. The Canadian National Railways from Sydney to
> Montreal is the most direct land artery available.[33]

The CCA also suggested that the crossing be built, or at least be promised, prior to Newfoundland's entry into Confederation. After all, 'this
antiquated bottleneck, on which all roads converge at Canso Gut,
[would not be] the most attractive reception that can be given to the
300,000 Newfoundland Canadians on their first setting foot in this
country.'[34]

The CCA's campaign had the desired effect, and Newfoundland's
entry was soon embraced by the public as justification for the Canso
crossing. A 25 February 1949 letter to the editor of the *Halifax Chronicle
Herald* from E.L. Gurney, an expatriate Cape Bretoner living in Quebec,
illustrates this trend. According to Gurney, Cape Breton had some
pressing problems that needed to be solved, 'not the least of which is
that long-dreamed-of and much-to-be-desired Strait of Canso crossing.'[35] For Gurney, Newfoundland's pending entry made it vital that
facilities at the Strait of Canso be improved. In words reminiscent of
the CCA memorandum, Gurney opined that

we are facing the prospect of having Newfoundland as a tenth Province of the Dominion. Will there be a consequent increase in the exchange of commodities with the new province and is it not to be expected that there will be a subsequent increase in rail transportation, both freight and passenger, between the Nova Scotia mainland and Cape Breton Island, as a result?[36]

The bridging of the Strait of Canso was 'not a matter of political expediency,' wrote Gurney, 'but rather a matter of national concern which deserves proper and immediate attention.'[37]

While the CCA conducted its successful public relations campaign in the country's newspapers, Premier Angus L. Macdonald negotiated with the federal Transportation Minister Lionel Chevrier about getting a link built.[38] A joint federal–provincial Board of Engineers appointed to investigate the matter issued a report on 14 March 1949 favouring the construction of a low-level bridge across the strait.[39] The provincial government readily endorsed the commission's recommendation and agreed to fund a portion of the cost of the project, 'details of which will be worked out later.'[40] In the end it was a causeway, not a low-level bridge, that on 13 August 1955 permanently connected Cape Breton to the mainland.

It is unlikely that Newfoundland's Confederation was the main factor convincing the federal government to build a crossing over the Strait of Canso, but certainly it added weight to the argument for one. With Newfoundland's entry into Confederation, a crossing over the strait began to be seen as a project of national importance, and could be linked to the broader nationalist weal that accompanied the union.[41] As L.J. Doucette wrote in his official history of the Canso Causeway, 'the new development in Newfoundland was indeed a break which the sponsors of the Canso Crossing Association had not anticipated or bargained for. It made the task [of securing a link] a little easier.'[42]

Support in Cape Breton: The Steel Industry

Another reason behind Cape Breton's support of Newfoundland's Confederation was the hope that the massive iron ore fields discovered in 1947 along the Quebec–Labrador border would revitalize the sagging Sydney steel mills. Cape Breton steel production had declined over the course of the Second World War, as the federal government gave steel contracts to Central and Western Canada at the expense of both the Maritimes and the war effort. The sole wartime industrial contract awarded by Ottawa to Cape Breton involved the temporary rehabilitation of a steel-plate mill in Sydney for ship construction.[43] As the war neared its end, Ottawa offered the plate mill's operators, the Dominion Steel and Coal Corporation (DOSCO), irresistible financial incentives to close the plant. This plant closure necessitated the cutting of DOSCO's sizable workforce, and by May 1947 about half of Nova Scotia's 20,000 unemployed resided in Cape Breton.[44]

Newfoundland's entry promised to aid the faltering Sydney steel industry. Newfoundland had long supplied the iron ore converted into steel in the Sydney mills. The Wabana ore field on Bell Island in Newfoundland's Conception Bay shipped about 5,700 tons of iron ore weekly to DOSCO's Sydney steel mills, even after the closure of the wartime steel-plate mill.[45] The discovery of Labrador ore was soon being viewed by Nova Scotia workers and industrialists as a potential boon to the province's industrial sector, and they used the discovery to lobby for the expansion of the Cape Breton steel industry.

In June 1948 the United Mine Workers (UMW) District 26, headquartered in Glace Bay and representing all of Nova Scotia and New Brunswick, sent a ten-page memorandum to Minister of Trade C.D. Howe urging the expansion of the Nova Scotia steel industry.[46] In this memorandum the UMW suggested that increased steel exports were the 'only cure for chronic unemployment in Nova Scotia.' To support its claim that the Cape Breton steel industry could be expanded, the UMW noted the discovery of iron ore in Labrador, '40 [sic] miles west of Sydney.'[47] This discovery, the UMW suggested, would lead to a shift of the North American steel industry from the Great Lakes region toward the Atlantic coast, in order to be situated closer to the Labrador ore fields. The allure of the Labrador ore fields to the steel industry was aided by depletion of the Mesabi Range in Minnesota, which had long supplied the mills of the continental interior with iron ore. In light of these events, the UMW argued that 'the Sydney industry is ideally placed, in relation to ore, coal, geographic position and ports, for export trade.'[48]

That same month, advocates for the expansion of the Cape Breton steel industry received unexpected good news. Faced with a hostile Republican-led Congress that viewed him as a lame duck, President Harry Truman put on hold plans to develop the St Lawrence Seaway.

A completed seaway, and the wider and deeper waters it would bring, would be an ideal way for ships laden with iron ore to travel to the steel mills of Ohio, Michigan, western Pennsylvania, and Ontario; it would also offset any geographical advantage held by the steel towns of the Atlantic seaboard. With the apparent shelving of the St Lawrence Seaway plan, without which there would be no cheap way to ship ore to the continental interior, Sydney's mills were seen by default as the place to refine Labrador ore.[49]

Unfortunately for advocates for the Cape Breton steel industry, the very same Labrador iron ore that they hoped would revitalize industrial Cape Breton was also being used to justify the reinstatement of the St Lawrence Seaway project. Prompted by his surprise victory in the 1948 U.S. election, and by the discovery of the vast Labrador iron ore fields, President Truman announced that he would force a showdown with Congress over the St Lawrence Seaway project and that he was 'more optimistic about it than he ever has been.'[50] Truman's optimism stemmed in large part from Newfoundland's pending entry into Confederation. After union was consummated, Newfoundland would be a province of Canada and the Canadian federal government would assume responsibility for negotiating Newfoundland's foreign agreements. That meant there would be only two governments involved in the discussions over American access to Labrador iron ore and that the chances of success would therefore be much improved.

It seems that Newfoundland's pending Confederation also soothed some of Truman's fiercest adversaries in the U.S. Congress. Senator Robert Taft, leader of the Congressional Republicans, stated in January 1949 that while he still was not fully committed to the seaway, he was 'looking with a great deal more favor upon it than [he] did a year ago.' Labrador ore was the reason for his improved opinion of the project. Taft represented Ohio, a major importer of iron ore. The depletion of Minnesota's Mesabi Range surely would have worried him. Without a steady supply of iron ore, Ohio's steel mills, along with the Port of Cleveland, 'would suffer tremendous economic loss which no other source could compensate for.'[51] American enthusiasm for the project was matched by that of Lionel Chevrier, Canada's transportation minister. In a speech that same month to the Marine Club of Toronto, Chevrier suggested that 'huge iron ore deposits discovered in Labrador and Quebec make the St. Lawrence seaway project not only feasible, but also a necessity.'[52] By January 1949 the St Lawrence Seaway project was back on.

With the reinstatement of the St Lawrence Seaway project, Cape Breton steel interests changed their tack. While still an important consideration, geographical proximity to Labrador was no longer the main argument for the revitalization of the Sydney steel mills. After all, once the seaway opened it would be just as easy to transport a load of ore to Cleveland as to Sydney. Instead, Nova Scotia's newspapers began to argue for the expansion of the Sydney mills in the name of 'sound national planning.'[53] It did not make economic sense, they suggested, to ship raw iron ore down the St Lawrence Seaway to be refined in the industrial American states of the continental interior only to purchase back from them finished steel at a higher price, especially while Canada was experiencing a steel shortage. The *Halifax Chronicle Herald* pointed out that since Sydney was already home to a large steel industry, conveniently located near coalfields, with the ability to easily ship to the continental interior via the St Lawrence or to world markets through ocean shipping, 'Nova Scotia has a strong claim to consideration in any plan to expand Canada's steel production.' This was a claim that no other Canadian steel mill could make.[54] What is more, the paper argued, it did not make sense from a national security standpoint to rely on foreign imports of finished steel when the capacity to produce it in Canada existed. Depending on American steel was more than financially inadvisable; it was not 'sound national policy.'[55] Despite their unrelenting lobbying, and despite their use of Newfoundland's Confederation, the Nova Scotia steel interests were unable to secure from Ottawa a commitment to rehabilitate or expand the Sydney steel mills.

Concern in Halifax: The Maritime Freight Rates Act Issue

In large measure, it was the benefits that would accrue to Cape Breton with Newfoundland's Confederation that prompted some people in Halifax to be cool to the coming union. Though the building of the Canso crossing was supported throughout Nova Scotia – indeed, as MP Percy Black stated in the House of Commons in 1948, 'there is one undertaking on which the 650,000 people of Nova Scotia speak with one voice, namely the construction of this bridge' – not all in the province were enamoured of the corollary benefits that the link would bring when coupled with Newfoundland's entrance into Confederation.[56]

North Sydney's designation as the hub for shipping goods to Newfoundland via the Canadian National Railway (CNR) was seen as detrimental to Halifax shipping interests. In particular, some in Nova Scotia were concerned that the Maritime Freight Rates Act (MFRA) – which gave a 20 per cent preferential shipping rate to goods shipped from Central Canada to the Maritimes – would be applied to Newfoundland only on the CNR's North Sydney–Port aux Basques route, and would not cover goods shipped via Canadian Pacific Railways or Dominion Atlantic Railways from the Annapolis Valley or Halifax. If the MFRA were applied solely to the CNR route, shippers would avoid shipping through Halifax, where costs would be higher. In other words, the non-application of the MFRA to Halifax-based shipping routes to Newfoundland would harm that city's shipping interests.

These issues were raised most strenuously in the House of Commons by Annapolis Valley Conservative MP George Nowlan.[57] Nowlan was concerned that only goods shipped on the CNR would qualify for the 20 per cent preference, as only the '"water hop" between Cape Breton port and the Newfoundland terminal has been declared to be part of the rail haul, whereas via Halifax is still considered to be an ordinary water route.' As Nowlan stated, 'I am afraid the amendment, as drafted, and I think perhaps narrowly drafted, will give the advantage in such traffic to the Canadian National Railways.'[58]

Transport Minister Lionel Chevrier shied away from directly addressing Nowlan's concern. According to Chevrier, the freight rates structure had been extended to include Newfoundland, and 'he felt sure the Canadian National Railways would file new tariffs and tolls with the Transport Commission on the basis of the general structure of the Maritime region.' If, after that had been done, it was still felt that the MFRA was discriminatory, those affected could 'make application to the board.'[59]

Unsatisfied with the minister's response, Nowlan pressed the attack. 'Frankly,' he stated, 'my particular concern is for the people who were not consulted in this connection, the people who operate and serve the Canadian Pacific Railway and the Dominion Atlantic Railway, who now obtain employment in connection with the movement of goods through Halifax for Newfoundland.'[60] The introduction of the workers of Halifax into his argument prompted Prime Minister Louis St Laurent to join the debate. The prime minister informed Nowlan that since the government had only agreed to supply water transportation between North Sydney and Port aux Basques, water rates from Halifax to Newfoundland were not covered. With regard to those shipping goods from Halifax to Newfoundland, the prime minister stated that 'they are private enterprises and they make their freight rates on a competitive basis.'[61]

Nowlan, still unsatisfied with the government's response, again posed the question. According to him, his concern was to ensure that the preference granted goods under the MFRA would also apply to goods shipped from Halifax. He contended that if preference were not granted to Halifax, shipping from that port to Newfoundland would dry up. The prime minister replied rather feebly that the Board of Transport Commissioners would have to consider this: 'I do not think we can go beyond that.'[62] This response prompted even Liberal members from Nova Scotia to voice their concerns. Halifax Liberal MP Gordon Isnor asked whether Halifax would 'lose anything' upon Newfoundland's entry. St Laurent replied, 'I hope you will not.' But, he continued, Newfoundlanders might prefer to ship goods to Canada via the shorter North Sydney–Port aux Basques route, and 'I do not think we can prevent that.'[63]

The amount of interest in this question prompted former Progressive Conservative leader John Bracken to ask the prime minister flatly if 'there [were] anything in the agreement which prejudices the position of Halifax as compared with Sydney in the matter of business going through those ports respectively?' St Laurent responded that he could not predict which route would be more popular. Cape Breton CCF MP Clarie Gillis saw a good chance to score a few points with his constituents, arguing that shippers would still prefer Halifax over Cape Breton because of the 'outmoded railroad' to Sydney. In Gillis's view, goods shipped from Central Canada would still be routed through Halifax, largely owing to the lack of a permanent link across the Strait of Canso.[64]

Still others joined the debate. According to Halifax Liberal MP John Dickey, there was nothing in the Newfoundland Act that affected the MFRA. For Dickey, the long journey from Port aux Basques to St John's would prove to be the great equalizer; he suggested that the competitive position of Halifax-based shippers would remain strong as Newfoundland merchants on the Avalon Peninsula would likely choose to ship direct from Halifax.[65] Dickey believed that even if Halifax were discriminated against by the MFRA, it would be best to deal with it after Confederation was a *fait accompli*. Prime Minister St Laurent agreed, suggesting that the MFRA's applicability to goods shipped from Halifax would be further examined after Newfoundland joined Confederation.[66]

The *Halifax Chronicle Herald* was quick to offer its view on the MFRA's application to the North Sydney–Port aux Basques route. The paper opposed the move, claiming that it would harm the city's shipping interests. As a 19 February 1949 editorial stated:

> Some may say there is precedent for application of the Maritime Freight Rates Act to the North Sydney–Port aux Basques water link – application of the provisions of the act to the Prince Edward Island–Mainland water link. But there is no precedent there. What operates between Tormentine and Borden is a car-ferry, carrying loaded railway cars without breaking bulk. A more accurate comparison is the water link between Digby and Saint John – and to this water link the provisions of the Maritime Freight Rates Act do not apply.[67]

An editorial published two days later made the case even more forcefully:

> For the purposes of railway rate-making and the application of the provisions of the Maritime Freight Rates Act, a phantom railway line is being laid across the Gulf of the St. Lawrence connecting the raw termini on the Cape Breton and Newfoundland seaboards.

Feeling that the application of the MFRA to the North Sydney–Port aux Basques route discriminated against Halifax shippers, the editor asked,

> What of the non-Government railways and the private steamship lines which operate, say, to and from the port of Halifax? Where do they fit in this new situation?[68]

The editor again was using a suspect line of reasoning in comparing the route to Newfoundland with the route across the Bay of Fundy to Digby – after all, goods shipped to Digby did qualify under the MFRA if they were shipped along a solely land-based route, which was not an option for goods shipped to Newfoundland. Even so, it is clear that some Haligonians had concerns about the impact that Newfoundland's entry into Confederation would have on the city's economy.

Halifax shippers did not have to wait until after Newfoundland's entry to find out what the railway rates through North Sydney would be. On 22 March 1949, these rates were announced, and they surely did not please Halifax shippers. Rates for goods shipped from Port aux Basques to St John's on the Newfoundland Railway would drop, and be essentially on par with seaborne shipping rates from Halifax to the Newfoundland capital. Some goods, such as feed, onions, and carrots, would be cheaper if shipped by rail (though flour would be more expensive). With goods shipped by rail covered by the MFRA, there would seemingly be no reason for Canadian exporters or Newfoundland importers to ship through Halifax.[69]

The news that Halifax shippers would not be covered by the MFRA was greeted warmly in Cape Breton. As *Sydney Post-Record* editor Duchemin wrote about the freight rate controversy:

> The request of Mr. George Nowlan, Progressive Conservative member for Digby-Annapolis-Kings, and Mr. Gordon Isnor, Liberal member for Halifax, that the 20 per cent reduction be also applied to all-water shipments from Halifax to Newfoundland was rejected most emphatically by Prime Minister St. Laurent and Transport Minister Chevrier for reasons so obvious and sensible that they must carry conviction to any unbiased mind.[70]

In the editor's view, there was no reason for the federal government to subsidize a private shipping company that was carrying private freight for private profit. What is more, the editor sagely pointed out, if the MFRA were applied to goods shipped to Newfoundland from Halifax, it would also have to be applied to goods shipped from Saint John, Pictou, Charlottetown, Summerside – indeed, from any Canadian port east of Diamond Junction, Quebec.[71] The issue of the MFRA's applicability to the North Sydney–Port aux Basques route divided Haligonians and Cape Bretoners and tainted their respective views of Newfoundland's entry into Confederation.

Competition and Cooperation in the Fishery

One of the earliest expressions of Nova Scotian support for Newfoundland's entry into Confederation revolved around the fishery. Lunenburg pharmacist J.J. Kinley, a former MP and MLA who had been appointed to the Canadian Senate in 1945 by Prime Minister William Lyon Mackenzie King, endorsed Newfoundland's entry during the debate on the 1946 Throne Speech. 'In the Maritimes,' Kinley stated, 'there is a feeling that Newfoundland is a competitor with us in the fishing business. The very fact that we produce the same goods and compete in a world market is a reason why we should get together and work together.' Kinley believed that with union, the Newfoundland market would expand, resulting in 'a stronger Canada.'[72] With this statement he adroitly got to the heart of the fishery relationship between Nova Scotia and Newfoundland. While there was competition between fishers of the two jurisdictions, there was also a good deal of cooperation. Rather like the Halifax shipping industry in terms of its concerns regarding the MFRA, it seems that Nova Scotia's fishing interests did not view Newfoundland's Confederation unfavourably – they had, after all, long competed with Newfoundland. Some, however, worried about the actual ramifications of union and wanted steps implemented to protect their interests.

The fisheries of Nova Scotia and Newfoundland were intricately linked. Nova Scotians and Newfoundlanders fished for the same products and often with the same men. Newfoundlanders had long been crossing the Cabot Strait to work in the Nova Scotia fishery, and many Nova Scotia fishing settlements – such as Ingonish, Neil's Harbour, and New Haven – had large populations of Newfoundlanders. What is more, Newfoundlanders or their descendants formed the bulk of the fishers in industrial Cape Breton towns such as North Sydney and Glace Bay. The impact of Newfoundland fishers was felt as far south as Lunenburg. In 1920, only 3 of that town's 1,240 fishers hailed from Newfoundland.[73] Twenty years later, Lunenburg's fishing fleet included 170 Newfoundlanders, down from a peak of 400.[74]

The Nova Scotia fishery's reaction to Newfoundland's Confederation was rooted in the events of recent decades. The 1930s saw a precipitous drop in the value of fish. In 1924, saltfish sold for $8.60 per quintal; by 1939, the price was $4.00.[75] The disastrous downturn in the saltfishery during the 1930s was in large measure remedied by the Second World War, which drove up both the demand and the price for saltfish. The war also brought cooperation among saltfish-producing nations striving to supply the wartime market. The war's end, however, brought fears of a rapid downturn in demand for saltfish, which would increase competition among fishing countries and had the potential to recreate the hard times of the previous decade.[76]

Nova Scotia and Newfoundland responded similarly to the 1930s fishery crisis. In Newfoundland the 1933 Amulree Commission recommended a massive restructuring of the fishing industry. In its view, the fishery's decline had been caused by 'unrestricted individualism,' and government regulation and control of the industry was the only viable remedy. To this end, in 1936 the Newfoundland Fisheries Board was created to improve the quality of Newfoundland's fishery output through regular inspection and to oversee the marketplace to prevent price cutting.[77] Recognizing that Newfoundland was undercapitalized, the same commission did not lobby for modern infrastructure or for conversion to the emerging fresh/frozen fishing industry. While it viewed modernization favourably, the commission feared that modernization of the Newfoundland fishery would be too costly for a Newfoundland government that had only recently voted to suspend responsible government owing largely to financial concerns. So instead of subsidizing modernization, the Commission of Government provided Newfoundland's fishers with a series of loans to renovate and build new schooners.[78] Thus equipped, the Newfoundland fishery would remain geared mainly toward the saltfish trade.[79]

Nova Scotia, too, adopted a laissez-faire approach to the 1930s crisis. Between 1930 and 1937 the number of workers engaged in the fishery had expanded by 20 per cent, while the actual value of the fish caught had dropped by over 12 per cent – a development that troubled Nova Scotia Premier Angus L. Macdonald. So bad was the situation that Macdonald even contemplated government control of the fishery, but the scale of such a venture went against his liberal instincts.[80] In 1938 he instituted a modest government bonus program in an effort to revitalize the saltfishery, but to little effect. However, in a move that foreshadowed the direction that the Nova Scotia fishery would soon take, he did court a cold-storage plant deal with General Seafoods, a deal that fell apart amidst fears of a political backlash.[81]

Not until near the end of the Second World War – a conflict that stabilized the fishery – did Newfoundland and Nova Scotia begin to adopt markedly different approaches to the fishery. In 1944, when it was apparent the war would soon end, Nova Scotia Premier A.S. MacMillan commissioned Stewart Bates of the federal Department of Fisheries to prepare a study of the Canadian Atlantic fishing industry for the Nova Scotia Royal Commission on Provincial Reconstruction and Rehabilitation.[82] Bates's report recognized that the Nova Scotia fishery was poorly organized; but in light of the Canadian fishery's commitment to private enterprise, he did not view large-scale government regulation as the answer. To Bates, though, poor organization was not the cause of the malaise in the Nova Scotia fishery. At fault, rather, was the industry's failure to adopt modern food-processing techniques. Other food production industries had implemented systems that carefully graded their products and placed them in grocery store freezers in colourful and attractive packaging. The development of quick-freezing technology in the late 1930s meant that fish fillets could also be marketed in this manner. This, Bates argued, was the course that Nova Scotia's fishery should take, and he recommended the modernization of the Nova Scotia fishery complete with the development of large-scale fishing corporations focused around a half-dozen fishery centres and geared toward the fresh/frozen fish industry.[83]

Bates's recommendations were in line with the thinking of the Department of Fisheries. During the Second World War the Canadian government had embarked on a plan to increase fresh and frozen fish production. To develop the industry, Ottawa increased production by subsidizing the construction of modern fishing vessels. Ottawa's efforts were aided by an upswing in market value for fresh and frozen fish and saltfish. The fresh and frozen fish sector also allowed for greater profit margins, which meant that much of the fish that had previously been salted was now being frozen instead. The result was that by 1945, far more fresh and frozen fish was being produced in Canada than had been the case prior to the conflict; production was nearing what contemporary observer S.A. Beatty termed 'saturation' levels.[84]

The Canadian fresh and frozen fish sector was able to expand so readily in part because it experienced little competition from Newfoundland during the war. The Newfoundland fresh/frozen industry was relatively undeveloped, with the first frozen fillet plant opening only in 1938.[85] As British demand for frozen fish fillets grew during the war, three St John's–based saltfish exporters, prompted by a British contract for 10 million pounds of frozen fillets, began to invest in the new freezing technology and Newfoundland's exports grew from 1.5 million pounds of frozen fish in 1938 and 1939 to 10.5 million pounds in 1940 and 1941.[86] For most of the war, then, Newfoundland exports were destined for the British market. Some Newfoundland frozen fish also entered the American market, but these exports paled compared to the amount of Canadian product being shipped to the United States. In 1945, for example, Newfoundland supplied only 10 per cent of American frozen fish imports while Canada supplied the remainder.[87]

Despite these reassuring figures, the development of modern fresh and frozen fish plants in Newfoundland over the course of the war, combined with the closing of the British market to Newfoundland exports, amplified the perceived threat of Newfoundland fish to Nova Scotia fishers. The Amulree Commission's commitment to the saltfishery had been born of financial necessity, so when private capital was found to develop new fish plants on Newfoundland the Commission of Government was well pleased. These new fish plants were seen as a threat to the Nova Scotia fishery and had the potential to foment division between the two jurisdictions. As some contemporary observers warned, the modern Newfoundland plants 'may lead to intense competition between Nova Scotia and Newfoundland in the event of a general decline in the salt fish trade,' as more fishers would shift production to the fresh/frozen industry.[88] It was feared by many in the Nova Scotian fishery that Newfoundland could potentially supply North America with an additional 100 million pounds of fresh/frozen fish. Such a large influx of Newfoundland fish into the North American market could affect prices drastically, and a 'very serious decline in prices during the summer of 1947' was predicted.[89] Some also feared that the lower standard of living on Newfoundland meant that the operational costs (i.e., salaries) of the Newfoundland plants 'would be abnormally low and therefore more highly competitive.'[90] Confederation, with its promise of improving the standard of living in Newfoundland, would thus offset the advantage enjoyed by the Newfoundland plants because of the island's lower living standards.[91]

Faced with the spectre of unfair competition from Newfoundland, some in Nova Scotia turned their hopes and attentions to the construction of a new, modern fresh/frozen fish plant outside Louisbourg. Convinced by Bates's 1944 modernization recommendations, the Nova Scotia government secured fourteen acres of waterfront land outside Louisbourg on which to build cold storage containers and deep freezing facilities. This 'million dollar' fish processing plant was to be financed jointly by the provincial government and private capital, with 'at least one American firm [having] expressed the desire to come into the scheme.'[92] It was expected that this new plant would greatly increase the province's production of fresh and frozen fish. As contemporary commentators R.D. Howland and D.M. Fraser suggested shortly after Newfoundland entered Confederation, 'in fresh and frozen fish lies the chief hope of future expansion of the Maritime fish products industry, and a degree of qualified optimism seems justified.'[93]

The development of the Louisbourg fish plant, however, met some opposition on Cape Breton Island. Cape Breton fishers who were engaged in the inshore fishery felt that this new plant, designed to serve factory trawlers, would undermine their livelihoods. They believed that the proposed plant would benefit fishing plant owners at the expense of the province's fishers. The fishers' dissent came to a head at a meeting in Louisbourg in October 1948, where they lashed out at the plan to build a modern cold storage plant in the community. Chief among their fears was that the proposed plant would serve 'the Pierces of Boston, the Gorton-Pew of Gloucester and a Halifax trawler fleet' at their expense.[94]

At their meeting, the Cape Breton fishers offered a number of reasons why the plant should not be built. First, they believed it would be the 'death-blow' to the inshore fishery because it would shift the focus from a small-scale, low-capital inshore fishery to a large-scale, high-capital ocean fishery characterized by factory trawlers and widespread foreign investment. Second, the fishers suggested that since responsibility for the fishery rested with Ottawa, the provincial government was overstepping its jurisdiction in agreeing to finance the venture. Third, if the plant were constructed it would have undesirable effects, since the factory trawlers that would be supplying the facility would be contributing to overfishing, to the detriment of all fishers.[95]

The fishers were also quick to use Newfoundland's Confederation as reason to oppose the new plant. Since negotiations were underway for Newfoundland's entry, the fishers suggested, 'it is a breach of faith with these people who when voting for Confederation had in mind the benefits of fishing from Canadian ports and belonging to a country which followed a same policy of conservation by its restriction of trawlers and draggers.'[96] In the end, the Cape Breton fishers blamed Halifax for their problems, as they 'generally agreed that The Minister of Industry acted in good faith but with his limited knowledge of the Fisheries he was easily deceived by the Halifax fish barons and their fellow-travellers in their get-rich-quick racket at the expense of the workers.'[97] Clearly, there was disagreement between the fishers of Cape Breton and those of the Halifax/South Shore area regarding the postwar direction of the fishery, and the Cape Bretoners were willing to use Newfoundland's entry to justify their demands.[98]

Despite the opposition from the Cape Breton inshore fishers, the modern fresh/frozen fish industry was here to stay. But as the Louisbourg fish plant example illustrates, this industry, reliant on technological innovations, was still trying to overcome a certain stigma. Modern trawling was seen as deleterious to the fish stock and fishers; moreover, the fish caught by this method were perceived as inferior. In the past, fish was frozen only when it had deteriorated in quality to such an extent that it could no longer be sold as fresh. Moreover, even when fish was frozen soon after being caught, if it took too long to come to market it lost much of its flavour. This meant that any area that could catch and freeze fish and get it to market quickly had an advantage. As S.A. Beatty contended,

> the east coast Canadian fishery is the only region on the North American continent that can fulfil these conditions throughout the year. The American fleet is too far from the banks to land fish of consistently high quality. The Newfoundland ... fish cannot be shipped to the market as fast as it is frozen without such small shipment as to increase transportation costs unduly.[99]

Thus the underdeveloped state of the Newfoundland fresh/frozen fish industry in the years preceding Confederation prevented it from being viable competition to the Nova Scotia product; this accounts for the latter industry's neutrality regarding Newfoundland's entry. As the minutes of an October 1948 meeting of the Halifax Board of Trade make clear, 'no official opinion has been expressed regarding the fish exporting situation should Newfoundland come into Confederation, but some shippers consider satisfactory arrangements can be made whereby prices can be made firm with very little more competition than at present.'[100] Unfortunately for Nova Scotia's fishing interests, it was only after Confederation – and as a direct result of the union and federal support for the expansion of the Newfoundland fresh/frozen fish sector – that Newfoundland emerged as strong competition to Nova Scotia in this sector.[101]

So, the Nova Scotia fresh/frozen fish industry seemed detached from its Newfoundland competitors. In contrast, the Newfoundland and Nova Scotia saltfish industries tried to cooperate during the postwar years. During a visit to Puerto Rico early in 1946, J.M. McKee, secretary to the Canadian Atlantic Saltfish Exporters Association (CASEA), established 'cordial relations' with representatives of the Newfoundland fishery, proposing that a Unity of Action arrangement be set up between the two jurisdictions. This arrangement simply meant that the Newfoundland Fisheries Board and CASEA would cooperate on matters of mutual concern. In McKee's words, Nova Scotia and Newfoundland would be compelled to make plans 'on the basis of understanding and co-operation ... instead of the basis of cut throat competition.'[102]

Inspired by the idea of mutual cooperation, representatives of the Canadian and Newfoundland saltfish industries met in St John's in early December 1946 for informal discussions. One idea put forward at the conference was for the establishment of a Central Office in London, where European markets for Newfoundland and Canadian saltfish could be courted. Another was for Newfoundland and Canada to cooperate in selling to the West Indies market, which was purchasing more and more of its saltfish from Norway and Iceland. While nothing concrete came from this meeting, the Canadians and Newfoundlanders pledged to foster cooperation in the saltfish trade.[103]

The roots of conflict between some Nova Scotia saltfish interests and those of Newfoundland may have been sown at this St John's meeting. While in Newfoundland, the Canadian representatives had a first-hand look at the operations of the Newfoundland Fisheries Board, the administrative unit recommended by the Amulree Commission and established by the Commission of Government to regulate the saltfish market. This regulatory system licensed all saltfish exporters, whose premises had to be inspected and meet certain standards. Moreover, contracts were entered into by the board – individual exporters were not allowed to sign contracts on their own. This ensured that the board regulated both shipments and prices to guarantee that Newfoundland saltfish did not flood the market in times of abundance. The market was thereby stabilized.[104]

Many of the Nova Scotians in St John's were intrigued by this system. Before his visit to Newfoundland, Lunenburg's F.H. Zwicker had not been 'altogether sold' on the Newfoundland marketing program; on seeing it in operation, he was '98% in favour of the scheme.'[105] Zwicker was supported on this issue by another Nova Scotian, Fletcher Smith of A.M. Smith & Co., who recommended that CASEA consider adopting a marketing plan similar to Newfoundland's. A potential flaw in the application of the Newfoundland marketing plan to Nova Scotia was pointed out by G.G. Harnish, a fisherman from Hubbards. Harnish predicted that some in Nova Scotia would oppose such a scheme. For example, many of the fish exporters operating in Lunenburg had their own sources of supply – they had their own fleets – and they would likely not favour a controlled selling environment. Their investment in their fleets allowed them to sell their processed fish at lower prices than their competitors while maintaining similar profit margins. A fixed marketing program would end their ability to undersell their competitors. Still others at the meeting were caught up in the postwar paranoia surrounding communism – this was, after all, the time of the Gouzenko Affair and of a bitter strike at Halifax-based National Sea Products[106] – and viewed the Newfoundland marketing program as 'complete government control' and therefore undesirable. Despite these concerns, CASEA moved that 'we recommend the principle of the Newfoundland marketing scheme of salt fish products in a form adaptable to Canada's needs.'[107]

Harnish's concerns were prescient. On 20 January 1947, O.F. MacKenzie, president of Halifax Fisheries Limited, wrote to his good friend Angus L. Macdonald to complain about the direction the province's fishery seemed to be taking.[108] In particular, MacKenzie did not like the prospect of applying the Newfoundland fish marketing system to Canada. He railed against the 'totalitarian practices in Nfld.' and pledged to fight the 'application of a so-called planned economy' to the Canadian fishery. Recognizing that the adoption in Nova Scotia of such a marketing scheme would require the premier's approval, he cautioned Macdonald regarding the dire effects of such a move, warning that it 'would probably mean the disappearance of salt fish export houses from the Halifax waterfront with the next decade.'[109] MacKenzie reiterated this point more forcefully in a late 1947 speech in which he strongly criticized the Newfoundland system: 'Whether you arrive at this goal [the Newfoundland marketing scheme] by a communist, socialist or fascist route, does not matter much as the end results will be the same, namely, complete loss of both your economic and political freedom.'[110] For some Nova Scotia fish exporters, Newfoundland's entry into Confederation – and the threat of Nova Scotia adopting its supposedly communist/socialist/fascist marketing system – would have undesirable consequences.

Nova Scotia, Newfoundland, and Provincial Rights

It is difficult to assess how much help Angus L. Macdonald was willing to give O.F. MacKenzie, for the Nova Scotia premier was careful not to express a public opinion on Newfoundland. Macdonald would have been concerned about the loss of the saltfish trade, but he was surely aware that the trend was toward modernization and the fresh/frozen fish industry. He was, after all, the premier who had approved the provincial government's investment in the modern Louisbourg fish plant.[111] And though he was no friend of undue government regulation – indeed, he was committed to decentralization and liberalism – it is uncertain that he would risk any action that might lead to claims that he was against the union.[112] There were too many expatriate Newfoundland voters living in his province for a politician as shrewd as Macdonald to publicly state his opinion on union one way or the other.

In private, however, Macdonald had some serious misgivings about the union. Though as a former professor of law at Dalhousie he was pleased that so many of that school's graduates were among the leaders of Newfoundland's pro-confederates – of the seven-man official delegation sent from Newfoundland to Ottawa to finalize the terms of union, five (J.A. Walsh, Philip Gruchy, John B. McEvoy, Gordon Bradley, H.G. Puddester) were graduates of Dalhousie's Law School – he remained concerned about some of the financial implications of the union.[113] Despite his reservations, Macdonald attempted to use Newfoundland's entry to further his fight against the centralization of power in Ottawa by claiming that the merger warranted consultation with the provinces at a dominion–provincial conference.

Following his return to the Nova Scotia premiership in the autumn of 1945, after his wartime tenure as Canada's Minister of War for Air Services, Macdonald became the country's most ardent and principled champion of provincial rights. As Stephen Henderson has suggested, Macdonald's 'career as premier, his federal war service, and his acknowledged understanding of constitutional issues' lent him an authority on the subject that belied his province's size and wealth.[114] Macdonald used this authority to try to counter the King government's centralizing tendencies during the years that followed the Second World War, and when Newfoundland began contemplating entry into Canadian Confederation, he was quick to use that development to reinforce his provincial rights arguments.

Perhaps Macdonald's greatest struggle with Ottawa over provincial rights revolved around the 1945–6 Dominion–Provincial Conference.[115] The federal government came to this conference with a sweeping set of initiatives in the fields of health, old age pensions, and unemployment relief. In return for the provinces allowing the federal government exclusive access to personal income taxes, corporation taxes, and succession duties – concessions the provinces had already temporarily made in the Wartime Tax Agreement – Ottawa put forward a substantial social welfare package, the 'Green Book,' which promised universal old age pensions and health insurance. As an added enticement to the provinces, Ottawa also proposed a fairly generous subsidy proposal based on population and taxation capacity. Under the proposed subsidy arrangement, Nova Scotia would receive a grant of $12 per capita, to be adjusted annually to account for growth in gross national product or provincial population. The guaranteed revenue from Ottawa, combined with the expansion of the social welfare net, made the proposals very attractive for the smaller provinces. A deadlock between the federal government and Ontario soon arose, however, prompting the conference to be adjourned *sine die*. With the failure of the conference, the dominion set out to negotiate tax agreements with the provinces on an ad hoc basis.

Most of the provinces quickly entered into tax rental agreements with the federal government, the sole hold-outs being Ontario, Quebec, and Nova Scotia. Ontario and Quebec's opposition stemmed from the lacklustre financial impact the agreement would have on their revenues; Nova Scotia's was rooted in something more principled. Even though the agreement would improve his province's coffers, Macdonald resisted signing a tax rental agreement for he did not want to surrender any of his province's constitutional rights. The conflict became one between the forces of centralization on the one hand and those of provincial rights on the other. In Macdonald's view, the postwar trend toward centralization was weakening the poorer provinces' autonomy.[116] As the *Halifax Chronicle* argued in words that the Nova Scotia premier would surely have endorsed, 'we want nothing to do with any proposal to exchange what remains of our birthright for a slightly increased mess of federal potage.'[117]

For fourteen months Macdonald refused to enter into an agreement with Ottawa; meanwhile, he put forward a series of counter-proposals. In return for granting Ottawa exclusive rights to income and inheritance taxes, Macdonald wanted guarantees that certain provincial fields of revenue – gasoline, electricity, and amusement taxes – would be vacated by the federal government. He proposed that fiscal need, and not a per capita formula, be the basis of all federal subsidies and grants to the provinces. Finally, Macdonald insisted on annual dominion–provincial conferences at which the parties could discuss matters of shared jurisdiction. Eventually Ottawa agreed to excuse itself from gasoline taxes – the only concession to Macdonald's demands – and in April 1947, Macdonald signed a tax agreement with Ottawa.

Despite having entered into an agreement with Ottawa, Macdonald continued to press his demands, and he soon incorporated Newfoundland's Confederation into his arguments. While he could not use the potential union to pressure the government to vacate such fields as electricity or amusement taxes, he *could* use it to try to get the idea of annual federal–provincial conferences back on the bargaining table. Macdonald had long supported the idea of fixed, annual dominion–provincial conferences. As early as 1938 he had proposed the idea to the Rowell-Sirois Commission, and in the late 1940s he began to use Newfoundland's pending Confederation as further justification.[118] The proposed union, Macdonald claimed, presented an ideal opportunity for provincial consultation. As the Nova Scotia premier detailed in a 26 August 1947 speech to the provincial legislature:

> There are now, and there have been for some time, discussions proceeding between a delegation from Newfoundland and representatives of the federal government. What stage these discussions have reached, I do not know, but before a final decision is reached I think that all the nine provinces should be consulted ... The Sirois Commission recommended yearly conferences between the Dominion and the Provinces, and the Provinces themselves, or most of them at any rate, have urged the holding of annual conferences. The admission of Newfoundland to Confederation is a subject that could well form a topic for discussion at such a conference.[119]

While Macdonald was careful to mention in this speech that he was neither 'for [n]or against' Newfoundland's admission to Confederation, it is clear that he did have some reservations about the merger.

Macdonald was concerned with the potential provincial cousin's debt allowance. He believed that Newfoundland's debt allowance would be based on faulty population estimates and on the artificial inflation of the colony's economy that had occurred as a result of the wartime boom in the fishery. 'Whatever is done in this regard,' he said, 'ought to be done realistically and not by the use of fictions as have been followed in certain cases, such as the assumption that the population of a province was greater than it really was, or that a province had a debt when it actually had no debt.'[120] Of even greater importance to Macdonald was Newfoundland's ability to meet its expected expenditures as a province if it were to join Confederation. He feared that Newfoundland would be able to raise only about $4,500,000 through local taxation, an amount far below its expected expenditures of $14,500,000. Unless Newfoundland was prepared to resort to unusually heavy local taxation – a virtual impossibility given that

Newfoundland had no income tax prior to Confederation and after entry only gradually introduced this tax – this deficit or gap of $10,000,000 between its total receipts and total expenditures could be made up only by the Dominion treasury. 'And a grant that size,' claimed the Nova Scotia premier publicly, 'would be larger, relatively, than the grants awarded to any other province under the Dominion-Provincial financial arrangements recently concluded.'[121]

In private, Macdonald had even harsher words for the proposed union. Writing to his close friend and former cabinet colleague Charles 'Chubby' Power, Macdonald posited that 'it is all very well if a young fellow wants to marry and move away from the family home and support his wife by himself, but if he proposes to bring the girl into the family and if the family has to support her, that is another matter.'[122] While Macdonald shrewdly refrained from explicitly endorsing or opposing the union in this letter, it seems clear that at the very least, he was not enamoured of the way the union was being carried out without provincial consultation or of its potential impact on the provinces. These concerns reinforced his conviction that 'the nine provinces now constituting the Dominion should be consulted before the 10th province is brought into Confederation.'[123]

Despite Macdonald's spirited fight, the federal government turned a deaf ear to his concerns. The provinces did not need to be consulted since the British North America Act had already made provision for Newfoundland's entry. What is more, the federal government had already investigated the necessity of consulting the provinces and concluded that since the provinces had not been consulted when Prince Edward Island or British Columbia were admitted to union, and since Section 146 of the BNA Act, which provided for the admission of Newfoundland into Confederation, made no mention of provincial consultation, a dominion–provincial conference to discuss the matter was unnecessary.[124] This line of argument held little sway with the Nova Scotia premier. 'It is all very well to point out as someone at Ottawa pointed out some time ago, that the British North America Act makes a provision for admission of Newfoundland,' said Macdonald, but 'the BNA Act makes provision for a great many things which in practice have only been done after consultation with provinces ... Failure to consult the provinces now will, I am afraid, lead to difficulties later.'[125] The premier's harsh words had little impact on his Ottawa confidant Chubby Power, who confessed to Macdonald that only real reason to 'annex' Newfoundland was for national defence and that the provinces need not be consulted on what was 'purely a defence matter.'[126]

Macdonald remained committed to the idea of a dominion–provincial conference to discuss Newfoundland's Confederation. In February 1949 he received an unlikely ally in the fight for such a conference. George Drew, who was premier of Ontario during the Dominion–Provincial Conference of 1945–6, had recently replaced John Bracken as leader of the federal Progressive Conservatives. On 14 February 1949, Drew moved in the House of Commons that the provinces be consulted 'before the Imperial Parliament was asked to amend the British North America Act to provide for Newfoundland's entry into Confederation.' Drew was concerned that amending the BNA Act to allow for Newfoundland's entry could set a dangerous precedent: that the constitution could be amended with a simple parliamentary majority. This motion was promptly attacked by both Prime Minister Louis St Laurent and CCF leader M.J. Coldwell. Likewise, Justice Minister Stuart Garson lashed out at Drew's motion, denying that there was any need or grounds to consult with the provinces on the matter, though Garson 'was hampered in his argument by a disposition evident on former occasion to give Newfoundland the new name of "New Zealand."'[127]

Despite Garson's proclivity for misremembering the new province's name, the Liberal government outmanoeuvred Drew. Near the end of the debate on Drew's amendment, two Quebec Liberal MPs, Wilfrid Lacroix and J.F. Pouliot, added a subamendment demanding not only that the provinces be consulted, but also that unanimous consent be secured from them before Newfoundland could enter Confederation. In essence, the Lacroix–Pouliot subamendment would have granted the provinces a veto over Newfoundland's Confederation only a month and a half before the union's consummation and would set a precedent for provincial consultation prior to any amendment to the BNA Act. Thoroughly outmanoeuvred, Drew was forced to vote against his own proposed legislation; and Newfoundland's Confederation was effected – much to Macdonald's chagrin – without a federal–provincial conference to discuss the matter.[128]

Conclusion

Though Macdonald had some misgivings about Newfoundland's entry, once union was complete he was quick to welcome his province's new North Atlantic cousin. Always the consummate politician, he was careful to state that 'he did not stand for or against Newfoundland's admission to Confederation,' and he emphasized the 'close bond between the Old Colony and this Province.' On 31 March 1949 the Nova Scotia premier introduced a resolution of welcome to the new province in his legislature. The resolution, seconded by the province's CCF Leader of the Opposition Russell Cunningham, passed unanimously. Said Cunningham on the union, 'let us hope that the entry of Newfoundland into the Canadian union will be conducive to an era of expansion and prosperity never before witnessed in our new island province and our Maritime region.'[129]

Macdonald's wary acceptance of Newfoundland's Confederation reflects that of Nova Scotia as a whole. Most Nova Scotians seemed reluctant to publicly endorse or oppose the pending union. Also, some parts of the province supported Newfoundland's entry to a greater extent than did others. Cape Breton, for example, with its large expatriate Newfoundlander population, seemed predisposed to favour the merger. That island's support seems even more understandable when one considers that many Cape Bretoners tried to use Newfoundland's Confederation to protect the inshore fishery and as justification for industrial development programs. Such efforts, however, met with mixed results. Cape Bretoners were able to secure a permanent crossing across the Strait of Canso, but their efforts to revitalize the Sydney steel industry fell short.

Likewise, Halifax had some concerns about the merger. The city's shipping interests worried that Newfoundland's entry, combined with the application of the MFRA to goods shipped only through North Sydney, would hurt both their trade with the new province and their bottom line. Similarly, some in the province's saltfish industry believed that Newfoundland's entry would lead to the application of Newfoundland's fish marketing system, which they feared could undermine their financial position. Despite these vested interests, most Nova Scotians, like their New Brunswick and PEI cousins, displayed a sense of interested ambivalence with regard to Newfoundland's entry into Confederation.

3 '... both islands would benefit': Prince Edward Island and Newfoundland's Entry into Confederation

On 4 April 1949, just four days after Newfoundland joined Canada, an editorial published in the *Summerside Journal* summarized Prince Edward Island's position on the union: 'The natural resources of Newfoundland are limited, and the population is small. Extensive agricultural development has not been possible due to the generally unfavourable soil and climatic conditions: Newfoundland, twenty times as large as Prince Edward Island, has only one-fifth of the croplands of this small province.' This, coupled with the new province's lack of industrialization, meant that 'for the bulk of its food and consumer goods, Newfoundland depends upon imports ... with Canada at present supplying almost two-thirds of Newfoundland's imports.' The editor recognized that despite Newfoundland's poverty and import dependency, its entry into Confederation might benefit Prince Edward Islanders: 'It is hoped with Newfoundland's entry into the Dominion that a new era of prosperity may begin with our own Island sharing largely as the result.'[1]

Prince Edward Island's support of Newfoundland's entry into Confederation stemmed from the belief of Walter Jones, premier of the province from 1943 to 1953, that union would benefit PEI economically. Newfoundland had long been a steady purchaser of PEI agricultural output, and Premier Jones wanted to keep it that way. During the Second World War, when it looked as if inter-island commerce would be sacrificed to wartime trade and shipping controls, Jones tried to manage the situation by appointing William Agnew, son of former Island Liberal MLA John Agnew, as the province's official trade agent in Newfoundland. Agnew would be kept busy courting the Newfoundland market, as issues relating to trade and shipping continued to define the postwar relationship between these two islands. While some Islanders had concerns regarding the union's impact on PEI, this opposition was small in scale and quickly muted; for most Prince Edward Islanders, Newfoundland was an important purchaser of PEI goods to be warmly welcomed into Confederation.

The PEI Report on Newfoundland's Confederation

The importance of the Newfoundland market to the economy of PEI is revealed by the simple fact that PEI was the sole Maritime province to commission a report on what effect Newfoundland's entry into Confederation would have on the provincial economy. In 1950, William Agnew, still PEI's trade agent in the new province, presented his report to J.O.C. Campbell, Deputy Minister of PEI's Department of Industry and Natural Resources. In five pages Agnew succinctly summed up the Island's past and predicted future trade with Newfoundland. He noted that Island exports to Newfoundland 'for the year 1949 compare favourably with 1948' and that beef and dairy cattle exports across the Cabot Strait continued 'at high level,' as did shipments of dairy products and, for much of the year, eggs.[2] In an approving tone, the PEI trade agent detailed how, 'when Newfoundland joined Confederation on March 31, 1949, all restrictions were removed, no export permits were required.'[3]

This change in tariff policy, combined with the fact that Confederation directly improved the purchasing power of Newfoundlanders by making them part of the Canadian social security net, prompted exporters from across Canada to flood Newfoundland hotels in search of new markets; and many Ontario, Quebec, New Brunswick, and Nova Scotia merchants offered to sell agricultural produce and dairy products at prices lower than those offered by PEI.[4] Despite this increased competition and the undercutting of PEI prices, Agnew was not overly concerned about Confederation's impact on PEI–Newfoundland trade. As he explained in his report, he was 'not at all alarmed that the other provinces will take away our trade, as I found that Newfoundland people liked trading with Prince Edward Islanders providing we give them what they want when they want it, quality, at competitive prices.'[5] PEI's optimism surrounding the continuation of the Newfoundland trade had much to do with the relationship that Jones and Agnew had fostered between the two islands during the Second World War.

The Wartime Experience

The interest in the Newfoundland market shown by Jones stemmed from changes that had occurred in both PEI and Newfoundland over the course of the Second World War. The middle decades of the twentieth century saw the rise of modern industrial agriculture in PEI.[6] As historian Wayne MacKinnon has suggested, mechanization and the use of fertilizers and pesticides increased production but had also resulted in larger, more specialized, highly capitalized farms that were vulnerable to external economic pressures.[7] Moreover, Island farmers were producing more with fewer people. The outbreak of the Second World War prompted Canadians to enlist in droves, and Prince Edward Islanders were no exception. With many able-bodied Islanders bound for the front, there were fewer people available to work Island farms. Between 1941 and 1951 the number of Islanders engaged in agriculture fell from 16,661 to 12,943.[8] This decline affected what Islanders produced. For example, with fewer hands on the farm there was a shift from labour-intensive dairy farming to less labour-intensive pursuits such as the raising of beef cattle. This increased the relative importance of the Island's beef cattle industry.[9]

Agricultural modernization also altered the shipping of PEI goods. To transport Island output to distant markets, larger, more modern methods of transport were needed; as a result, reliance on the traditional coasting schooners that sailed between various outports declined. Modern shipping, where bulk carriers concentrated at a central location with specially designed wharves, became an essential feature of agricultural trade. For Walter Jones the Newfoundland trade presented an opportunity to have his proverbial cake and eat it too. His government strove to reinvigorate the traditional PEI coastal trade with Newfoundland outports, while also seeking to secure modern shipping for the Charlottetown–St John's route. This quest proved to be one of the defining features of the PEI–Newfoundland relationship during the 1940s and early 1950s, one that contributed to Island support for Newfoundland's Confederation.

Newfoundland, too, underwent profound changes in the 1940s. As indicated in chapter 1, Canada and the United States invested heavily in Newfoundland during the war, building military bases across the island and employing many Newfoundlanders in well-paying jobs. This wartime investment increased the demand for foodstuffs in Newfoundland to unprecedented heights. The significant number of foreign service personnel placed stress on the colony's food supplies; moreover, the money spent by the military increased Newfoundlanders' capacity to purchase imported foodstuffs. Some PEI companies profited from Newfoundland's heightened wartime demand. For example, Summerside's Ideal Dairy shipped by U.S. military plane as much as 2,000 gallons of pasteurized milk per week to Harmon Air Base.[10] Most Islanders, however, found it difficult to take full advantage of Newfoundland's increased purchasing power because the war had created an unprecedented demand for ships, large and small; this in turn decreased the shipping capacity available to PEI–Newfoundland trade. Shipping demands curtailed PEI's ability to transport goods across the Cabot Strait; at the same time, the issuing of large numbers of 'essentiality certificates' – the wartime import/export permits required of almost all foodstuffs shipped from Canada to Newfoundland – to companies not entrenched in the Newfoundland market further eroded PEI's competitive position.[11] As a result, Central Canadian firms such as Canada Packers strengthened their hold on the Newfoundland market.[12] In part because of this decreased shipping capacity and increased bureaucratic regulation, 1945 saw PEI's cash income from farming decline by 2 per cent, whereas the rest of Canada witnessed a 25 per cent increase.[13]

The Farmer Premier

Fortunately for Island farmers, Walter Jones was their premier when wartime pressures threatened their access to the Newfoundland market. A well-educated farmer with experience in exporting beef cattle to Newfoundland, Jones was a shrewd and purposeful politician. After receiving his BA from Acadia University in 1904, he briefly taught on the Island, before furthering his education at the Ontario Agricultural College, from which he graduated in 1909. He then moved to the United States, where he taught at Virginia's Hampton Agricultural Institute, leaving that position to become Assistant Superintendent of the U.S. Government Experimental Agricultural Farm in Arlington, Virginia. In 1913, Jones returned to PEI eager to apply his formal scientific training to farming. He experimented with cattle breeding and was so successful that one of his Holsteins, Abegweit Milady, set world records for milk and butterfat production. His farming prowess was recognized in May 1935, when he was awarded the King's Silver Jubilee Medal for his contributions to agriculture.[14]

The same year, he was elected to the PEI Legislature. Though success-ful in the election, Jones was, for a time, relegated to the backbenches by a Liberal Party that was wary of his flirtation with the Progressives in the 1921 federal election. Not until he became premier in 1943 did Jones formally become part of the Liberal establishment. Casting himself as the 'Farmer Premier,' he soon earned the respect of many people on the agriculture-dependent Island.[15]

As the 'Farmer Premier,' Jones committed himself fully to a revital-ization of the PEI–Newfoundland trade. His success in this endeavour would prompt him to champion Newfoundland's entry into Confeder-ation. Indeed, one of the eighteen planks of Jones's Liberal platform for the 1943 PEI provincial election was that 'the Newfoundland trade ... will be encouraged vigorously.'[16] Two years later, PEI incorporated trade with Newfoundland into its postwar reconstruction plans.[17] In particular, Jones's government tried to assist small shippers in setting up businesses that used 'small, diesel-engine craft for coastal shipping, since these can slip in and out of the shallow harbors in the province and Newfoundland, where much of the trade is expected to develop.'[18] The Island government pledged as part of its reconstruction plan to secure cargos for the Newfoundland market, and it contemplated the development of a limestone quarry and crushing plant in Newfound-land so that Island shippers would not have to return empty-handed from their voyages. This plan had the added benefit of providing Island farmers with a cheap source of limestone for fertilizer.[19]

Jones's commitment to the Newfoundland export trade had merit, as agricultural exports were a pillar of the PEI economy.[20] Shortly after his victory in the 1943 provincial election, Jones took steps to make good on his promise to improve the Newfoundland trade. To that end he appointed William Agnew, author of the 1950 report on Confedera-tion, as the Island's trade representative in Newfoundland.[21] In the spring and summer of 1944, Agnew journeyed across Newfoundland attempting to convince importers, farmers, merchants, and grocers of the merits of buying from PEI. Though PEI cattle dominated Agnew's pitch, he also promoted PEI butter, pork, poultry, eggs, hay, and pota-toes. Over the course of his travels, Agnew discovered that many Newfoundlanders were amenable to purchasing PEI's agricultural products, especially cattle.[22] And Agnew did what he could to make the transfer of cattle from PEI to Newfoundland as easy as possible, by helping farmers and merchants interested in Island livestock to acquire the various permits and certificates necessary for importation.

As Agnew informed Jones with no false modesty, 'if Nfld. never knew P.E.I., it will when I leave.'[23] Agnew's hard work and face-to-face dealings with Newfoundland merchants and importers helped consolidate the PEI–Newfoundland trade relationship. The close economic and personal relationships that Agnew cultivated between the two islands would, it was expected, give PEI a leg up on the competition when Newfoundland entered Confederation. This contributed to PEI's strong endorsement of the union.[24]

The Problem of Shipping

Agnew's success at selling Newfoundlanders on Prince Edward Island produce meant little, however, without a reliable means of transporting goods across the Cabot Strait. The struggle to secure adequate shipping capacity between PEI and Newfoundland was one of the defining features of the mid-century relationship between the two islands, one that persisted into the postwar era. During the war, Island farmers were increasingly obliged to rely on the North Sydney–Port aux Basques ferry, which made three trips weekly. Because most goods shipped from the Canadian mainland to Newfoundland also took this ferry, and because it operated on a first come, first served basis, delays inevitably developed that took a toll on both live cattle and produce. The obvious solution, as the PEI Federation of Agriculture made clear in 1945, was for the provincial government to institute 'a special Prince Edward Island–Newfoundland service under such controls as will insure every shipper, farmer, dealer or cooperative, an opportunity of utilizing the space so provided.'[25] The prolonged quest to secure federal funding for a direct PEI–Newfoundland route occupied much of Jones's time and effort during the 1940s. The energy he expended on this crusade spoke to the importance of Newfoundland in PEI's economic planning and helped consolidate his support for Newfoundland's entry.

In 1944 the absence of a dedicated steamer for the PEI–Newfoundland route prompted Jones to approach Canadian National Railways for assistance in securing such a vessel. Arthur Day, the CNR's Industrial Representative for the Atlantic Region, informed the PEI premier that a Newfoundland Railway boat, chartered from the Montreal Shipping Company, made regular trips from Montreal, was usually about 1,000 tons light, and stopped in North Sydney to take on freight.[26] Jones contacted the Montreal Shipping Company to see whether its boat could call at Charlottetown; unfortunately, the services of the steamer *Henry W. Stone* failed to live up to his expectations. It was unable to carry even 300 tons of Island potatoes, and – contrary to promises – it did not have a deck load and therefore had difficulty accommodating live cattle.[27] Fearing that this poor service would provoke an electoral revolt, Jones again attempted to secure a dedicated ship for the trade. In February 1945, Jones wrote to Oliver Master, Assistant Deputy Minister of Trade and Commerce, making the case for an increased subsidy of between $50,000 and $100,000 for the Charlottetown–St John's route. Jones also requested a $10,000 subsidy for a diesel schooner to trade with Newfoundland's western outports. Despite this active lobbying, Ottawa was content to maintain the status quo, though it did convince the Newfoundland Railway to replace the unsatisfactory *Henry W. Stone* with the steamer *John Cabot*, which would make three trips every two months for a subsidy of $4,500 per voyage. Unfortunately for the PEI premier, the *John Cabot* did not solve the Island's shipping woes. By November 1945, Jones was complaining to Minister of Reconstruction C.D. Howe that the $4,500 subsidy per voyage for the *John Cabot* was simply too high for a steamer of such limited use. What is more, delays were common, with the result that PEI livestock 'arrives in very poor condition.'[28]

With the conclusion of the war in Europe, Jones began to look at soon to be decommissioned military supply ships for the PEI–Newfoundland trade. He wrote to the Minister of Reconstruction urging him to allocate just such a vessel to the Charlottetown–St John's route. Jones had even selected two he felt were appropriate: the *Mohawk* and the *Beaver*. Jones offered $25,000 for the *Mohawk*, an amount that P.A. Belanger of the Wartime Assets Board's Marine Section considered 'an extremely low price for such a vessel.'[29] Jones ultimately failed to purchase the *Mohawk*, but he did gain something from his discussions with Ottawa – a four-year extension of the previous year's subsidy and Ottawa's commitment to support twelve trips between the two islands at $4,500 per voyage, or an annual subsidy of $54,000. This subsidy was granted without competition to Desmond Clarke, a Toronto-born and Montreal-based businessman with a record of receiving federal assistance to ship to Newfoundland. Clarke soon founded the Inter-Island Steamship Company and began operation of the aptly named *Island Connector*, a diesel schooner that travelled the Charlottetown–St John's route for four years commencing in 1946.[30]

Clarke's *Island Connector* should have improved PEI's ability to ship across the Cabot Strait. It was, after all, a brand new 1,000-ton ship specifically designed to transport livestock, with a top speed of 11 knots. The ship, however, got off to an inauspicious start as Clarke had considerable difficulty getting the vessel up and running. The *Island Connector* was supposed to be ready by early May, but owing to delays at the Vancouver shipyard where it was being built, the vessel did not begin its first Charlottetown–St John's trip until 5 June – something that led Jones to contract with alternative shipping in order to clear up the backlog.[31] This prompted Agnew, PEI's trade agent, to write to J.A. Heenan in February 1947 with some suggestions on how to improve service to PEI for the coming season.[32] Key among his recommendations was that the *Island Connector* should sail from Charlottetown every two weeks rather than every three, at least 'until freeze up.' Once winter made sailing in the Northumberland Strait impossible, the *Island Connector* should load PEI cattle in Halifax every three weeks in order to get the livestock to the Newfoundland market. Heenan responded that the contract could not be altered until it expired in 1949, though he did assure Jones that he would bring the premier's remarks to Clarke's attention.[33] This unsatisfactory experience only strengthened Jones's resolve to secure his own ship for the PEI–Newfoundland route.

Postwar Expansion of Trade

The *Island Connector*'s insufficiencies for the conduct of trade between PEI and Newfoundland was a pressing concern, for it was expected that 1948 would see an increase in agricultural trade between PEI and Newfoundland since Ottawa had agreed to increased allocations of Canadian foodstuffs to Newfoundland for that year.[34] Given the anticipated expansion of PEI–Newfoundland trade, Jones felt it necessary to secure another vessel for this important market, and he began to use Newfoundland's pending entry into Confederation as his justification. On 5 January 1948, Jones was quoted in the *Summerside Journal* as stating that 'if Newfoundland should join Canada ... a weekly and bi-weekly ferry to Corner Brook should be established,' a view the premier later put before his fellow Island politicians.[35] As the PEI premier told the March 1948 session of the PEI legislature, 'a good boat ought to be able to make two trips a week,' and it 'would give the Cornerbrook vicinity a chance to get fresh produce and other commodities

Table 6
Exports from Prince Edward Island to Newfoundland, 1947–50

	1947	1948	1949–50
Swine (head)	6,994	5,938	5,311
Cattle (head)	5,454	4,516	3,993
Calves (head)	1,274	1,112	1,647
Horses (head)	209	88	104
Live poultry (head)	29,500	27,092	28,635
Feed/flour (lbs)	255,000	2,425,100	448,990
Potatoes (bushels)	267,797	347,241	301,000
Vegetables (lbs)	635,900	867,700	1,069,700
Turnips (bushels)	23,877	20,873	32,145
Fruit (lbs)	41,100	338,100	239,400
Cheese (lbs)	42,100	321,500	252,100
Butter (lbs)	39,000	156,400	263,460
Eggs (cases)	6,480	10,593	12,367
Hay (tons)	–	881	826
Milk (gallons)	–	37,000	34,551
Oysters (barrels)	–	89	83
Apples (barrels)	–	138	292
Canned goods (cases)	–	7,877	16,687

Source: Compiled from *Charlottetown Patriot*, 10 March 1949, *Summerside Journal*, 1 April 1949, and Annual Report of the Department of Industry and Natural Resources, Prince Edward Island, *Journal of the Legislative Assembly of Prince Edward Island* (Charlottetown: King's Printer, 1951).

previously lacking because they entered the colony at St. John's.' Moreover, the Corner Brook trade would not be as one-sided as that which was shuttled through St John's. Jones had heard that the lumber camps of western Newfoundland had many horses that were idle during the summer months and that had to be fed hay 'at a cost of $50 a ton.' As Jones told his fellow Island politicians, 'if Newfoundland becomes a province we could ship these horses here, work them and put them in the pasture, and return them in the fall all fattened up. This wouldn't cost anything and both islands would benefit.'[36]

Island export statistics reveal that predictions for increased trade between PEI and Newfoundland in 1948 were prescient. In 1947, PEI shipped 255,000 pounds of flour and feed across the Cabot Strait. In 1948, this grew to 2,425,100 pounds, an approximately 850 per cent increase. Likewise, from 1947 to 1948, potato shipments to Newfoundland increased from 267,797 to 347,241 bushels, vegetable shipments rose from 635,900 to 867,700 pounds, fruit shipments grew from 41,100 to 338,100 pounds, cheese shipments jumped from 42,100 to 321,500 pounds, and butter shipments expanded from 39,000 to 156,400 pounds.[37] In contrast, shipments of livestock declined from 1947 to 1948. The number of PEI swine shipped to Newfoundland dropped from 6,994 to 5,938, cattle from 5,454 to 4,516, calves from 1,274 to 1,112, and horses from 209 to 88.[38]

These trade statistics were a source of optimism for Islanders. After all, Newfoundland was buying large amounts of PEI produce. As a May 1947 editorial in the *Charlottetown Patriot* made clear, 'Newfoundland is rapidly becoming one of our best customers, people in this province are naturally very much interested in the suggestions that the Old Colony may become a tenth Canadian province ... During the past few years our aggressive trade developments have really been bearing fruit, and the outlook for the future is brighter than ever.'[39] The *Patriot* had reason for optimism; in 1948, Newfoundland bought over $3,000,000 worth of agricultural products from PEI, approximately six times the per capita amount purchased from the rest of Canada.[40]

Jones made clear in his 1948 Labour Day speech that he agreed with the *Charlottetown Patriot*'s favourable prediction for PEI–Newfoundland trade by suggesting that agricultural shipments to Newfoundland 'may well ... increase after entry into the Dominion of Canada.'[41] By the 1949 session of the legislature, the 'Farmer Premier' was even suggesting that when Newfoundland entered Confederation there would be a revival of 'the oldtime schooner traffic between Prince Edward Island and Newfoundland.' The anticipated revitalization of trade brought by Newfoundland's Confederation would benefit the Island farmers whom Jones saw it as his duty to represent. As the premier predicted, Newfoundlanders 'will want our farm products in increasing quantities as they begin to handle more money.' And in an example of truly circular trade, Jones forecast that schooners that carried Island produce to Newfoundland could return from Newfoundland laden with limestone, which could be used to fertilize PEI's farmlands.[42] This sentiment was reiterated in the PEI Legislature on 25 March 1949, when Jones made perfectly clear his reasons for supporting Newfoundland's Confederation:

Because we are an island and because they are an island, and have to trade in ships, we have an excellent opportunity of trading in close association with Newfoundland; and in addition we produce those agricultural products which Newfoundland desires, and we are the nearest place by hundreds of miles from which they can purchase such commodities. We hope to develop a reciprocity of trade over the years that will make us both prosperous.[43]

With these words Jones confirmed his conviction that Newfoundland's entry into Confederation would prove economically beneficial to the people of Prince Edward Island.

Fleeting Opposition

Not everyone on PEI shared Jones's positive outlook on Newfoundland's entry into Confederation. However, opposition to the union was fleeting and had largely disappeared by 31 March 1949. Only PEI Conservative Opposition Leader W.J.P. MacMillan harboured serious concerns. As the date for the union's consummation approached, he 'expressed doubt whether Newfoundland's entry into Confederation would benefit this Province.' He noted the potentially detrimental effect that union might have on Island fishers, for it would bring unwanted competition to PEI fishermen, 'who could not find proper markets now.'[44] The PEI fishing industry was facing difficult times in the late 1940s – a number of European countries had effectively closed their markets to Island fish by means of a high tariff. Even so, the impact of Newfoundland's Confederation on the Island's fisheries would likely be of little concern to most Islanders, for PEI and Newfoundland focused their fisheries on different catches.[45]

In Newfoundland the cod fishery was of paramount importance, accounting for approximately two-thirds of the total fishery.[46] PEI, for its part, was equally dependent upon the lobster fishery, which accounted for roughly two-thirds of its fisheries revenue.[47] In truth, provincial sibling New Brunswick, home to both St Andrews, the 'Live Lobster Capital of North America,' and to numerous fishing communities along the province's north shore, posed a much greater threat to the profits of PEI fishers than did Newfoundland.[48] Some Islanders even suggested the Newfoundland's entry could benefit PEI fishers. Island Liberal MLA George Seville predicted that Newfoundland would prove to be a source of bait for PEI fishermen during times when bait from other sources was scarce.[49] Opposition Leader MacMillan himself may have come to the same conclusion; his opposition to Newfoundland's entry was not so resolute that it prevented him from seconding Premier Jones's motion in the PEI Legislature formally welcoming the new province into Confederation.[50]

Of more pressing concern than the impact of Confederation on the PEI fishery was the effect that union would have on the Island butter industry. The one issue that might have altered the Island's favourable opinion of Newfoundland's entry into Confederation was the legalization of margarine in Canada. Until the late 1940s the production and sale of margarine was illegal in Canada, whereas in Newfoundland, which lacked a firmly entrenched dairy industry, it had long been an important industry.[51] At the time negotiations for Newfoundland's entry into Confederation were being conducted, a shortage of butter, and the resulting high prices on what butter was available, prompted Ottawa to remove the federal ban on margarine production – an action that had the added benefit of facilitating Newfoundland's union – leaving it up to the individual provinces to decide whether they would allow the sale of the butter substitute.[52] PEI newspapers were quick to connect the legalization of margarine with Newfoundland's Confederation. As early as May 1947 an editorial in the *Charlottetown Patriot* pointed out:

> One of the problems that would have to be solved [before Newfoundland entered Confederation] concerns oleomargarine. Banned in Canada owing to opposition from Canada's dairymen, the butter substitute is manufactured and sold in sizable amounts in Newfoundland. Were she to come to as a tenth province one problem that would arise would be what to do about oleomargarine in Canada, would the position here be reconsidered, or would Newfoundland be told that she could not continue to manufacture and sell it at least for export to the other nine provinces.[53]

The *Patriot*'s fears appeared to be realized when, on 14 December 1948, the Supreme Court legalized the sale and production of butter substitutes in Canada.[54]

The threat of margarine competing with PEI butter was short-lived. On 13 January 1949 the PEI legislature banned the sale and manufacture of margarine on the Island, making PEI the first province to explicitly do so.[55] The Jones government's actions restricting margarine sales proved effective. In early 1949, Island butter production was above that of the previous year, even with the added threat of margarine.[56] Said the *Summerside Journal*, 'although butter sales are reported down in Canada, which is believed due in part to the sale of margarine, there is no change here. Margarine is not sold in this province.'[57] Part of the reason for the continued productivity may even have been derived from Newfoundland's purchasing power. Shipments of Island butter to Newfoundland increased from 39,000 pounds in 1947, to 156,400 pounds in 1948, to 263,460 pounds in 1950, Newfoundland's first year in Confederation.[58]

Financial concerns about the union also caused some Islanders to be wary of Newfoundland's entry into Confederation. The staunchly conservative *Charlottetown Guardian*, for example, was initially apprehensive about the merger, maintaining that the cost of union would outweigh any benefits. These apprehensions came to the fore when rumours surrounding Newfoundland's terms of entry began to swirl in October 1947. Newfoundland was reportedly being offered 'subsidies ranging somewhere between $15,000,000 and $20,000,000' as inducement to enter – an amount, the *Guardian* pointed out, that was well in excess of what PEI had been granted in the recently concluded dominion–provincial tax agreement, under which the provinces had agreed to cede their right to levy corporation, income, and succession taxes in return for an annual grant. If PEI were to receive similar consideration as Newfoundland, the Island would receive roughly three times the $2,100,000 it had been granted in the 1947 Tax Rental Agreement. When the reputed terms of entry were viewed through the lens of that agreement, the paper claimed, 'it will be seen the alleged Federal offer of between $15,000,000 and $20,000,000 is not only generous but prodigal.'[59]

Yet within a year, after Newfoundland's entry into Confederation was a certainty, the *Guardian*'s opposition to the financial terms of union had begun to wane. A 2 August 1948 editorial 'Another Island Province?' began with the requisite recitation of Newfoundland's financial inducements to enter Confederation but soon progressed to a discussion of how these terms might actually benefit PEI. It detailed a speech given by Jones in the provincial legislature. 'Newfoundland's Ottawa bargain was on a much more generous scale than ours,' Jones stated, and he wondered 'whether this Province, which is in a somewhat similar position, could not base a claim for more subsidy on that account.' With the tax agreement set to expire in 1952, Jones thought the time was right to 'begin to make a study of this matter and help the Government in getting facts together which would assist us in getting more liberal terms in the next five years than we now enjoy.'[60] By October 1948, while a Newfoundland delegation was in Ottawa trying to finalize the terms of entry, the *Guardian* was practically cheering for them to raid the federal cupboard:

> Judged by what the Maritime Province obtained under the existing Dominion-Provincial tax agreements, the terms offered to Newfoundland as an inducement to enter Confederation would appear to have been generous ... Now, however, it is reported that the Newfoundland delegation have presented financial statements to the Canadian Government showing the need for still higher provincial revenues and therefore the necessity of reopening negotiations on the financial proposals made by the Dominion last year ... No one will blame the Newfoundland delegates for getting everything they can in their negotiations with Ottawa. The Maritimes, however, have a right to insist on equal terms, and even to have these terms made retroactive.[61]

From this passage it is clear that the *Guardian* had come to view Newfoundland's entry as potentially beneficial to PEI, for it was hoped that whatever financial considerations Newfoundland received to join Confederation would potentially be applied to the rest of the under-developed Maritimes.

The Freight Rates Issue

Financial justifications for PEI's endorsement of Newfoundland's Confederation came to the forefront when Canada's Board of Transport Commissioners increased railway freight rates. Early in 1948, after more than a year of contemplation, the Board of Transport Commissioners approved a 21 per cent horizontal increase in rates, effectively removing the regional subsidies that had helped offset the geographical disadvantages faced by shippers from outside Central Canada. The increase caused much concern in PEI; as an editorial in the *Charlottetown Guardian* written when the rate increase was first being considered put it, 'if the blanket increase goes into effect the Maritimes and particularly P.E.I. will be in the doldrums of permanent depression.'[62] This rate hike prompted Jones to join with the other two Maritime premiers and their four Western counterparts to protest what was seen as an unfair and unreasonable hike. The 'seven premiers,' as they came to be known, lobbied Ottawa to appoint a

Royal Commission to investigate the problem of freight rates to the outlying provinces.[63]

Despite the general concern among the have-not governments, the *Charlottetown Patriot* was optimistic that Newfoundland's entry would offset any difficulties occasioned by the increased railway rates. Newfoundland's Confederation would surely bring increased waterborne trade activity at the Charlottetown waterfront – trade not subject to the 21 per cent rate increase. Not only would the increased volume of waterborne trade give PEI stevedores 'regular employment with a steady and sizeable income,' but it would also make 'the freight rate problems and the battle with the railways ... of much smaller importance to P.E. Island.'[64] The importance of shipping in alleviating the hardships of a rate increase was clear to Premier Jones, who stated in July 1947 that the proposed increase 'would kick back on the rail carriers themselves because the Province's traffic ... would shift to ships.'[65] Moreover, despite the 1948 increase on mainland railway freight rates, Newfoundland's rates actually declined following Confederation when the Canadian National Railways assumed control of the Newfoundland Railway – a move that further opened, and enticed competition for, the Newfoundland market. As Agnew noted, lower freight rates meant that 'far more products started moving by rail at cheaper than water rates, with all other Provinces of Canada making an all out effort for Newfoundland trade – competition became very keen.' Despite this 'keen' competition, Agnew remained confident that increased waterborne shipping for the Newfoundland trade, combined with his work cultivating the Newfoundland market over the previous years, would allow PEI to maintain its market share.

It is likely that the concern over freight rates was at least in part responsible for both the *Charlottetown Guardian*'s and the *Charlottetown Patriot*'s advocacy of a direct steamship connection between Georgetown, PEI, and a 'convenient port in Newfoundland.' Such a connection, the papers claimed, had much to recommend it. Unlike Charlottetown, the Port of Georgetown was ice-free through the winter months, and this would remove the need to route goods destined to Newfoundland by rail through Halifax when the Northumberland Strait was frozen over. Moreover, Georgetown already had railway facilities adequate to handle the increased volume of trade that could be routed through its harbour. All that was needed, so the *Patriot* claimed, was a federal subsidy to support the route. And the *Patriot* was confident that such a subsidy would be forthcoming, as 'the benefits that would undoubtedly result would amply justify the necessary expenditure.'[66] While a winter port at Georgetown was not forthcoming, the mutual support of the plan shown by the *Guardian* and *Patriot* speaks to the importance of a year-round Island port for PEI–Newfoundland trade, and more generally of PEI–Newfoundland trade itself.

Post-Confederation Trade

The continued importance of PEI–Newfoundland trade following Confederation, even with increased competition from Central Canada, was the result of Premier Jones's actions. Throughout the 1940s he had steadfastly courted the Newfoundland market, and he personally took steps to foster the relationship between the two islands. As a sign of the close relationship between the two provinces, Jones was invited in April 1949 to speak at the first Newfoundland Liberal Convention. Championing the cause of Newfoundland–PEI cooperation in front of Newfoundland's political and economic elite, Jones 'received a tremendous welcome upon entering the Convention Hall ... and kept the attention of the audience during his oration.'[67] As Agnew would later detail, 'from all the favourable comments which I received [while meeting with prospective Newfoundland customers] I have no hesitation in saying that this visit did more to bind the friendly relations between our two Provinces than anything that has taken place in years past.'[68]

Jones's dedication to maintaining and developing inter-island connections is revealed by the fact that within two months of Newfoundland's entry into Confederation, Prince Edward Island finally acquired its own vessel for the Newfoundland trade, something for which PEI trade agent William Agnew had long lobbied and which the Charlottetown Board of Trade strongly endorsed.[69] The *Eskimo*, a '200-ton motor vessel equipped with refrigeration,' had been built in 1942 for the Air Force and had been purchased by PEI from the Hudson's Bay Company. The ship would make 'weekly trips with meat, poultry, and other perishable products from Charlottetown to various ports in Newfoundland not now provided with steamer service,' with Corner Brook serving as the first Newfoundland port of call.[70] The launch of the ship in June 1949 heightened Jones's optimism for inter-island trade. In the premier's own words, 'the possibilities for a tremendous expansion in trade between Prince Edward Island and Newfoundland were never brighter than at the present time.'[71] And Jones's optimism was apparently well placed. As Agnew outlined in his 1950 report, the launch of the *Eskimo* 'opened up a direct trade with these out-ports [along the South Coast of Newfoundland] – which we did not have before. And, therefore, it was a means of greatly increasing our trade to that part of Newfoundland.'[72] And increase trade it did. During seven months of operation in 1949, the *Eskimo* shipped over 1,900 tons of PEI cargo to Newfoundland.[73] In addition, the *Island Connector* and 'many privately owned Prince Edward Island diesel vessels that operated to Newfoundland from Summerside, Souris, Montague and Murray Harbour, as well as a great number of Newfoundland owned vessels' continued to facilitate inter-island trade.

Though the addition of the *Eskimo* to the fleet of trade steamers sailing between PEI and Newfoundland assisted Island exporters, Agnew maintained that for PEI to fully exploit the Newfoundland market even more ships would be needed, and he recommended the allocation of additional refrigerated boats for the St John's route. Moreover, he believed that PEI needed to develop more cold storage space and abattoir facilities on the Island, as the 'trend is more and more going towards chilled beef for the Newfoundland trade.' The experience of the Island government with the newly acquired *Eskimo* confirmed for Agnew the importance of refrigerated ships, cold storage facilities, and meat processing plants. As he suggested, the 'necessity of this refrigeration space was well proved by the amount of perishable products shipped to the South Coast of Newfoundland by the M/V "Eskimo" with her limited cold storage space.'[74] If the *Eskimo* could capitalize on shipping perishables to the relatively sparsely populated south coast, then great profits could surely be made shipping them to the much more populous Avalon Peninsula, site of the Newfoundland capital of St John's. Were these things to be done, then 'trade will continue to improve with Confederation and it is up to our exporters to take every advantage at their disposal to increase their trade with Newfoundland.'[75] In other words, if PEI were to secure more shipping capacity, the Island's support for Newfoundland's entry into Confederation would be well placed.

Conclusion

During the 1940s the relationship between Prince Edward Island and Newfoundland grew increasingly close. In an effort to foster the economic relationship between the two islands, PEI Premier Walter Jones appointed a trade representative to Newfoundland. Throughout the late 1940s Trade Agent William Agnew travelled the length and breadth of Newfoundland, cultivating intimate face-to-face relationships with Newfoundland's numerous importers and merchants. As Jones stated in late 1948, 'the established contacts made with the farmers and consumers in the Ancient Colony have been of outstanding benefit and should place us at considerable advantage when the final inclusion of Newfoundland as a province of Canada is consummated.'[76] Perhaps Jones was looking at the situation through rose-coloured glasses, but he had worked too long and too hard to secure the Newfoundland market for Islanders to have it taken away by Central Canadian interests the moment the clock tolled midnight on 31 March 1949. The long fight for the Newfoundland market and the optimistic view that it would remain theirs led Prince Edward Islanders to support the entry of a second island province into Confederation.

4 '... for the general expansion of the economy': New Brunswick and Newfoundland's Entry into Confederation

The 1 April 1949 edition of the *North Shore Leader*, a small community newspaper in Newcastle, New Brunswick, contained no mention of Newfoundland's entry into Confederation. Instead, the paper gave prominent front-page coverage to the coming of wireless communications to northern New Brunswick. On that day, CKMR 1340 took to the airwaves, bringing the residents of the Miramichi their very own radio station.[1] This indicates New Brunswick's reaction to Newfoundland's Confederation: it was, in large measure, a non-event for New Brunswickers, with many provincial newspapers generally ignoring the subject. In the postwar period, with New Brunswick striving to improve its outdated infrastructure by building highways, hydroelectric plants, and modern communications, it seems that a new provincial cousin did not generate much interest.[2]

This is not to say that Newfoundland did not factor into New Brunswick's discussions regarding postwar reconstruction. Throughout the recently concluded war, the federal government had been reluctant to place wartime contracts in New Brunswick, maintaining that the province's lack of hydroelectric facilities and its proximity to the Atlantic justified the concentration of investment in Central and Western Canada.[3] New Brunswickers took note, and after the war, infrastructure development became key to Liberal Premier John McNair's industrial strategy. A prominent component of that strategy was to build the Chignecto Canal to link the Gulf of St Lawrence with the Bay of Fundy. When Newfoundland's Confederation was being discussed, elites in New Brunswick used the potential new province as further justification for the canal's construction. Likewise, New Brunswick senator and fisheries magnate A. Neil McLean, an advocate of the canal, tried to use union to expand his fishery operations on Newfoundland. This chapter provides an overview of New Brunswick support for Newfoundland's entry into Confederation by focusing on the ways the province's elites publicly and privately tried to use the merger to further personal and provincial development programs.

Distant Cousins

In large part, New Brunswick's general disengagement with the Confederation issue can be explained by the fact that the province did not have as close a relationship with Newfoundland as did Prince Edward Island or Nova Scotia. Geographically, New Brunswick is farther from Newfoundland, and it did not have Prince Edward Island's long history of supplying Newfoundland with agricultural products. Nor was New Brunswick home to as many expatriate Newfoundlanders as Nova Scotia. As a result, relations between New Brunswick and Newfoundland had historically been more limited than those between Newfoundland and Prince Edward Island or Nova Scotia. What is more, Newfoundland and New Brunswick were not major economic competitors. The rocky soil of Newfoundland meant that the island did not compete with New Brunswick's agricultural producers, and the two provinces engaged in different fisheries. Only in the pulp and paper industry was there the potential for serious rivalry, but the Second World War's end brought a high demand for pulp and paper and, as a result, postwar competition in this area was minimal. As J.A. Guthrie, an economics professor and expert on the pulp and paper industry, projected in 1942, 'the post-war outlook for the Canadian newsprint industry ... is relatively favorable [and] the Maritime mills appear to occupy a favorable position in the Canadian industry.'[4] Canadian Minister of Trade and Commerce C.D. Howe concurred, informing Newfoundland Premier Joey Smallwood in December 1950 that 'present production of newsprint is proving inadequate to meet demand, not only in North America but also in any overseas countries.'[5] Canadian mills were running at a seemingly impossible 103 per cent of capacity in their efforts to meet the demand. So profitable were the forest industries that New Brunswick's Bathurst Power and Paper Company recorded its most successful year in 1948, with profits of $1,685,186.[6] Moreover, when Newfoundland formally entered Confederation the island's giant Bowater Paper Mill would be subject to Canadian laws and corporation taxes, thereby levelling the playing field and abrogating some of the competitive advantages enjoyed by the Corner Brook mill, which paid much lower stumpage fees than did its mainland Canadian competitors.[7]

The York-Sunbury By-Election

The lack of economic connections between New Brunswick and New-foundland meant that, initially, New Brunswick's politicians seemed largely uninterested in Newfoundland's entry into Confederation, with the extent of their concern seemingly confined to the possibility that Newfoundland would get better financial terms to enter the union than those enjoyed by New Brunswick in Confederation. This inequity, Liberals feared, would have an impact on their prospects in the late 1947 York-Sunbury federal by-election, necessitated by the unexpected death of Frank Bridges, Minister of Fisheries and New Brunswick's sole cabinet minister. Prime Minister William Lyon Mackenzie King was reluctant to publicize the terms of union offered Newfoundland prior to the by-election as he was certain that, if announced, they would prove a contentious issue. He recognized that Ottawa was offering Newfoundland better financial terms to enter Confederation than New Brunswick was receiving in Confederation, and he worried that, were the terms released before the election, New Brunswickers might show their disapproval at the ballot box by rejecting Liberal candidate Milton Gregg. As King confessed to his diary, 'we would be asked why we were treating strangers better than our own people and supporters.' He feared that New Brunswick Premier John McNair 'might prove very difficult in agreeing to the terms being suggested.'[8]

King had good reason to suspect that McNair would be intractable if Newfoundland were to receive better terms than New Brunswick. Less than a year earlier, McNair had proven to be a thorn in King's side during the negotiations surrounding the 1947 Tax Rental Agreement. New Brunswick had been the first province to enter a deal with the federal government to rent corporation, personal income, and inheritance taxes to Ottawa in return for an annual subsidy; but when it became known in December 1946 that British Columbia had brokered a much more lucrative arrangement than had New Brunswick, McNair wrote to King to inform him that his province would suspend relations with Ottawa until it received a similar deal. Though the situation was smoothed over within a few weeks by a renegotiation of New Brunswick's agreement, McNair was not shy about letting the prime minister (and the public) know when he thought his province had been treated shabbily.[9]

If King had any fears of a repeat hardline performance by McNair, they were misplaced. The New Brunswick premier was little concerned about Newfoundland's entry into Confederation largely because he did not think it would affect his province's finances. Included in McNair's papers regarding the proposed terms of union between Canada and Newfoundland is an unsigned document that compares Newfoundland's position were it to enter Confederation with that of New Brunswick. According to the calculations, Newfoundland's total subsidies from the federal government upon entry would be $1,542,000 – less than the $1,632,000 New Brunswick would receive.[10]

Despite these reassuring figures, McNair shared King's inclination to suppress the terms of union until after the by-election. In a letter to the prime minister detailing Liberal prospects for the by-election, McNair asked whether the proposals for Newfoundland's union with Canada were going to be made public before the 20 October contest. He felt that the Liberals would certainly win a majority, but he also cautioned that 'should this break before the by-election I will not predict what the outcome will be here.'[11] J.W. Pickersgill, Special Assistant to the Prime Minister, displayed no such reservations. As Pickersgill opined, 'New Brunswick was dead against Newfoundland coming in on practically any terms,' and Gregg's chances for election would be hurt 'if anything were said which indicated we were keen on having Newfoundland brought in.' McNair had little to worry about, however, for Pickersgill guaranteed that 'ways and means will be found to keep the Canadian terms offered to Newfoundland secret until after the 20th of October.'[12] With the terms of union suppressed, Gregg won a strong majority in the by-election.

Neil McLean and the Newfoundland Fishery

Fredericton seemed little concerned about Newfoundland's Confederation. The same cannot be said for Blacks Harbour, a small fishing community 50 kilometres west of Saint John. The Blacks Harbour newspaper, *The Fundy Fisherman*, was New Brunswick's earliest and staunchest advocate of Newfoundland's entry into Confederation. Its wholehearted support of union stemmed from two main considerations. First, the Newfoundland and New Brunswick fisheries were substantially different. Second, and more important, Neil McLean, the Liberal senator who owned both *The Fundy Fisherman* and Connors Brothers, Blacks Harbour's large sardine cannery, strongly favoured Newfoundland's entry for his own economic reasons.

Though both Newfoundland and New Brunswick derived substantial revenues from the sea, there was little direct competition between the two fisheries. The Newfoundland fishery was based largely on cod, while in New Brunswick sardines and lobsters were the most important catches. Fished mainly in the Charlotte County area, which runs from the Maine border to the Saint John County line, sardines are young herring caught using elaborate stationary weirs built of stakes and twine in the fertile waters of Passamaquoddy Bay and the Bay of Fundy. Blessed with these rich waters, Charlotte County accounted for 98 per cent of New Brunswick's annual sardine catch in 1948.[13] In 1947 the sardine was New Brunswick's most lucrative fish resource, with the market value for the province's canned sardines being $5,683,213. When the $926,339 received for the fresh and salted sardines is added to that figure, the total value of the New Brunswick sardine fishery in 1947 was $6,609,552, displacing the lobster industry as the province's most lucrative fishery.[14]

Charlotte County was also home to much of the province's fresh lobster fishery. St Andrews, touted as the 'Live Lobster Capital of North America,' was the site of the world's first lobster 'ranch,' which was capable of holding 1,000,000 pounds of lobster, enough to ensure a steady year-round supply of the tasty crustacean. Despite the success of the lobster ranch, the bulk of the catch still came from the open sea. In 1946, New Brunswickers caught 9,135,800 pounds of lobster, worth a total landed value of $2,589,057. This catch was then marketed for $4,627,203, making it the most profitable ocean catch for that year.[15]

While sardines and lobsters jostled for the position of New Brunswick's most lucrative catch, the cod fishery occupied an important, but by no means integral, part of the province's overall fishing economy. Though the quantity of codfish caught during the late 1940s steadily increased as the result of the use of modern draggers, the market value of the fish declined. New Brunswick had its most successful cod catch in 1948, when it landed 24,349,700 pounds. Yet the marketed value of the 1948 harvest was only $1,270,942 – more than $200,000 less than the value of the sparser 1947 catch.[16] Three-quarters of this amount came from the sale of dried and salted cod, a sector of the fishery that was in decline. At this time, fresh fish markets in New

England and Central Canada were expanding, and government officials in New Brunswick hoped that the province's cod fishers could adapt to the changing times by abandoning the green salted and dried cod trade, for they doubted that the province's fishers could compete in this market with either Newfoundland or Iceland.[17] Given the relatively insignificant and diminishing dried cod industry in New Brunswick, Newfoundland's codfish supremacy posed little threat.[18] What is more, since the cod fishery was largely based out of Caraquet on the province's Acadian north shore, any concerted opposition to Newfoundland's Confederation that arose among New Brunswick's cod fishermen would likely have been ignored by both Ottawa and Fredericton, as Acadian concerns would have counted for less in 1940s New Brunswick than the endorsement of a prominent senator and industrialist.[19]

Ottawa and Fredericton need not have been concerned about Acadian opposition to the union, since French-language newspapers in New Brunswick displayed the same general disengagement with the issue of Newfoundland's Confederation as did most of the province's English print media. Throughout 1947 and 1948, for example, coverage of Newfoundland's Confederation negotiations in the Acadian newspaper *L'Evangeline* tended to be translations of Canadian Press stories concerning the political process. Not until the eve of Newfoundland's entry did Emery LeBlanc, editor of *L'Evangeline*, directly address the subject of union. In a 31 March 1949 editorial, LeBlanc welcomed Newfoundlanders into Confederation. Not only did he feel that it made sense, as it would allow Canada to consolidate its hold on the northern part of North America, but he also believed that the merger would benefit the new province's French-speaking population. As LeBlanc stated, 'en souhaitant la bienvenue à nos nouveaux frère canadiens, nous n'oublions pas la population acadienne de Terre-Neuve … Esperons que leur entrée dans le Canada, pays officiellement bilingue, leur aidera à conserver leur langue et leur foi.'[20]

With Acadian concerns about the merger seemingly non-existent, McLean's enthusiasm for Newfoundland's union with Canada was irrepressible. A Liberal senator since 1945, McLean was perhaps the most important businessman in Charlotte County and one of the most influential in the province. In 1923 he led a number of Saint John businessmen in purchasing a controlling interest in Connors Brothers, one of New Brunswick's premier sardine canneries. McLean oversaw the expansion and modernization of the business, with the result that by 1949 Connors Brothers was believed to be the largest single sardine cannery in the world, with exports to 96 countries under 150 different brand names.[21]

Connors Brothers employed the bulk of Blacks Harbour's 1,500 townspeople, and it had done much to modernize the community, which was touted as 'one of America's most progressive small towns.' The prosperity of Blacks Harbour during the 1940s was directly attributable to McLean and his sardine cannery.[22] As the 1945 *Canadian Fisheries Manual* stated, Blacks Harbour

> is practically a company owned community, with all modern municipal conveniences – cement sidewalks, paved roads, fire department, water, light, churches, schools, theatres, and all those material things which cater to the working and social life of its people. From their employment in the company's fleets, fish canneries, can-making and lithographing plants, cold storage, lumber mill and box-making shop, the majority of Black's Harbor workers derive a comfortable income and the whole economic life of the town revolves around the catching, processing and marketing of the canned sardines, herring, clams, haddock, etc., which Connors Bros., Ltd., produce and ship to all parts of the globe.[23]

As this rose-coloured description suggests, Connors Brothers had an enormous influence on the town. As a result, the town's newspaper, *The Fundy Fisherman*, pushed the agenda of its owner and the town's influential benefactor.

As early as September 1945, *The Fundy Fisherman* was introducing its readers to Newfoundland and promoting McLean's pro-Confederation stance. After detailing the composition of the Commission of Government, the editor identified the strategic importance of both Newfoundland and Labrador to Canada, arguing that 'the position held by both Labrador and Newfoundland was of the greatest importance to the defence of all Eastern North America.' The editor noted that both Canada and the United States recognized the vital place of Newfoundland in continental defence, and had therefore spent over a hundred million dollars on wartime expenditures on the island, with the result that 'some of the finest defence bases in the world are to be found there.' Despite this massive military investment in Newfoundland, the province was still resource rich and capital poor, a situation that Canada would be wise, the editor claimed, to remedy:

Newfoundland and her possessions are rich in natural resources. Lumber, fish, minerals etc., are found there in abundance. They are wonderful neighbours and buy the majority of their needs in Canada. We in turn should take a very great interest in these good neighbours, so near at hand and extend all the aid possible in helping them to develop their great country, also in assisting them in finding markets for what they produce.

The editor concluded that given these realities, 'Canada should welcome Newfoundland to join Confederation.'[24]

It was not just the musings of the editor that were presented to the people of southwestern New Brunswick by *The Fundy Fisherman*. On 7 November 1945, Senator McLean was the first Canadian parliamentarian to endorse union, suggesting in his paper's pages that Canada should begin negotiations for Newfoundland's entry into Confederation.[25] Less than two years later, on 19 June 1947, McLean delivered a speech in the Senate that formally endorsed opening negotiations with Newfoundland on the matter of union; that speech was published in *The Fundy Fisherman*. While McLean recognized such important considerations as Newfoundland's strategic position vis-à-vis continental defence, the main benefit for Canada, he argued, would be the addition of 320,000 'good, British citizens.' Since Newfoundlanders were a 'stalwart, hardworking people,' the island's entry into Confederation would be a 'great addition to Canada.' Moreover, Newfoundland's entry would benefit Canada because the island contained vast untapped supplies of important natural resources. These resources – 'lumber, metals, fisheries, water power, etc.' – would soon be 'sought after by the nations of the world far more than ever before.' As McLean made clear for his fellow senators, 'Newfoundland, considering its size, including Labrador, has proportionately just as great natural resources as Canada has.' Unfortunately, the island did not have the necessary capital to develop these resources. Canada did, however, have the money required for the necessary infrastructure for resource exploitation and could 'set aside a considerable sum for the development of transportation and natural resources over there.'[26]

McLean's advocacy for the development of Newfoundland and Labrador's natural resources stemmed from his personal beliefs concerning the nature of prosperity. In a book penned by the senator, undated but clearly written in the immediate postwar period, he declared that the only true wealth is that derived by resource extraction. In McLean's own words: 'We cannot emphasize too strongly, that all wealth originally comes from the land, sea or forest. We get it by the application of brawn and brain, with the help of power and machinery. There is not a balance sheet in the land that has any income, surplus earnings or profits thereon, which cannot be traced directly or indirectly to what someone dug from land or sea.'[27] Given this disposition, it should come as no surprise that the New Brunswick senator viewed Newfoundland as an untapped source of riches ripe for the picking and that he soon began to invest heavily in the island.

Though McLean also had family ties to the island – his son Dougall lived in Corner Brook, and his two grandchildren were Newfoundlanders – he backed the entry of Newfoundland into Confederation primarily because he had considerable economic investment in the island. As an expert on the herring fishery, McLean had testified before the Newfoundland National Convention's Fishery Committee in 1946. Part of the Fishery Committee's plan for Newfoundland was to 'eliminate antiquated canning procedures' by 1948 in favour of more modern canning methods that relied on the presence of cold storage facilities to keep fish fresh.[28] This 'new deal in the Canning Industry' would likely result in the industry being centralized at 'a number of up-to-date Canning Plants.' The commissioners then trumpeted that one such modern canning facility – 'one of the most modern canning plants in the world' – was already under construction in the Bay of Islands.[29] The entrepreneur building the plant was Neil McLean. Given McLean's close ties to the Fishery Committee, it seems likely that he would have received early word of the island's plans to modernize its fishery and canning industries. This may account for his jump on the competition by finishing construction of his 'very large and modern fish cannery' near Corner Brook on 26 March 1947.[30]

McLean had set plans in motion for the construction of his canning plant at Curling in late 1945 or early 1946. A 29 January 1946 letter from L.N. Brookes, Secretary of the Newfoundland Fisheries Board, to the Newfoundland Secretary for Natural Resources made it clear that Connors Brothers 'recently purchased an area of land at Petries Point, Bay of Islands known as "The Petrie Property,"' where McLean planned to construct a plant that would produce between 500 and 1,000 cases of herring daily. The construction of the canning plant would also necessitate cold storage facilities, warehouses, and a waterfront pier suitable for shipping. McLean's initial investment in the Bay of Islands totalled $200,000; it would eventually amount to as much as $750,000.[31]

Given the scope of McLean's investment in the western part of Newfoundland, it should come as no surprise that the Newfoundland government was willing to grant him a number of concessions to facilitate
the construction of the canning plant. The first concession sought by
McLean was the closing of a road that bisected the Petrie Property
location of his cannery and that was used as a public thoroughfare to
the beach. Newfoundland Fisheries Board Secretary L.R. Brookes took
up McLean's cause, writing to the Department of Natural Resources
about the matter.[32] That department was quick to respond. Its Assistant Secretary wrote to the Secretary for Public Works on 12 February
1946: 'This Department strongly recommends that the present public
road running through the property purchased by Connors should be
closed and henceforth be declared a private one. This firm proposes to
develop the fisheries in the Bay of Islands on an extremely large scale
and it is important that they should be facilitated in doing so in every
way possible.'[33] When the matter was further investigated by Assistant Magistrate T.J. Wade, it was discovered that the road was a public
one, the Newfoundland Supreme Court having 'ruled it as such eight
or ten years ago.'[34] This led officials in the Department of Public Works
to conclude that 'it would appear from this judgement that any action
by Connors Bros. to close this road will be met by opposition which the
Court will uphold.'[35]

This setback prompted the Department of Public Works to find
other reasons to justify privatization of the road. As Deputy Crown
Land Surveyor W. Verge made clear, 'the road skirts a Grove of Trees
a favourable resort for reputable [sic] characters, and I consider it a
calamity to this community if when this Firm builds an expensive
plant there and establishes an Industry, some hobo or otherwise sets
fire to the whole place and the plant and Industry is lost to this
country.'[36] And despite being a public road, it was little used by the
public, prompting Wade to propose that if Connors Brothers were to
build a new access road to the beach, the potential problem could be
averted.[37] This idea had the support of prominent local citizens and
of Connors Brothers, which agreed to bear 'some if not all the cost of
such a change.'[38] The archival record does not make clear whether
Connors Brothers was able to privatize the access road that bisected
the Petrie Property; it seems likely, though, that some mutually beneficial arrangement such as that proposed by Wade was put into place,
for construction on the canning plant commenced in the summer of
1946.

Connors Brothers also sought assistance from the Commission of Government in getting Liverpool salt from Great Britain to use in the canning process. Liverpool salt, it was contended, was the best salt for the canning of herring, and Canada received a 'substantial annual allocation of it.' Connors Brothers asked the Newfoundland Fisheries Board for help in acquiring a yearly supply of 700 tons of Liverpool salt from the British government for use in its Bay of Islands cannery. L.R. Brookes again helped McLean by writing to the Department of Natural Resources on the matter. That department in turn sought the assistance of S.R. Raffan, the Trade Commissioner for Newfoundland in the United Kingdom.[39] Raffan was pessimistic of his chances, as the British had recently curtailed exports of salt in order to meet domestic demand.[40] Despite his concerns, Raffan took the matter up with the British Salt Federation, which informed him that there was 'no immediate prospect' of filling Connors Brothers' Newfoundland salt needs.[41] While McLean failed to acquire Liverpool salt, the Newfoundland government's efforts to assist him illustrates both the importance of his fish cannery to the island's economic future and the Canadian senator's access to Newfoundland's corridors of power.

Other concessions granted McLean by the Commission of Government are more clear-cut. When Connors Brothers wanted to dam Petries Brook, which ran through the plant's property, the Department of Natural Resources quickly investigated the matter. Forest Inspector E.L. Stratton told his superiors that the brook was used only for limited drainage from a 'few homes standing near the brook,' but that these accommodations were well outside the area to be dammed and 'in no way would the water supply be contaminated.' Stratton also informed the department that the people of the Petries area were 'very much in favour of making the use of the water and the brook available to Messrs Conners [sic] Brs. Ltd. and are over anxious that no obstacle be placed in the way of the proposed operation.'[42] Permission was soon granted to build the dam.

Similarly, Connors Brothers' desire to have certain goods imported into Newfoundland duty free was met with agreement from the Commission of Government. On 11 July 1946, the Commissioner for Finance wrote the Commissioner for Natural Resources detailing customs concessions desired by the New Brunswick–owned cannery. In addition to duty-free importation of 'all machinery, fixtures and materials required for and used in the construction of plants, buildings, water, sewerage and lighting systems, piers, harbour installations and warehouses required by the Company in the canning of fish and fishery products,' Connors Brothers asked for a draw-back in the duty on the tomato and mustard sauce used in canning herring and on the cans themselves for a period of fifteen years.[43] The Commissioner for Finance made it clear to his compatriot that 'we have granted Customs concessions in respect to the improvements and extensions of the fishery plant undertaken during the war period' and that the 'Department of Customs is prepared to consider favourably the application made by Connors Brothers.' Moreover, the commissioner presented the added carrot of hinting that Connors Brothers intended to develop other canning facilities in Newfoundland, 'if the Curling venture proves successful.'[44] The Commissioner for Natural Resources took the bait, replying that he believed the cannery to be 'an industry deserving of every encouragement consistent with normal practice and the concessions enumerated ... should be granted the company.' That the Chairman of the Newfoundland Fisheries Board was strongly in favour of assisting Connors Brothers also helped influence the commissioner's decision; thus McLean was free to import without duty any material used in any aspect of building or expanding his Curling fish plant for a period of fifteen years.[45]

This heavy investment in the Bay of Islands' fishery seems to be the most pertinent factor in explaining McLean's support for Newfoundland's entry into Confederation. If Newfoundland entered Confederation, Canada's $2 per case duty on sardines would no longer apply to his Newfoundland packed fish, allowing him free access to the Canadian market.[46] His support of the confederate cause was no secret; it was well known among Newfoundland's labour advocates. In August 1948, pro-confederate leader Joey Smallwood wrote to the senator, asking for financial help. 'We are working on a hand-to-mouth basis,' Smallwood stated, '[and] we can't even hope to pay our way with less than $200,000.' In a likely reference to McLean's plans to build a cold storage facility for his Curling cannery, Smallwood went on to suggest that 'we have very fine plans that have to lie in *cold storage* for lack of funds.'[47] Smallwood's letter must have been persuasive, since McLean apparently donated $50,000 to the confederate cause.[48]

The money that McLean gave Smallwood to support the pro-confederates is best viewed as an investment and not as a donation, since after Newfoundland's entry, the senator would benefit from his generosity. One of McLean's projects for the Bay of Islands involved the construction of a cold storage facility for his cannery; by keeping landed fish fresh for an extended time, it would allow him to substantially increase his cannery's output. McLean had hoped to have the only cold storage plant in the Corner Brook area, but two competing projects were also being developed. By 3 November 1949, McLean's newly incorporated Western Cold Storage Co., Ltd., had been approved by Newfoundland's Department of Fisheries; meanwhile, Smallwood and Newfoundland Senator Ray Petten were conspiring to hinder the development of any competition. In reference to the proposed construction of two other cold storage facilities in the Corner Brook area – facilities that would be direct competition to McLean – Petten informed Smallwood that 'this upsets the apple-cart completely, and definitely will hinder our plans for the larger project at Cornerbrook.' Petten further implored Smallwood to 'allow those two smaller projects to remain in abeyance until we get the other and larger project finished.'[49] McLean's $50,000 investment in the pro-confederates seemed to be paying off.

The Chignecto Canal

Another way in which Newfoundland's Confederation was incorporated into New Brunswick's postwar industrial plans was through the drive to build the Chignecto Canal, a project that Senator McLean believed would be 'one of the greatest things ever accomplished in the Maritimes.'[50] The proposed canal was simple enough – a channel about nineteen miles long would be dug across the Isthmus of Chignecto, the narrow strip of land linking New Brunswick and Nova Scotia and separating the Bay of Fundy from the Gulf of St Lawrence. Such a passage would shorten the water route from the continental interior to the eastern seaboard of the United States by roughly 640 kilometres.

The Chignecto Canal was not a new idea: various proposals for a canal had been bandied about for nearly three hundred years. As early as 1686, Jacques Meulles, the Intendant of New France, mused that 'the portage of one league from Baie Verte on the way to Beaubassin can easily be cut by a canal because all the land is low, and thus water communication could be established between the Gulf of Saint Lawrence and the French Bay.'[51] In 1822 the province of New Brunswick surveyed a possible route for the proposed canal.[52] An 1871 Royal Commission on Canadian Canals favoured the canal's construction, while another Royal Commission in 1875 recommended against the project.[53] The closing years of the nineteenth century saw calls, not for a canal, but for a railway to be built from the St Lawrence to the Bay of Fundy.[54] Finally, a 1933 Royal Commission emphatically argued against building a Chignecto Canal, concluding that there was no 'pronounced or general demand for the construction of the canal [and] the proposal to construct a canal at Chignecto offers no national or local advantages at all commensurate with the estimated outlay.'[55] With that, support for the project would lie dormant for over a decade.

During the late 1940s the Chignecto Canal plan received renewed attention. A committee to investigate the feasibility of building the canal was struck on 2 July 1947, and numerous Boards of Trade in the Maritimes endorsed the project.[56] The greatest support came from those areas that would benefit most materially from the increased seaborne traffic the canal would bring. While New Brunswick's Sackville area was the most enthusiastic advocate of the canal, since the route would pass a mere stone's throw from the town, support for the project also came from along New Brunswick's Northumberland shore and from the city of Saint John.[57] And support was not confined to the western side of the Bay of Fundy – Amherst, Nova Scotia, and the Annapolis Valley were also actively involved in advancing the project.

Renewed interest in the canal project in the postwar period was part of a larger context in which construction projects were high on every government's agenda. The proposed St Lawrence Seaway provided renewed justification for the Chignecto Canal's construction; in the minds of Maritime developers, it also fostered the idea of tapping the canal for hydroelectric power. The experience of war had shown Maritimers the necessity of developing hydroelectric power – power that could come from harnessing the tides that would be passing through the proposed canal. As in the 1930s and earlier, the fact that the canal would shorten the travelling distance between the eastern seaboard and the continental interior was used to promote the proposal. With Newfoundland's pending entry into Confederation, along with the discovery of massive amounts of iron ore in Labrador, the improved communications corridor could now be touted as necessary for Maritime defence, economic modernization, and regional prosperity.

The St Lawrence Seaway figured prominently in the early cries of Maritimers for the Chignecto Canal's development.[58] The massive St Lawrence project, a joint venture of the Canadian and American governments, called for the dredging of a channel along the St Lawrence

River sufficient to allow large oceangoing tankers access to the Great Lakes and continental interior. Given the scale of the project, costs were extremely high, and Canada's share was to be paid for in large measure from federal coffers. This was seen by many in the Maritimes as only the most recent example of Ottawa spending national revenue on a project of regional importance, and led some New Brunswickers to demand the Chignecto Canal as a matter of right. As C.C. Avard, a former municipal politician from Sackville and the owner and editor of both the *Sackville Tribune-Herald* and the *Maritime Advocate and Busy East*, wrote in an April 1946 editorial, 'we have contributed our full share to the cost of canals elsewhere in Canada. If the St Lawrence waterway goes through, as currently seems likely, we will also have to contribute to that.' This prompted him to ask, 'Ontario has its canals, why not the Maritimes?'[59]

Avard went so far as to state that the Chignecto Canal was warranted, if only because there had been tremendous expenditures on canal construction in Central Canada without any corresponding investment in Maritime waterways – a view later endorsed by New Brunswick Conservative MP Alfred J. Brooks and by Amherst, Nova Scotia, Conservative MP Percy Black in the House of Commons.[60] Speaking in the House on 9 June 1948, Brooks opined that 'it was all very well for Ontario to have pleasure excursions, scenic beauty and places for the boys to go swimming, but we in the maritime provinces are asking for canals which would be of some benefit to the maritime provinces and to the whole of Canada.'[61] A year later, MP Black admonished his colleagues for their inaction regarding the Chignecto Canal. 'The members of this house are not averse to spending $500 million in order to build the St. Lawrence canal,' he declared, 'but Nova Scotia, Prince Edward Island and New Brunswick are given the brush-off.'[62]

Associated with the St Lawrence argument for the building of the Chignecto Canal was the idea of using the ebb and flow of the Bay of Fundy's massive tides through the waterway as a means of providing New Brunswick with much-needed electricity, just as the St Lawrence River's current was to be used to power Central Canada. Though it had not specifically called for the building of the Chignecto Canal, the Report of the New Brunswick Committee on Reconstruction had advocated the construction of hydroelectric power facilities in the province.[63] Indeed, much of the New Brunswick government's reconstruction program would be geared toward the expansion of hydroelectric generating facilities. The scarcity of electric power in the province during the postwar period led canal supporters to trumpet the economic boom that a hydroelectric plant affixed to the canal would bring.

It was in this context that Avard's *Sackville Tribune-Herald* carried news on the front page of a 1948 speech delivered by R. Herbert Cooper. A native of Springhill, Nova Scotia, Cooper was a member of the Professional Engineers Association of Ontario and had served during the war with the Department of Reconstruction. He had since become an engineer attached to the Public Projects Branch of the Department of Trade and Commerce, and it was in this capacity that he had been brought to Sackville on 29 October 1948 to discuss the merits of the proposed Chignecto Canal in terms of the hydroelectricity it could generate. Cooper's plan was to construct a dam across the Cumberland Basin and then use hydraulic dredges to dig from the dam through to Tidnish, where the power facility would be located. Cooper believed that because the canal and the hydro facility were tightly intertwined, they should not be conceived of as separate projects. In Cooper's estimation, the finished project would bring the region 'industrial prosperity, increased population and far-reaching hydro developments to bolster the economy of the Maritime Provinces.'[64] As the *Sackville Tribune-Post* pointed out: 'The tremendous boost which would be given to new industries in the Maritimes by the availability of ample electric power, is, in itself full justification for serious consideration of this new ... scheme. Add to that the inland water route ... and the whole scheme assumes an importance which cannot be denied and which cannot be assessed only in dollars and cents.'[65] Noted New Brunswick industrialist K.C. Irving, who was also present at the Sackville presentation, was convinced by Cooper's plan, and he used the language of entitlement to show his support. 'We all should get together,' Irving declared at the meeting, 'and convince Ottawa that this is a contribution they owe to this part of the country.'[66]

Another prominent line of argument used to support the construction of the Chignecto Canal was that it would shorten the distance by sea between the industrial centres of the American eastern seaboard and the continental interior. Given the emerging Cold War, continental defence figured into this line of reasoning. By giving ships a direct path from the Gulf of St Lawrence to the Bay of Fundy, the Chignecto Canal would allow Canadian and American warships travelling from the continental interior to lessen their exposure to hostile forces in the Atlantic; at the same time, it would reduce the distance from the Great Lakes to the eastern seaboard of the United States. The Bay of Fundy could then be used as a holding area for the staging of the massive trans-oceanic convoys such as those that had been used during the Second World War.[67] Left unexplained by those who used defence as the rationale for building the canal was why the federal government, which had been reluctant to place war industry in Saint John because it believed that city was vulnerable to German attack, would now see the Bay of Fundy as a safe harbour for the gathering of convoys.

Perhaps owing to this logistical shortcoming, canal advocates quickly displaced the defence line of justification with other, more regional and economically centred reasons for the project's construction. The Nova Scotia Fruit Growers' Association, for example, endorsed the Chignecto project, noting that the canal would help counter a shrinking British market for Maritime fruit by facilitating exports to hungry consumers in central and western Canada. Nova Scotian apples could be loaded onto ships in the Bay of Fundy and then make the relatively short voyage through the Chignecto Canal and up the St Lawrence to Montreal and points farther west. At the same time, it was suggested that the shorter route offered the Chignecto Canal would decrease transportation costs.[68] When the federal government increased railway freight rates from the Maritimes to Central Canada in 1948, the construction of the canal took on added urgency for the region's fruit growers, who depended on the markets of Ontario and Quebec. As Secretary to the Nova Scotia Fruit Growers Association R.D. Sutton made clear at a 1947 meeting of the Chignecto Canal Committee, 'at present time 300,000 barrels of apples are being shipped from Nova Scotia to the Central Canadian provinces and the proposed increase in railway freight rates makes all growers and shippers extremely interested in other forms of shipping.'[69]

The Saint John Board of Trade was convinced of the Chignecto Canal's merits. In particular, it argued that the canal would bring Newfoundland closer.[70] As early as 1946 the board was trying to secure shipments of lumber from Newfoundland to help offset a shortage of birch in New Brunswick. K.C. Irving in particular was keen on Newfoundland lumber, and was reportedly 'interested in the Chignecto Canal because of the virgin mines and forests of Labrador.'[71] In addition, members of the Saint John Board of Trade, along with 'some very influential citizens,' were trying to secure a direct sailing between the New Brunswick city and St John's in order to expand trade between the two jurisdictions.[72] Since Saint John was relatively close to Newfoundland, and because Newfoundland was one of Canada's best trading partners, New Brunswick's port city stood to profit from increased Newfoundland trade should the island enter Confederation, and that trade would be of even greater volume if the Chignecto Canal were built.[73] As the editor of *The Fundy Fisherman* made clear, 'if Saint John desires to carry on a prosperous seaborne trade with Newfoundland, the first thing to do is to get behind the building of the Chignecto Canal.'[74] Conservative Toronto-Davenport MP John R. MacNicol, a longtime friend of the region and advocate of Maritime issues in Parliament, made the case for the canal even more forcefully when speaking to a 1947 meeting of the Maritime Board of Trade. MacNicol said that if the canal was built, Newfoundland ships would have 'an almost inland water route to Bay of Fundy ports and the United States Atlantic coast ports.'[75] To this end, the Saint John Board of Trade in 1947 endorsed the construction of the Chignecto Canal. By 1948, Board of Trade President A.F. Blake was on record that 'the Canal would undoubtedly benefit Saint John.'[76]

Members of the New Brunswick legislature, who had been essentially silent on the issue of Newfoundland's Confederation, also began to view the construction of the Chignecto Canal favourably and incorporated the pending union as justification for the canal's construction. In March 1948, Liberal MLA Harry Greenlaw of York County implored his fellow politicians to endorse the canal, since it would shorten the water route to Central Canadian markets and help offset the painful railway freight rate increases.[77] The canal received bipartisan support in a 1948 session when Liberal MLA Owen Morse of Charlotte County and Conservative MLA Ralph G. McInerney of Saint John endorsed it. Not until the following year, however, would Newfoundland's Confederation be factored into the discussion.[78]

On 29 March 1949, just two days before Newfoundland officially joined Canada, Moncton Liberal MLA E.A. Fryers strongly endorsed the Chignecto Canal in the New Brunswick legislature, using Newfoundland's Confederation as justification for the canal's construction. 'Even if we were to forget the tremendous value of this canal as a traffic artery,' Fryers stated, 'and only consider the electric power potentialities, this alone would warrant this Legislature taking immediate action to ensure its development.' Moreover, Newfoundland's pending entry into Confederation made the canal 'more vital and essential.'[79] This line of argument was repeated less than a week later by Saint John Liberal MLA E. Roy Kelly. Immediately after welcoming Newfoundland into 'our national family circle' and wishing the citizens of the new province 'happiness, progress and prosperity,' Kelly launched into a lengthy speech endorsing the canal, which would not only 'bring us nearer to our new citizens' but would also transform the economy of the Maritimes.[80]

Perhaps the clearest linking of the Chignecto Canal to Newfoundland and Maritime industrial development appeared in *The Fundy Fisherman*. A 12 January 1949 article, 'The Four Maritime Provinces and the Chignecto Canal,' began by painting anyone who may have opposed Newfoundland's entry as being 'those with reactionary minds and whose interest is centred on self rather than on the good of the country and its people.' These reactionaries did not see that Newfoundland would strengthen the political position of the Maritimes through increased representation in the House of Commons and the Senate and that the economic position of the region would be improved through increased interprovincial trade – trade that would depend, so the article claimed, on the construction of the Chignecto Canal. The Maritimes could anticipate a 'bright outlook for the general expansion of the economy of the four maritime provinces through the creating of a waterway through the Chignecto Isthmus that will permit a flow of exports from Newfoundland's basic production to Bay of Fundy Ports in New Brunswick and Nova Scotia and to the United States on the one hand and that of manufactured goods from these ports to Newfoundland on the other.'[81] Moreover, since the Chignecto Canal would shorten the distance that goods needed to be shipped between Newfoundland and the Maritimes, prices would inevitably fall. Newfoundland, the article claimed, would be the big winner if the Chignecto Canal were built: 'Perhaps it would not be amiss to say that the Chignecto Canal offers benefits equal to or even greater than those expected for the neighbouring three provinces separated ... by a stretch of water quite easily traversed as compared to the long hard route around the province of Nova Scotia.'[82]

Use of Newfoundland's entry into Confederation as justification for the building of the Chignecto Canal took on an added significance with the discovery of massive iron ore deposits in the Quebec–Labrador trough. In 1947, exploratory drilling indicated that as much as 150,000,000 tons of iron ore were embedded in this mineral-rich region along the Quebec–Labrador border; that was more than enough to pique the interest of steel producers in the United States. With the 1949 incorporation of the Iron Ore Company of Canada – a consortium of four U.S. steel companies – the exploitation of these iron ore fields was soon underway.[83] Advocates of the Chignecto Canal argued that these U.S. steel companies would welcome a project that shortened the shipping distances between the Quebec–Labrador trough and the industrial centres of the eastern seaboard. As Amherst MP Percy Black made clear in a 29 March 1949 address to the House of Commons supporting the canal's construction, Labrador's 'hundreds of millions of tons of iron ore' could be transported to the markets of New England via the Chignecto Canal.[84] Northern New Brunswick's *Northern Light* concurred, suggesting that the canal would 'benefit Newfoundland as well as the Maritime Provinces, and the coming of Newfoundland into Confederation adds further importance to the project. Also, the discovery of huge iron ore resources in Quebec and Labrador means that a continuous future traffic of ore-carrying freighters en route to United States Atlantic ports could each save hundreds of miles by using the canal.'[85]

Eventually such ore freighters were able to shorten their journey, but not in the manner that either Black or the *Northern Light* desired. In 1954 the first shipments of ore set sail from Sept-Îles, Quebec, and journeyed around Nova Scotia and down the Atlantic coast on their voyage to the Pennsylvania steel mills. With the completion of the St Lawrence Seaway, however, the route changed. In June 1959, the ore freighter *E.G. Grace* sailed west from Sept-Îles to Ashtabula, Ohio, from which point its cargo would be shipped by rail to various mills around the United States.[86] That Labrador iron ore was travelling along the recently completed St Lawrence Seaway – a seaway that Maritimers had used to justify the construction of their own canal – on its way to the American industrial heartland was a bitter pill for proponents of the Chignecto project to swallow.[87] Longtime proponent of the Chignecto Canal Alfred Brooks felt that Labrador's iron ore deposits were the primary reason for the development of the St Lawrence Seaway. 'In developing the St. Lawrence seaway,' Brooks claimed, 'we are supplying transportation for the conveyance of this great asset to the mills of the United States,' a situation abetted by American ownership of the Labrador iron ore fields.[88] Canadians, Brooks believed, would be much better served if the iron ore were processed in the Maritimes and then exported to the eastern U.S. seaboard via the Chignecto Canal. But by this time the New Brunswick MP was tilting at windmills. The fix was in, and plans for construction of this Atlantic Canadian canal were permanently shelved.

Three issues account for the failure of the Chignecto Canal movement in the postwar era. First, the powerful Minister of Transport Lionel Chevrier did not support the project and consistently used the 1933 Chignecto Commission Report as his justification. Chevrier's influence must not be ignored: a powerful cabinet minister from Quebec, he no doubt saw the St Lawrence Seaway as of paramount importance – it would, after all, lead to greater seaborne trade through his province – and he gave the Central Canadian project his unwavering support.[89] Second, at the same time that New Brunswickers were petitioning for the Chignecto Canal, Nova Scotia was lobbying for a crossing over the Strait of Canso, and it was highly unlikely that the federal government would approve both costly infrastructure projects. Third, there was a lack of consensus among the region's provincial governments regarding the need for a canal. Though by June 1950, Newfoundland, Prince Edward Island, and New Brunswick supported the project, the failure of the Nova Scotia's provincial government to join them relegated the canal to the status of another failed development scheme.[90]

It was with the goal of gaining the Nova Scotia government's endorsement of the Chignecto project that former Moncton mayor and New Brunswick Liberal MLA C.H. Blakeny, a staunch advocate of the Chignecto Canal, wrote to Nova Scotia Premier Angus L. Macdonald in June 1950. Blakeny reminded Macdonald of the support given by the other three Atlantic provinces, and implored him to do the same. He told the Nova Scotia premier that he hoped he could 'count upon Nova Scotia co-operating with the other Atlantic provinces.'[91] Likewise, Martin J. Kaufman, Nova Scotia Liberal MLA for the Cumberland constituency that bordered the proposed canal route and a former mayor of Amherst, wrote his leader that same month to inquire about the possibility of getting 'an endorsement in principle only of the Chignecto Canal project from the Premier of Nova Scotia.'[92]

An 'endorsement in principle' from Angus L. Macdonald was not forthcoming. Though the Chignecto Canal project had the support of Nova Scotia's Amherst and Annapolis Valley regions, the city of Halifax was staunchly opposed to it. At the 1947 meeting of the Canadian Chamber of Commerce, the Halifax Board of Trade went on record against the Chignecto Canal; many of Halifax's shipping interests believed that the canal would hurt their business.[93] Put simply, such a canal would benefit Saint John at the expense of Halifax, thereby diminishing the Nova Scotia capital's status as the leading Atlantic Canadian port.[94] The Nova Scotia premier made no mention of these issues in his reply to Kaufman. Even so, his dismissive response is quite telling: 'As you know, the Government here has not joined in this matter, because with the two bridges at Canso and Halifax, we felt we could not very well ask the Government to do something more.'[95] With these words, Macdonald put the interests of his native Cape Breton and those of the provincial metropolis of Halifax ahead of those of Amherst, the Annapolis Valley, and, indeed, the entire region. This lack of regional solidarity stymied the construction of the Chignecto Canal in the late 1940s.

Though interest in the Chignecto Canal project would resurface a decade later as part of the Atlantic Revolution's 'three Cs' of development – the corridor road through Maine, the Chignecto Canal, and the Prince Edward Island Causeway – the Chignecto Canal's death knell was for all intents sounded with the publication of the 1951 Report of the Royal Commission on Transportation. Anticipating the high cost of building the waterway, the growth of trucking, and the flurry of highway construction that was to come later that decade, the commission recommended against the canal's construction – a move that irked the many Maritime MPs who had long lobbied for the canal.[96] Perhaps MP D.A. Riley best summed up the feelings of his fellow New Brunswickers in the House of Commons. Speaking before the House on 23 April 1951, he stated 'that the finding of the [Turgeon] commission in respect to the Chignecto canal leaves me with a cold feeling toward the St. Lawrence seaway.'[97]

Conclusion

In the late 1940s, New Brunswick elites tried to use Newfoundland's pending entry into Confederation to add weight to calls for industrial development. One of the staunchest supporters of Newfoundland's Confederation was Liberal Senator Neil McLean, who used his newspaper, *The Fundy Fisherman*, to publicize his views. In large measure McLean's support of union stemmed from his having invested in Newfoundland's Bay of Islands fishery – Confederation would eliminate pesky tariff barriers – and from the personal and political connections he had made through this investment. Moreover, McLean was one of a number of New Brunswick political and economic power brokers who used Newfoundland's pending entry as justification for the Chignecto Canal. Building this waterway would, they claimed, improve the New Brunswick economy through an increase in trade and by tapping the tides to supply the province's hydroelectric needs. The failure of the canal movement illustrates the degree to which provincial cleavages persisted in the 1940s. Though the Chignecto Canal was promoted as a regional development project, it was New Brunswick that would have benefited most from it, with few if any dividends accruing to Halifax. A lack of support for the scheme from the Nova Scotia capital, coupled with a thoroughly uninterested federal Minister of Transport, relegated the canal to the scrapheap of failed Maritime development projects. New Brunswick's hope that Newfoundland's Confederation would promote provincial development proved to be misplaced.

5 '... preaching a dangerous gospel': Regional Union and Newfoundland in the 1940s

The preceding three chapters have examined the reactions of Prince Edward Island, New Brunswick, and Nova Scotia to Newfoundland's entry into Confederation in isolation, focusing largely on the perceived ways in which union would benefit or harm each province financially and the ways each province attempted to use the union to further provincial development programs. This chapter adopts a different approach, shifting the focus from provincial economies to regional politics with an examination of the arguments that were put forward in the late 1940s for Maritime union – arguments that would be expanded to include union with Newfoundland once it entered Confederation. Atlantic union, some believed, could strengthen the region's representation in Ottawa and thereby secure more federal support for regional development programs. The failure of Atlantic union is as much a testament to the supremacy of provincial loyalties as it is to the questionable benefits that amalgamation would bring. Proponents of unity offered little beyond vague predictions in their efforts to overcome entrenched political institutions and inertia. The words of economist David Amirault, speaking at a 1995 roundtable discussion on the merits of regional union, seem particularly apt in describing the 1940s movement for regional unity: 'Putting four buckets of problems into one bucket only makes one great big bucket of problems.'[1]

That some Maritimers began to push for regional union in the 1940s should not be surprising. This idea had been raised since the 1860s, and if regional union was likely to have occurred at any time in the twentieth century, the 1940s were the most propitious historical moment. The region was politically aligned, with Liberal governments ensconced in Charlottetown, Fredericton, and Halifax, and a Liberal victory was expected in the provincial election that would follow Newfoundland's entry into Confederation. Moreover, the Maritimes had been hit hard by the Depression, and their shared economic and political marginalization – the bedrock on which many felt the union could be built – increased during the early 1940s as the federal government consolidated regional disparities by concentrating wartime investment in the central provinces. Though the idea of regional cooperation of any kind remained at a low point for much of the decade, the region's failure to catch Ottawa's attention in postwar reconstruction efforts prompted some Maritimers to see united action as the only way to ensure that their voices would be heard. The failure of their quest for regional union, even when presented with such seemingly ideal circumstances, illustrates the degree to which provincial self-interest persisted.

This chapter does not argue that regional union in the 1940s – or any kind of coherent regional approach during this period – would have solved the Maritimes' economic problems. That sort of 'alternative history' falls outside the scope of this study. Instead, this chapter examines the late 1940s push for Atlantic union occasioned by Newfoundland's entry into Confederation with an eye to assessing the nature of regionalism during that important decade by focusing on what the Maritimes hoped to gain from such a merger. An analysis of this abortive quest for Atlantic union shows that politicians and private citizens from all three Maritime Provinces tried to use Newfoundland's entry to promote schemes of supposedly regional importance. While these few advocates of union do not a movement make, that regional amalgamation was even being considered points to the difficulties that the Maritimes – and ultimately Newfoundland as well – faced during the postwar years. The fact that the regional union movement bore no fruit illustrates both the questionable benefits that a merger would have brought and the political fragmentation that characterized the Maritimes during the postwar years.

Maritime Union on the Agenda

The late 1940s was not the first or only time that some Atlantic Canadians lined up behind the cause of regional union.[2] Indeed, Maritime union had been presented as a policy option for well over a century. The 1864 Charlottetown Conference was originally intended as a forum for the discussion of Maritime union before the broader platform of British North American union took centre stage. With Confederation in 1867, the push for Maritime union fell by the wayside. It reared its head intermittently – most notably in the 1880s and again in the 1920s – before reaching its apex with the Deutsch Commission on Maritime Union of the late 1960s and early 1970s.[3]

One of the earliest proponents of Atlantic union in the 1940s was Prime Minister William Lyon Mackenzie King. Writing in his diary in 1943, King confessed that the Second World War had confirmed Newfoundland's strategic importance, and he thought that Confederation might prove an ideal way to prevent Newfoundland from drifting into the American orbit. But King did not just want Newfoundland to join Canada – he also had his eye on Bermuda and the British West Indies. As the prime minister considered such possibilities, he concluded that 'what would really be best would be to have all of these and the three Maritime provinces made into one provincial entity.'[4] Though nothing ever came of King's speculations, his comments suggest several things. First, that ideas of 'Atlantic' union were in the air during the 1940s, even before Newfoundlanders began seriously contemplating Confederation. Second, and more important, that as early as 1943 Prime Minister King conceived of the Maritimes and Newfoundland regionally – a status that would be formally entrenched under King's successor Louis St Laurent with Term 29 of the Newfoundland Act.

Two years after King's diary musings, the first local support of Atlantic union began to emanate from the tiny New Brunswick fishing hamlet of Blacks Harbour. A 12 September 1945 editorial of Blacks Harbour's newspaper, *The Fundy Fisherman*, strongly endorsed the idea of Newfoundland's union with Canada, suggesting that Confederation might be the impetus for the amalgamation of Newfoundland and the Maritimes under one government.[5] 'Canada should welcome Newfoundland to join Confederation,' stated the editor, but he believed that such an offer would be rebuffed, as the people of Newfoundland would have no interest in 'just becoming another Maritime Province.'[6] The editor here was suggesting that Newfoundland saw the Maritime Provinces as the weaker partners in Confederation and that the island would be wary of entering a union where it would assume this same position.[7] As a later editorial made clear, 'many of the people of this fine island [Newfoundland] are shrewd political observers and they have the feeling that the present Maritime provinces have had a poor deal from the Federal Government.'[8] Yet this poor deal was not, the editor argued, entirely Ottawa's fault. The Maritime Provinces themselves were equally responsible.

According to *The Fundy Fisherman*'s editor, a lack of Maritime solidarity had allowed the region to be thrust into a position of political and economic marginalization. As he observed, the people of Newfoundland 'see too much division among the Atlantic Provinces.' The advanced solution to this problem – a solution the editor believed would benefit the Maritimes and be attractive to Newfoundland – was for the Maritimes to unite as a single political entity: 'If the Maritime provinces were to join up with Newfoundland in forming one large Maritime Province of the Dominion we are inclined to think the people of Newfoundland would be interested.' It made sense, the editor claimed, because 'the interests of these territories are almost identical,' and if the Maritime Provinces and Newfoundland were united, it would then be the third-largest province in Confederation, trailing only Ontario and Quebec. A political body such as this 'combined [Atlantic] group would have such a large representation in the federal House of Commons and Senate, they would be able to hold their own very well with the rest of Canada.'[9] In other words, Atlantic union would kill two birds with one stone: it would entice Newfoundland to enter Confederation, even while increasing the region's sway in the political arena.

Andrew Merkel, a prominent Maritimer and the former Atlantic Superintendent of the Canadian Press, lent his voice to the cause of regional union.[10] Upon his retirement from the press, he began a regular radio broadcast on the CBC's Halifax station, which he used to promote regional union. The show's format included letters from Merkel's friends and colleagues, which were read on air. Apparently, Merkel often solicited letters that served his purposes. In this vein, on 7 February 1946 he wrote to C.R. Blackburn, an old friend and the Washington correspondent for the Canadian Press, asking him to submit a five-hundred-word article to be read on air. Merkel even offered a topic for Blackburn's piece: 'Several of thos [sic] with whom I have discussed the project have emphasized the Maritime unity angle. Well you are a Maritimer.' Despite this appeal to Blackburn's Maritime status, the Washington correspondent ignored the suggested topic and submitted an article examining just one of the provinces, Nova Scotia, trumpeting it as a vacation destination.[11]

Despite Blackburn's Nova Scotia–centric article, the idea of Atlantic union remained on the agenda, receiving further notice at the 1947 Mount Allison University convocation, when John Fisher made it the subject of his address to graduating students. Fisher was a native son of Sackville who had gone off to Dalhousie University to study law. After graduation, he was a legal counsel for the Rowell-Sirois Commission, which had been called to investigate the financial relationship between the Dominion and the provinces, before becoming an award-winning journalist. It is likely that Fisher's experience working with the Rowell-Sirois Commission contributed to the tenor of his remarks to the 1947 graduating class. In his view, regional union would improve the region's economy and psyche; it would also be in keeping with contemporary political trends.[12] Fifty years from now, Fisher predicted, there would be no separate provinces in the Maritimes. The potential entrance of Newfoundland into Confederation gave added weight to his call: 'A great opportunity knocks at this hour. If Newfoundland decides to link with the Canadian family, let us ask her to join the Maritimes and form one grand province.' As separate provinces, Fisher argued, the Maritimes had been speaking with a 'divided and feeble' voice. In a united Maritimes, such division would be impossible. 'Let us speak as one,' Fisher implored the graduates:

> Let us revive the ancient name of Acadia and have one great province of Acadia embracing the three Maritime provinces and Newfoundland. Such a move will not only be in keeping with the trends of the times, but, with modern transportation we can weld it into a powerful voice. Such a union would give the Atlantic provinces the psychological boost we have needed for so long ... Together we could do things now denied us.[13]

In Fisher's view, some form of political and economic consolidation was inevitable, and the coming of Newfoundland presented the Maritimes with an opportunity ripe for the picking. Indeed, Fisher claimed that 'such an offer might be the turning point in Newfoundland's discussion of Confederation.'[14]

Politicians Weigh in on Union

The idea of Atlantic union entered the political realm on 7 April 1947, when James R. Burnett, editor of the *Charlottetown Guardian*, reported that a Canadian parliamentarian 'in close touch with affairs of Newfoundland' had suggested that Newfoundland join with the Maritimes to form one large province. This prompted the *Guardian* to solicit responses from the provincial premiers. While Nova Scotia

Premier Angus L. Macdonald was unavailable for comment, New Brunswick's John McNair and Prince Edward Island's Walter Jones readily offered their opinions of the proposed merger. 'Maritime Union has been suggested at various times,' said McNair, who did not 'think there is any marked degree of opinion in this province on it.' Jones agreed with McNair, pointing out that the idea had been around since the 1864 Charlottetown Conference. He doubted, though, that the subject would 'become a live issue.'[15] Only Newfoundland pro-confederate leader Gordon Bradley came out in support of the idea, and even Bradley's endorsement was rather muted. While on his way to Ottawa to participate in negotiations for Confederation with the federal government, Bradley told the *Sydney Post-Record* that it was 'possible that from the viewpoint of administrative costs it [Atlantic union] would be more economical than for separate provincial governments.' Moreover, Bradley suggested that 'if Newfoundland were to join Canada this might be the occasion for them all agreeing to such a formation.'[16]

The next summer, regional politicians again addressed the idea of union when, in June 1948, PEI's Walter Jones clarified his position. Regional union, he claimed, would be an 'excellent step,' but for the merger to truly be effective, Newfoundland would also have to join.[17] Within two months, Jones was tempering his enthusiasm for the project. In an August 1948 letter to radio commentator Andrew Merkel, Jones recognized that Newfoundland's entry into Confederation would alter the position of the Maritimes and could possibly provide the impetus for some form of union. The PEI premier was careful, however, not to come out in favour of a formal political union, suggesting instead that 'at least we should form some kind of an economic union to ascertain and develop our resources.' Moreover, he suggested that cooperation in the federal sphere could greatly assist the region: 'If the four eastern provinces were developed into a block, they might have a considerable influence in Parliament and effect legislation which would tend to develop the Maritime Provinces, and resist the encroachments of large Dominion corporations which would tend to centralize industry in Central Canada.'[18] Though the PEI premier was 'greatly interested' in Maritime union, he doubted very much whether Newfoundland would share his enthusiasm. 'It may be a little early to expect Newfoundland to join with us in promoting such an economic union,' Jones acknowledged with considerable understatement, 'but it could be proposed to them.'[19]

Jones's support of some form of union was mirrored by New Brunswick Progressive Conservative Opposition Leader Hugh John Flemming. Put off by the lack of regional cooperation that he saw in the ongoing tax rental negotiations, Flemming used his response to the 1947 New Brunswick Speech from the Throne to throw his support behind the idea of regional union. As he told his fellow legislators on 17 March 1947, 'personally, I am in favour of Maritime union if it could be arranged.'[20] Flemming believed that had New Brunswick and Nova Scotia presented a united front on the issue they would have effected a more generous tax rental agreement from Ottawa. This did not happen, which underscored for Flemming the importance of regional integration. As Flemming explained, 'down here in the Maritimes we speak with three divided voices. New Brunswick tells its story, Nova Scotia presents its case and Prince Edward Island does likewise.' And this allowed the federal government to play one province off against another. This regional division prompted the opposition leader to ask, 'When will we realize that we can build up a larger unit by simply working together, cease being divided against ourselves, but speak as one?'[21]

As Flemming saw it, regional union would bring many benefits to the Maritime Provinces. Not only would the region speak as one in federal–provincial negotiations, but it would also be able to trim expenditures by eliminating the cumbersome duplication of services. In Flemming's words, regional union would 'reduce the expense per person affected by increasing the unit and likewise render duplication unnecessary.' The New Brunswick opposition leader continued with obvious enthusiasm: 'What an advantage it would be to work with Prince Edward Island on potatoes, with Nova Scotia on many things. The ramifications of working together are almost endless.'[22] One ramification of his plan that Flemming overlooked was the political backlash that his call to erode provincial boundaries would create, and within a month's time he was backpedalling on the issue.

A Political Backlash

The day following Flemming's remarks in the New Brunswick legislature, the *Sydney Post-Record* came out strongly against any form of regional amalgamation. As editor H.P. Duchemin, a noted politico whose influence was felt both on and off Cape Breton Island, made clear:

These arguments for Maritime union are as hoary as they are fallacious. There would be no assurance in a union of Nova Scotia, New Brunswick, and Prince Edward Island that either the administrative costs, public expenditures, or taxation would be reduced. Experience rather goes to show that the larger the area of Government is, and the more important the administered interests are, the more costly all branches of the public service become.[23]

For Duchemin, talk of union displayed a basic misunderstanding of the purpose of Confederation itself. According to the editor, the British North America Act made provision for a strong central government to deal with international affairs, national defence, and other matters that required a dominion-wide response. The provinces were meant to deal with the administration of local affairs in a 'legislative jurisdiction small enough to insure close contacts between the people's elected representatives and their constituents.' The three Maritime Provinces, claimed Duchemin, all had widely different economies and ways of life, and therefore each needed its independent legislature to serve its widely divergent constituents. As Duchemin saw it, 'for these unanswerable reasons ... the bundling of the Maritimes and Newfoundland together under a single "local government" is miles outside the range of practical politics.'[24] What is more, the *Post-Record*'s editor believed that the inclusion of Newfoundland would actually hinder the prospects of union. As a later editorial articulated, Newfoundland's Confederation 'makes such a union less desirable than it ever has been, and indeed removes the question entirely from the realm of even speculative politics. For it makes Maritime Canada far too expansive and economically diverse to be ever governed acceptably by a single local government.'[25]

Perhaps because of this unfavourable media coverage of his remarks in the legislature, Flemming began to qualify his endorsement of regional union. While not opposed to the idea of union, Flemming concluded that political amalgamation was not feasible at that time. As the New Brunswick opposition leader stated on 9 April 1947, 'some day, possibly, there may be a certain advantage in effecting a legislative union of Prince Edward Island and Nova Scotia with this province, but I do not think the day has come for it.' While Flemming continued to believe that union would prove to be a cost-saving measure, any financial benefits that came from the plan would be offset by the loss of provincial autonomy. In short, he concluded, 'the disadvantages of a legislative union, at the present time, would be far greater than the possible advantages.'[26]

This did not mean, however, that the idea of Maritime cooperation need be rejected. In Flemming's view, if Prince Edward Island, Nova

Scotia, and New Brunswick were to cooperate on matters of common concern, they could 'improve their national position and directly attack the grave problems of their economic life.'[27] Maritime cooperation, Flemming contended, was a worthwhile goal, one that had 'infinite possibilities.' Already the three provinces were cooperating in a number of ways, the Maritime Lumber Bureau and the Maritime Board of Trade being Flemming's foremost examples. What is more, the time was ripe for regional solidarity. The three Maritime Provinces had all recently concluded reports on reconstruction, and they could use these documents to pinpoint shared areas of need to be jointly developed. At the same time, the differing experiences of New Brunswick and Nova Scotia in the negotiation of tax rental agreements with Ottawa illustrated for Flemming the problems of not acting in concert and reinforced his belief that the Maritime Provinces could come to an informal agreement to cooperate on matters of regional concern.[28]

Flemming's reversal on the issue of union undoubtedly pleased Charles R. Allen, editor of the *Hartland Observer*, a small New Brunswick newspaper published in the heart of Flemming's own Carleton County constituency. In a 17 April 1947 editorial, Allen addressed the linked issues of Newfoundland and Atlantic union. While Allen acknowledged that 'there is room for Newfoundland as part of the Dominion of Canada,' he was adamant in dismissing the prospect of regional union. Allen suggested that most Maritimers would be against such a proposition, as the provincial divisions 'made many years ago have [existed] too long to effect a change now.' And even if provincial traditions could be overcome, there would still be troublesome financial details to work out, details that would make it 'next to impossible to reach a solution satisfactory to all.'[29] Allen welcomed Newfoundland to join Confederation as a tenth province, as it would be the easiest sort of union to effect, and it would have the added benefit of leaving the provincial status of New Brunswick, Nova Scotia, and PEI unchanged.

From Regional Union to Regional Solidarity

Flemming's qualification of his statements regarding regional union serve as a useful demarcation point between the desire among some Maritimers for Atlantic union and the less ambitious goal of developing some form of regional cooperation. It also seems likely that the clamour for formal Maritime political amalgamation began to subside in part because the entry of Newfoundland into Confederation had become a political certainty and the impracticality of merging the Atlantic region into one provincial body became more readily apparent. Nevertheless, the talk of Newfoundland's entry inspired hope that provincial political leaders would act in concert to improve conditions in the region. As the editor of *The Fundy Fisherman* observed in an editorial assessing the existing political relations between the Maritime Provinces, 'few families grow up with the children consistently harmonious [but perhaps] Newfoundland will be the catalyst that will finally resolve us into some united mass.'[30] As a 'united mass,' Maritime politicians would be better able to represent the interests of the region.

Perhaps the most enthusiastic advocate of Maritime regional cooperation during the late 1940s and early 1950s was New Brunswick businessman C.C. Avard. Well educated, articulate, and a respected former municipal politician, Avard served on a number of business boards in the Sackville area and emerged as the spokesman for the cause. Avard's spokesman status was aided by his strong ties to the New Brunswick Liberal establishment – he had been the director of publicity for Premier A.A. Dysart's 1939 provincial election campaign. Most important, however, as owner of the Tribune Printing Co., publisher of both the *Sackville Tribune-Post* and the *Maritime Advocate and Busy East*, Avard had a ready forum for disseminating his views both locally and across the region.

Notwithstanding his continued support for New Brunswick Liberal Premier John McNair, events in the federal sphere had cooled Avard's enthusiasm for the Liberal Party. Disheartened by the increasing marginalization of the Maritimes under the long rule of the King government, Avard observed as early as 1944 that

> we are victims of conditions over which we seemingly have little control, but one thing is sure and that is that we can't have a united Canada if some sections are weak and ailing, while other sections are strong and vigorous. From many stand points the Maritime Provinces would be better off to hoe their own row but we can't disrupt Canada. There must be some way out but I don't know what it is.[31]

By 1947, Avard was suggesting that Confederation had failed the Maritime Provinces, since the trend toward centralization ensured that 'the smaller provinces have not always received fair treatment.' He laid the blame for regional problems squarely on the shoulders of the region's Liberal MPs.[32] As Avard saw it, the Maritimes' Progressive Conservative MPs were increasingly becoming the champions of regional causes, while the Liberal representatives for the region were constantly hamstrung by party loyalty. Avard argued that Maritime Liberals' fear of the party whip was impeding regional development.[33]

This philosophy was ably illustrated in an article written by an author using the pseudonym Grant Evans that was published in the January 1949 *Maritime Advocate and Busy East*.[34] In a piece titled 'What's the Matter with the Maritimes?' Evans argued that years of centralist federal policies had hindered Maritime economic development. But instead of laying all the blame at Ottawa's feet, Evans, like Avard, admonished Maritime federal representatives for not adequately protecting the region's interests. He was especially critical of the Maritimes' recent Liberal MPs under Mackenzie King, who had failed to adequately defend the region. Maritimers had given King a large number of seats in the House of Commons, but this support was not returned by the prime minister. As Evans saw it, 'for the past 10 years Maritime members have had the King government in a corner where they could have squeezed out any concession they chose. But did they do so? You know the answer as well as I.'[35]

The key to solving the problem of regional representation, according to Evans, was to form a de facto regional bloc among the Maritime MPs in the House of Commons. This would not require any large-scale integration of the provincial governments, nor would it even necessitate discussions among Fredericton, Charlottetown, and Halifax regarding how to cooperate on matters of common concern. All that was required was a desire among the region's representatives in Ottawa to think regionally and not along party or provincial lines. In Evans's words, Maritimers should 'resolve to be masters in our own house and elect and retain control of a Maritime delegation of sufficient ability and practical experience to form a powerful bloc at Ottawa.' Since Maritimers would 'pledge all candidates of all parties in advance to vote against the party where necessary on each and every Maritime measure that arises from time to time,' this Maritime bloc would not be shackled by the customary bounds of party loyalty and would be expected to vote against the party line on matters of regional importance.[36] In so doing, the regional politicians would be looking after the interests of their constituents rather than the interests of the Liberal Party machinery.

Just a few months later, Avard used Newfoundland's recently concluded entry into Confederation to again promote regional solidarity. In a fiery June 1949 editorial, he trumpeted the cause of regional cohesion and cooperation, with Newfoundland as his catalyst:

> Now that Newfoundland has become Canada's tenth province, the Maritimes comprise four provinces instead of three. This has possibilities for solidarity, for unanimity of action, for a united Atlantic front. If all the representatives from this section of Canada would stand firmly together there would be formed a solid block that could demand Maritime rights from Ottawa instead of being men with their hats in their hands seeking favors from the bigwigs, who for a brief time occupy the seats of the mighty.[37]

Avard went on to recognize that though he 'may be preaching a dangerous gospel … if a man, a province, a group of provinces don't stand up for their rights then no one else will do so for them.'[38] For Avard, a regional front was needed to gain concessions that were due to the Maritimes as a matter of right, and the addition of Newfoundland would strengthen this claim by providing the Atlantic region with increased political representation. This added clout, he believed, would curb the governmental monopoly held by Liberals in Central and Western Canada. As Avard argued, 'the entrance of Newfoundland into the Canadian Confederation will give Nova Scotia, New Brunswick and Prince Edward Island a stronger voice in he government of Canada. Newfoundland should work with us and perhaps the tendency towards centralization in Ottawa can be checked.'[39] Newfoundland's Confederation, he believed, could only strengthen the Maritime region.

The *Maritime Advocate and Busy East*'s sentiments regarding the positive impact that Newfoundland's entry would have on the region were replicated in other Maritime news sources. The *Charlottetown Patriot*, for example, had suggested as early as June 1948 that Newfoundland's Confederation would make the Maritime voice in Ottawa better heard. Nova Scotia, New Brunswick, Prince Edward Island, and Newfoundland had many identical interests, contended the *Patriot*, and by acting together they would make their concerns better known in the federal sphere. This would be aided by Newfoundland's entry, as the new province would add seven members to the House of Commons, creating a 'bloc of 33 votes,' in addition to six new senators. As the *Patriot* argued, 'once the Newfoundland representatives are elected to the Commons and appointed for life to the Senate, the demands of the Atlantic provinces will carry more weight.'[40]

A similar take on the importance of Newfoundland's entry into Confederation to the Maritimes was offered in the pages of *The Fundy Fisherman*. On 3 November 1948, in one of the most politically astute editorials to appear in that paper's pages, the editor examined the Maritime role in federal politics. In the editor's eyes, the coming years should see the Maritime Provinces wielding greater say in federal affairs and Ottawa should be more than willing to assist Canada's eastern provinces. As the editor stated,

> The Maritime Provinces are now the stronghold of Liberalism in Canada. There are only three Liberal Provincial Governments and all three are located in the Maritimes. This places our Atlantic Provinces in a favourable position politically and the Federal Liberal Candidates should not be slow to call the attention of the present Federal government to the political loyalty of the Maritimes and ask for greater consideration of Maritime needs.[41]

The editor went on to recognize that within a year's time there would in all likelihood be a fourth Liberal government in Newfoundland, giving the region even greater say with the federal government.

Even H.P. Duchemin, editor of the avowedly anti-union *Sydney Post-Record*, endorsed the idea of regional cooperation, as such a tack had in the past born 'fruitful results.' The successes of the Maritime Rights movement, claimed the editor, were proof of what the Maritimes could accomplish when they acted in concert. Moreover, the time was right for a united front. The Board of Transport Commissioners had recently raised railway freight rates, which had brought the three Maritime Provinces together – along with the four western provinces – to oppose the measure, illustrating that when issues of common concern arose, the Maritime Provinces could act together to make their voices heard. Such actions, Duchemin maintained, did not warrant a new regional legislature.[42]

The regional solidarity espoused by Maritime papers almost occurred at the Liberal Party's national convention in 1948. At the convention, plans were made for New Brunswick Premier McNair to nominate Angus L. Macdonald for the Liberal leadership, guaranteeing Macdonald a chance to speak to the assembled delegates. During his speech, Macdonald would be able to articulate Maritime concerns, and in so doing he would spearhead a united Maritime front that would capture the attention of the convention, the press, and the public at large. After his address, Macdonald would withdraw his name from candidacy. As journalist and political operative Dalton Camp later described it: 'It seemed an entirely plausible, effective, and even dramatic way to make our views known and to demonstrate the unity and strength in which they were held.'[43] What is more, Newfoundland's pending entry added to the impact the Maritime politicians could have. As the *Charlottetown Patriot* trumpeted in its coverage of the convention, 'our three Maritime premiers are making them sit up at Ottawa and we also will have the Newfoundland premier with us – that's the idea!'[44] Despite the PEI paper's enthusiasm, the unity and strength of the Maritimes failed to appear. Nova Scotia MP Robert Winters, who was destined for a cabinet position under Louis St Laurent, caught wind of the scheme and managed to dissuade Macdonald from going through with it. With the Maritime threat extinguished, Louis St Laurent easily won the leadership on the first ballot.[45]

While Maritime unity fell prey to party politics at the 1948 Liberal convention, the idea of the Atlantic Provinces acting in concert stuck a chord with some Nova Scotia politicians. For example, during the 1949 Nova Scotia Throne Speech, Amherst Liberal MLA Martin Kaufman proposed the formation of a Maritime–Newfoundland Council that would discuss common interests in business and government among the soon-to-be four Atlantic Provinces. This council, Kaufman suggested, would then be able to present a united front to the federal government on matters of common concern.[46] Again, the added regional representation occasioned by Newfoundland's entry into Confederation was particularly important. As the *Charlottetown Guardian* stressed in discussing Kaufman's proposed council, 'it was important to have a "united Maritime bloc" for the welfare of the Provinces concerned or this advantage of increased strength would be lost.'[47] PEI Premier Jones seemed convinced of the plan's merits, and pledged that the Prince Edward Island government would 'heartily co-operate' in setting up an 'unofficial Maritime-Newfoundland Council' to be comprised of various regional business and government leaders.[48] But Jones may have unwittingly doomed the plan, when he declared it 'most proper' that Nova Scotia, as the oldest Maritime province, take the lead in setting up this cooperative body, for it was doubtful that Nova Scotia Premier Angus L. Macdonald would endorse any form of binding regional economic or political union.

Macdonald Says No

Macdonald's staunch support of provincial rights made him particularly ill-suited to spearhead any sort of union or cooperative movement. Given his spirited defence of provincial rights in 1947, it was unlikely that he would play the key role in galvanizing regional solidarity only two years later. The premier of the largest and wealthiest of the three Maritime Provinces, Macdonald certainly had a vested interest in maintaining provincial autonomy. As shown in the preceding chapter, he surely suspected that, given the federal government's reluctance to invest in the Maritimes during the war, the chances of Ottawa agreeing to both the Chignecto Canal and the Canso crossing were slim. Moreover, he recognized that these development programs could be viewed as at odds with each other – for example, the Chignecto Canal would benefit New Brunswick at the expense of Nova Scotia – and this led him to doubt the feasibility of regional union or even the practicality of regional cooperation. Thus, while PEI's Jones and New Brunswick's Flemming seem to have endorsed the ideas of union and cooperation because of the benefits to their respective provinces, Macdonald opposed these plans for the very same reasons.

Macdonald's opposition to Maritime union is clearly illustrated in an exceedingly brief interview he granted the *Sydney Post-Record*. When asked in June 1948 by the Cape Breton newspaper whether he saw regional amalgamation as a possibility, the Nova Scotia premier simply replied 'no.'[49] He elaborated on his negative opinion of union in a 1948 letter to pro-unionist Andrew Merkel: 'I doubt very much whether any great gain would be effected by Maritime Union.' The Nova Scotia premier, recognizing the region's long history of disunity, also rejected arguments that union would give the region a greater voice in Ottawa. 'Would we speak with one voice,' he pondered, 'and, if so, would the voice be in the proper pitch? I am not sure.' Even if the Maritime Provinces did unite, he contended, provincial cleavages would persist within the larger provincial entity. As he informed Merkel, 'there have been instances not so very long ago where I had hoped that Nova

Scotian members, and perhaps members from the other two Maritime Provinces, might have taken a stand, but they did not. I do not think that an amalgamation of the three provinces would change our natures.'[50] Merkel's reply admonished the premier for his limited perspective, suggesting that 'the thing that has wrecked Maritime Union has been a narrow provincialism of which no doubt we are all guilty.'[51]

Despite Macdonald's dismissal of Maritime union, Merkel did not give up hope for his cause. If Macdonald doubted the feasibility of Atlantic union on a broad scale, Merkel was prepared to push for union writ small. Betraying a weak grasp of the motivations and concerns of Newfoundlanders in the days leading up to their union with Canada, Merkel asked the Nova Scotia premier 'why would it not be possible at this juncture to have Newfoundland apply to Nova Scotia as a sort of big brother, to smooth the way by joining Confederation as part of Nova Scotia.' For Merkel, a Nova Scotia–Newfoundland merger would likely be the first step on the road to a broader Atlantic union in the near future. As the newsman made clear, 'my own feeling if this [Nova Scotia–Newfoundland union] were done Prince Edward Island and New Brunswick would subsequently ask to be admitted too. And even if either did not it would be okay.'[52]

Merkel seemed oblivious to what would have surely been a frosty response from Newfoundland to such a proposal. Many Newfoundlanders had been put off by the prospect of surrendering their independent dominion status in favour of Canadian provincehood. Indeed, some St John's advocates of responsible government had raised black flags on 1 April 1949 as a muted protest to Newfoundland's union with the 'Canadian wolf.' They surely would have objected even more vociferously to what would essentially be annexation by Nova Scotia. Merkel ultimately tempered his enthusiasm with realism, noting that a Nova Scotia–Newfoundland merger might carry few benefits. As he conceded to Macdonald, 'if there is nothing to be gained by such a union, we would do well to let sleeping dogs lie.'[53] Macdonald wisely ignored Merkel's ill-conceived suggestions, and Newfoundland entered Confederation at the stroke of midnight on 31 March 1949 without a Nova Scotian big brother holding its hand along the way.

Conclusion

During the late 1940s some Maritimers came to view their region as a community with similar problems and similar interests and began to agitate for regional union. They believed that with such a merger the Maritimes would be better able to petition Ottawa for greater assistance. Advocates of regional union were willing to welcome Newfoundland into this community, believing that the inclusion of the new province, with its added seats in the House of Commons and the Senate, would strengthen calls for federal aid to prevent further regional underdevelopment. Some Maritime and Newfoundland politicians even considered union to be a policy worth pursuing. But by the time Newfoundland formally entered Confederation in 1949, the push for formal political amalgamation had been replaced by the blossoming of a more limited and informal regional cooperation movement, one that grew into the 'Atlantic Revolution' of the 1950s.

Atlantic union did not occur in the 1940s because provincial loyalties and concerns invariably superseded regional ones and because no one could point to any real benefits of such a merger. With no guarantees that a union scheme would actually improve the region's economic prospects, Maritime politicians were highly reluctant to upset the political apple cart for a program that would be a tough sell to their constituents. As a result, regional politicians concluded that their best chances for economic improvement lay in the maintenance of separate provinces. Individually, Prince Edward Island could lobby for increased shipping capacity to Newfoundland, New Brunswick could demand the Chignecto Canal, and Nova Scotia could fight for the Canso crossing with equal vigour. These were important development programs for the individual provinces, and if union were effected, they would have to be prioritized by a new regional government. Moreover, there was surely an element of political self-preservation to be considered. With but one legislature for what had been four separate governments, the number of positions for politicians would likely decrease. What ultimately undid the Atlantic union drive of the 1940s was that the region's politicians, much like their 1970s counterparts, had simply concluded that Atlantic union – or even Atlantic solidarity – would not serve their purposes. They believed they could accomplish just as much individually without the disruption that union would bring. Not even the prospect of Newfoundland's added representation and clout could alter this simple fact.

Epilogue:
Term 29 and the Atlantic Revolution

During the late 1940s, as Newfoundland contemplated entering Confederation, Maritime politicians hoped that the pending merger could improve the regional situation by alleviating underdevelopment. Yet despite the existence of a Maritimes-wide rhetoric that connected Newfoundland's Confederation with improved economic and political prospects, differing assessments of provincial self-interest prevented the emergence of a regional front in response to the new province's entry and blunted efforts to alter the region's depressed position in Confederation. In large measure, the lack of regional purpose at the time of Newfoundland's Confederation stemmed from events of the previous few decades – events that had gradually eroded Maritime regionalism. The limited gains promised by the Maritime Rights movement gave way to the harsh realities of the Great Depression, the Second World War, and the protracted negotiations around dominion–provincial relations that privileged provincial needs rather than regional ones. By the end of the Second World War the regional front of the 1920s was a distant memory, with each Maritime province using Newfoundland's pending entry to champion schemes that would largely help itself, and reluctant to endorse development plans in a neighbouring province that would not bring corollary benefits.

Emblematic of this provincial mindset were the development programs that the Maritime Provinces proposed when Newfoundland was contemplating entering Confederation. Prince Edward Island focused its efforts on securing federal subsidization for the expansion of trade with the potential new province; New Brunswick tried to use the pending merger to add weight to its calls for the construction of the Chignecto Canal; and Nova Scotia argued that the inclusion of Newfoundland in Confederation warranted the construction of a fixed link across the Strait of Canso. Created largely in isolation and geared primarily toward provincial rehabilitation, these programs prevented the formation of a regional front, thereby weakening the Maritime lobby. As a result, only in Nova Scotia did Ottawa assist with a province's Newfoundland-based development plan, and even in this case the degree to which the new province influenced the ultimate decision is debatable. Maritime regionalism – a political phenomenon that ebbs and flows in relation to perceived political benefit – was thus at a low point on the eve of Newfoundland's entry into Confederation. Only during the mid-1950s 'Atlantic Revolution' – a term coined by historian W.S. MacNutt to describe the joint action undertaken by the four Atlantic Provinces during that decade to try to collectively alter the region's position within Confederation – did regionalism begin to reassert itself, and even then the bonds were not strong.

The cooperative spirit would emerge by mid-decade as the Atlantic Revolution coalesced slowly after Newfoundland's entry into Confederation. One of the first opportunities for the newly minted region to display a sense of solidarity was at the 1950 Dominion–Provincial Conference, which had been called to discuss Old Age Security. At this meeting, Nova Scotia, New Brunswick, and Prince Edward Island argued for a plan that would meet the needs of all provinces and that would bring the standard of living and services in the Maritimes closer to the Canadian average. PEI premier J. Walter Jones made the Maritime case most strenuously. 'The basis for any satisfactory agreement between the federal and provincial governments,' he argued passionately, 'must make possible at least an adequate average Canadian standard of services in every province' without impeding the rights of the richer provinces to provide a higher standard if they were so able.[1] Jones was hopeful that the addition of Newfoundland would strengthen his case. As he stated in his opening remarks, since the last time the federal and provincial governments had met 'there has been a new province created with its dynamic leader who sits here and takes part in our deliberations. As he likes to say, he belongs to one of our Atlantic provinces.'[2]

Unfortunately for Jones, Newfoundland Premier Joey Smallwood may have taken Newfoundland's new status as an 'Atlantic Province' a little too much to heart – to the detriment of the slowly coalescing new region. While the PEI premier and his Maritime counterparts lobbied Ottawa for more money to bring the regional situation more in line with the national average, Smallwood took a different approach. Though he acknowledged that 'the maritime provinces are regarded in Canada as the backward area of Canada,' Smallwood – perhaps motivated by Newfoundland's unenviable status as Canada's poorest province – maintained that his 'fondest ambition' was to raise Newfoundland's level of services 'up close' to what prevailed in the Maritimes.[3] That the average Maritime standard, not Canadian, was the Newfoundland premier's benchmark undercut Maritime desires for greater economic and social parity with the rest of the country, while revealing the influence that Term 29 had in Newfoundland's early post-Confederation political discourse. At this conference – the first since Newfoundland's entry into Confederation – Newfoundland seemed at odds with the Maritime Provinces. Though a regional front was clearly not entrenched at this point, from this inauspicious beginning the Atlantic Revolution would soon emerge.

The Atlantic Revolution, much like the Maritime reaction to Newfoundland's entry into Confederation, was rooted in events of the 1930s and 1940s, when the Maritime Provinces competed against one another for scant federal assistance. During the Great Depression and the Second World War, Nova Scotia, New Brunswick, and PEI acted in isolation when lobbying Ottawa – a strategy that proved ineffective. In the end, this fractured front, combined with federal concerns regarding defence of the region, led Ottawa to largely ignore the Maritime Provinces and to concentrate investment in the central provinces. The effects of such actions and policies on the Maritimes were readily apparent by war's end, when per capita income in the region stood 24 per cent below the Canadian average. Things did not improve in the 1950s. By 1955, per capita income in the region had dropped to 33 per cent below the Canadian average. In other words, the decade following the war's conclusion saw per capita income in the Maritimes drop from 76 per cent to 67 per cent of the Canadian average. Moreover, the net value of secondary manufacturing in the Atlantic Provinces was only $94 per person, far below the national average of $405.[4] Declining incomes relative to the Canadian standard prompted more and more Maritimers to leave their farms and fishing villages for the region's urban centres in search of secure work in expanding sectors such as construction, banking, and (particularly) government. The result was an increasingly urban Maritime population.[5]

The expansion of government in the postwar era points to a fundamental reconceptualization of the state that was occurring during these years – a reconceptualization that contributed to the birth of the Atlantic Revolution. This was the era of Keynesian economics, with government elites calling for such things as countercyclical financing and a greater role for the state in regulating the economy. After the war, governments across Canada turned their attention to massive reconstruction efforts – efforts that required them to play a far more interventionist role. The Maritimes was no exception. New Brunswick's road-building efforts, PEI's expansion of its Newfoundland trade, and Nova Scotia's modernization of the fishery, to cite but a few examples, all placed additional pressure on provincial treasuries, which in turn led to heightened expectations among Atlantic Canadians regarding what the state could do to remedy underdevelopment. The federal government had, after all, overseen the centralization of industry in Ontario and Quebec during the war; and the postwar years had seen expenditures of huge sums of money on projects deemed important to the central provinces, such as the St Lawrence Seaway. Perhaps, then, concerted action by the Maritime governments could counter this centralizing trend and bring federal largesse east of the Quebec border.

Also contributing to the Atlantic Revolution was a change in political will and leadership. Conservative Hugh John Flemming's victory over Liberal John McNair in New Brunswick's 1952 election brought to the premier's office a leader more committed to regional action and less beholden to the federal Liberals. Equally important was the ascension of Henry Hicks as premier of Nova Scotia following the death in 1954 of Angus L. Macdonald. Macdonald had been at the forefront of the 1940s battles between the provinces and the federal government over provincial rights, and his steely commitment to that crusade made him ill suited to the regionalist cause. Hicks, on the other hand, was quick to embrace the potential of regional action. Within two weeks of becoming Nova Scotia's premier in 1955, he oversaw the creation of the Atlantic Provinces Economic Council (APEC), a region-wide organization tasked with surveying, studying, stimulating, and coordinating activities related to the economic well-being of the Atlantic Provinces.[6] Not to be outdone, that same year Flemming inaugurated a series of Atlantic Premiers' Conferences (APCs), where the four Atlantic premiers could discuss matters of common concern. Through initiatives such as APEC and the APC, the cooperative movement of the 1950s enabled the premiers of the four Atlantic Provinces to meet on matters of common interest without being compelled to

commit to any plan that might prove harmful to their own provinces –
a luxury the regional union movement of the 1940s did not provide.[7]
These 1950s regional initiatives performed as expected, allowing the
Maritime Provinces to act in concert in lobbying the 1955 Royal Commission on Canada's Economic Prospects and in making the regional
case at the 1955 Dominion–Provincial Conference. These regionally
minded actions seemed to have succeeded when the 1956 federal
budget was released with plans for a more equitable equalization
formula based on the average income of the two wealthiest provinces.

An important – and often overlooked – catalyst of the Atlantic Revolution was Newfoundland's entry into Confederation and the connections that developed between the Maritimes and the new province.
Though the Maritimes and Newfoundland had operated in some
important ways in close proximity prior to 1949, since the earliest days
of European settlement there had been a distance between the two.
Newfoundland's formal political links tended to be with either
London or Ottawa, bypassing Maritime political and economic
centres. The ties that did exist between the Maritimes and Newfoundland were often between private individuals or interests and did not
involve strong connections between states. As a result, broad regional
connections between Newfoundland and the Maritimes were extremely rare in the years preceding Newfoundland's entry into Confederation, for there was no strong institutional base on which to
develop such linkages.

This situation changed at midnight on 31 March 1949, when Term 29
of the Newfoundland Act formally bound Newfoundland and the
Maritimes together. This rather pathetic clause from Newfoundland's
terms of union tied the new province's standard of living to that of the
Maritime Provinces rather than to that of Canada, in the process
inventing 'Atlantic Canada' as a political entity while simultaneously
ensuring that this new entity remained economically distressed. Term
29 grouped the four provinces as one region in federal eyes; also, with
the addition of an impoverished new province, it made the discrepancy in standards between Atlantic Canada and the rest of the country
all the more striking. For example, when Newfoundland was factored
into the calculation of 1955 per capita income, the Atlantic Canadian
average dropped to a mere 63 per cent of the Canadian average.[8] At
the same time, the entrance of Newfoundland quadrupled the geographic area of the region, leading many Maritimers to believe that the
new province's additional seats in the House of Commons and Senate

would allow the region to more forcefully make its case for federal assistance. As a result, Newfoundland became an integral part of the Atlantic Revolution's cooperative push. Soon after its entry into Confederation, for example, the new province was warmly welcomed into the Maritime Provinces Board of Trade, whose Transportation Commission coordinated the Atlantic effort to halt increases in freight rates to the region – an effort that Newfoundland supported.[9]

As the 1950s rolled on, Newfoundland premier Joey Smallwood – notwithstanding his performance at the 1950 Dominion–Provincial Conference – became a spirited advocate of Newfoundland and Maritime development. He was quick to criticize the federal government for the centralist policies that had strengthened Ontario and Quebec seemingly at the expense of Atlantic Canada, and he pledged that 'every bit of [Newfoundland's] strength and energy as a government will be used in this great work of development.'[10] As the fiery Newfoundland premier told a 1955 meeting of the Atlantic Association of Broadcasters, 'before we become second-class citizens of Canada we will show the other Maritime provinces how to get out of Confederation.'[11] Yet despite Smallwood's braggadocio, secession was never a viable option for the Newfoundland premier, and his trenchant support of regional development stemmed from factors unique to his province. According to Term 29, within eight years of Newfoundland's joining Confederation a Royal Commission was to be called to determine 'the form and scale of additional financial assistance, if any, that may be required' to ensure that the Newfoundland standard of services was equal to that prevailing in the Maritimes.[12] With Confederation, the Newfoundland government would have to impose new taxes, such as a general sales tax, and increase existing taxes, such as gasoline levies, in order to remain financially viable while providing an acceptable level of social services. Term 29 mandated a transitional grant for eight years to help the provincial government fulfil this obligation during the early years of its integration into Canada. The end of this eight-year period would culminate in a promised Royal Commission to investigate Newfoundland's financial position and to recommend any future grants that might be owed the province. It was over Term 29 and this Royal Commission that Smallwood would come into conflict with his fellow Atlantic premiers, leaving the Newfoundland leader profoundly disappointed and splintering the neophyte Atlantic Revolution before it could bring about any meaningful changes to the region's position within Confederation. In a somewhat ironic twist,

Term 29 helped invent the political region of Atlantic Canada even while it prepared the ground for a splintering of regional cooperation as a political strategy.

The importance of Term 29 to the Newfoundland premier cannot be overstated. Smallwood had long viewed this clause of the Newfoundland Act as the key to his province's economic future. Indeed, he claimed that without the guarantees offered by Term 29, Newfoundland would never have entered Confederation.[13] The perceived importance of this clause led Smallwood to begin preparing as early as 1953 to lobby for a generous federal grant under Term 29. That year he appointed a Newfoundland Royal Commission to ready itself to make the province's case before the federal Royal Commission that was to follow within four years. Smallwood was optimistic that Newfoundland's special status as Canada's newest and poorest province would result in a financial windfall when the Royal Commission mandated by Term 29 was finally called. And the Newfoundland premier had an additional reason for optimism: he had an amiable relationship with the Liberal government of Louis St Laurent, which gave him much confidence that Newfoundland federal politician and Liberal insider J.W. Pickersgill would ably champion the province's interests with regard to the Term 29 Royal Commission. Indeed, Smallwood was certain that St Laurent 'would have died rather than deny the moral obligation created by Canada's signing of Term 29.'[14] Unfortunately for the Newfoundland premier, St Laurent did something far worse than dying: he lost the 1957 federal election. Smallwood's carefully laid plan for Term 29 imploded when John Diefenbaker, a Progressive Conservative, was elected prime minister.

Smallwood initially had reason to be optimistic about Diefenbaker. As Smallwood's memoirs make clear, during the 1950s the Newfoundland premier had performed a number of 'favours' for the Saskatchewan-born prime minister. He hoped that such small gestures as (quite by accident) being the first Newfoundlander to greet Diefenbaker on his initial trip to the new island province would pay off down the road.[15] Moreover, Diefenbaker had originally been a supporter of the Atlantic cause, largely for political reasons. During the 1957 federal election, in an effort to increase the Progressive Conservative vote in Atlantic Canada, Diefenbaker readily adopted the Atlantic Manifesto, a program for regional economic development created by the five Maritime Progressive Conservative MPs, which called for such things as the decentralization of industry, adjustment grants to assist the poorer provinces, and reductions in freight rates.[16] The manifesto did what it was designed to, and in the 1957 campaign Diefenbaker and his party won a minority government with a slim seven-seat majority over the Liberals, largely on the support of Atlantic Canadian voters. Though the Liberals tried to jump on the regional development bandwagon during the 1958 election, Atlantic Canadians again voted for Diefenbaker.[17] Yet while the new prime minister appeared committed to regional development – he did, after all, loan $29.5 million to New Brunswick for the Beechwood power plant and provide more than $25 million in Atlantic Adjustment Grants – he proved reluctant to entertain Smallwood's claims to special status under Term 29.

In the fall of 1957 the Royal Commission to investigate Term 29 was appointed. Headed by former New Brunswick Premier John McNair, and featuring commissioners such as Queen's University economist John Deutsch and Newfoundland Chief Justice Albert Walsh, the commission reported remarkably quickly on the status of Newfoundland's finances, tabling its report on 25 July 1958. The McNair Commission, as it came to be known, recommended that the transitional grant paid to Newfoundland be raised to $8 million annually – an amount particularly galling to Smallwood, who viewed $15 million as a more viable sum. Never one to hold his tongue when he felt he had been wronged, Smallwood freely aired his discontent, a tactic that greatly annoyed Diefenbaker – who already looked unfavourably on Newfoundland because that province had elected only one Progressive Conservative MP in the recently concluded election – and that backfired when the prime minister rose in the House of Commons to declare that the $8 million grant recommended by the McNair Commission was the 'final and irrevocable' settlement of Newfoundland's terms of union and would only be paid until 1962. Diefenbaker's hardline stance incensed Smallwood, and the Newfoundland premier began to disassociate himself from his Atlantic counterparts and from the politics of regionalism. At the 1959 Atlantic Premiers' Conference, Smallwood publicly stated that he would not ask the other premiers to take an official stance on Term 29. His fear was that their position might be at odds with his and lead to frosty relations between Newfoundland and the other Atlantic Provinces. 'It would be a pity if the Atlantic front were broken,' he told his counterparts.[18] Yet the fact that Smallwood was wary of asking his fellow premiers to support Newfoundland's position meant that, for all intents and purposes, the front had already begun to splinter.

Though the Atlantic Revolution would persist into the 1960s, by the end of that decade Atlantic Canadian regional collaboration was once again on the wane. The defeat of New Brunswick's Flemming – the de facto leader of the Atlantic Revolution – in the 1960 New Brunswick election led to the ascension of Louis J. Robichaud, who as premier of that province continued the fight for the Chignecto Canal, while also advocating in 1964 for the union of the Atlantic Provinces.[19] While Smallwood, along with Robert Stanfield, the Nova Scotia premier who had replaced Hicks, promised to 'study' the proposal, new PEI Premier Walter Shaw refused to commit his province to the idea.[20] Despite the Deutsch Commission's subsequent endorsement in 1970 of Maritime Union, just as in the late 1940s, nothing tangible came out of the 1960s union movement. What is more, the Deutsch Commission did not even consider Newfoundland in its study, which makes clear that by the end of the 1960s Newfoundland had begun to distance itself from its Maritime cousins. By the time the Deutsch Report was tabled, regional union was essentially a non-starter and the coopera- tive spirit of the Atlantic Revolution had faded, a victim both of a lack of public involvement – women, labour, and rural voters in particular had little say in shaping the movement's principles – and of the oppo- sition of other provinces.[21]

The Atlantic Revolution was an attempt by Atlantic Canada to act regionally, but its gains were limited. A lasting sense of regionalism and solidarity did not take root among the four Atlantic Provinces during the 1950s and 1960s, and the region's economic position remained below the Canadian average. Term 29 of the Newfoundland Act was one area on which the Atlantic premiers could surely have found common ground, as that issue saw a convergence of provincial and regional interests. Term 29 not only 'invented' Atlantic Canada as a functional political designation by formally linking Newfoundland's development to the Maritime average, but also ensured that the new region would remain economically marginalized.[22] Instead of accept- ing economic status below the Canadian average as was mandated by this clause, the four Atlantic premiers could have lobbied Ottawa together to ensure that Newfoundland and the Maritimes reached national levels of wealth and well-being. Unfortunately, the seeds of division sown during the Depression and the Second World War remained strongly rooted, and provincial ambitions continued to trump regional concerns even during the heady days of the Atlantic Revolution.

In his study *The Rise of Regional Europe,* historian Christopher Harvie
has compared the historiography of European regionalism to 'a badly
organised dinner party' at which the guests 'somehow contrive to
speak not to but alongside one another.'[23] The same could be said of
the Maritime Provinces' response to Newfoundland's Confederation.
Their long experience since colonial times of dealing with Newfoundland on an individual basis meant that by the postwar years they were
well accustomed to operating in isolation. Because of this, when Newfoundland contemplated joining Confederation the Maritime
Provinces did not act in concert; instead, three separate but similar
provincial responses emerged as each province reacted to Newfoundland's entry individually and provincial leaders took it upon themselves to try to use the union to remedy underdevelopment in their
respective provinces, with generally disappointing results. This lack of
a regional response to Newfoundland's entry into Confederation
speaks to the lack of ties more generally among the three provinces
that constitute the Maritimes and Newfoundland, and foreshadowed
later problems that would arise to fragment the cooperative spirit of
the Atlantic Revolution. Instead of speaking together with one clear
voice, the Maritime Provinces offered a discordant chorus. Perhaps the
ensuing chatter made it easier for Ottawa to ignore them.

Notes

Introduction

1 I have chosen to use Newfoundland rather than the current political designation of Newfoundland and Labrador as this study deals almost exclusively with relations between the island of Newfoundland and the Maritime Provinces. In the 1940s Labrador did not factor into the relationship; it was viewed merely as a resource-rich extension of the island. James Hiller has noted that 'for many years, Labrador was treated as a subordinate dependency of Newfoundland, and the territory did not develop its own effective and separate political and cultural consciousness until the late 1960s and after.' James K. Hiller, 'Robert Bond and the Pink, White, and Green: Newfoundland Nationalism in Perspective,' *Acadiensis* 36, no. 2 (Spring 2007), 113.

2 This study does not analyse the relative merits of Newfoundland's entry into Canadian Confederation, nor does it detail Newfoundland's efforts to negotiate a Confederation agreement. Those subjects have already received much coverage. See, for example, H.B. Mayo, 'Newfoundland's Entry into the Dominion,' *Canadian Journal of Economics and Political Science* 15, no. 4 (November 1949), 505–22; and idem, 'Newfoundland and Canada: The Case for Union Examined' (DPhil thesis, Oxford University, 1948). More recently, Newfoundland's Royal Commission on Renewing and Strengthening Our Place in Canada produced a number of background studies detailing the province's position within Confederation. These backgrounders include Jerry Bannister, 'The Politics of Cultural Memory: Themes in the History of Newfoundland and Labrador in Canada, 1972–2003'; Christopher Dunn, 'Federal Representation of the People and Government of Newfoundland and Labrador'; and Roger

Gibbins, 'Assessing Newfoundland and Labrador's Position on Canada's Evolving Federalism Landscape.' There are also a number of monograph-length studies of Newfoundland's Confederation. David Mackenzie has provided a thorough study of Canada's role in bringing about Newfoundland's union. Peter Neary has offered insight into British motivations for Newfoundland's entry into Confederation; he has also considered whether Confederation was a 'conspiracy or choice.' Raymond Blake has extended the study of Newfoundland's Confederation past the 1949 merger by exploring the bureaucratic and political difficulties associated with incorporating Newfoundland as a province. See David Mackenzie, *Inside the Atlantic Triangle: Canada and the Entrance of Newfoundland into Confederation, 1939–1949* (Toronto: University of Toronto Press, 1986); Peter Neary, *Newfoundland in the North Atlantic World, 1929–1949* (Montreal and Kingston: McGill–Queen's University Press, 1988); idem, 'Newfoundland's Union with Canada, 1949: Conspiracy or Choice?' *Acadiensis* 12, no. 2 (Spring 1983), 110–19; and Raymond Blake, *Canadians at Last: Canada Integrates Newfoundland as a Province* (Toronto: University of Toronto Press, 1994). Newfoundland's Confederation has also been the subject of a number of graduate theses. See, for example, John E. FitzGerald, 'The Confederation of Newfoundland with Canada, 1946–1949' (MA thesis, Memorial University, 1992); and Jeff A. Webb, 'Newfoundland's National Convention, 1946–48' (MA thesis, Memorial University, 1987). The journal *Newfoundland Studies* devoted an entire issue to Confederation. See *Newfoundland Studies* 14, no. 2 (Fall 1998).

3 Canada, 'Term 29,' *An Act to confirm and give effect to Terms of Union agreed between Canada and Newfoundland*, assented to 23 March 1949.

4 W.L.M. King Diary, 18 July 1947, MG 26, LAC.

5 Dominion of Canada, *Official Report of Debates, House of Commons*, 1949 (Ottawa: King's Printer, 1949), 289.

6 House of Commons, *Debates*, 1949, 297.

7 Paul Bridle, ed., *Documents on Relations between Canada and Newfoundland*, vol. 2: *1940–1949, Confederation*, Pt I (Ottawa: Minister of Supply and Services Canada, 1984), 1187; J.G. Channing, Secretary of the Newfoundland Delegation, to Cabinet Committee on Newfoundland, 23 November 1948, in ibid., 1215. See also Minutes of a Meeting of the Cabinet Committee and the Newfoundland Delegation, 26 November 1948, in ibid., 1224.

8 Emphasis added. Winters's use of the term 'greater Maritime region' suggests the inclusion of Newfoundland in that designation. *Sydney Post-Record*, 20 April 1949.

9 Maritime opinion of Newfoundland's entry has been neglected by schol-

ars of Atlantic Canada. For example, the two most prominent general surveys of Atlantic Canadian history, E.R. Forbes and D.A. Muise's *The Atlantic Provinces in Confederation* (Toronto and Fredericton: University of Toronto Press and Acadiensis Press, 1993) and Margaret Conrad and James Hiller's *Atlantic Canada: A Concise History* (Toronto: Oxford University Press, 2006), make no mention of what Prince Edward Island, New Brunswick, and Nova Scotia thought of Newfoundland's Confederation. This oversite has been corrected in the most recent edition of the Conrad and Hiller survey. See Margaret Conrad and James Hiller, *Atlantic Canada: A History* (Toronto: Oxford University Press, 2010).

10 J.W. Pickersgill and D.F. Forster, *The Mackenzie King Record: Volume 4, 1947–1948* (Toronto: University of Toronto Press, 1970), 75–6. See also Neary, *Newfoundland in the North Atlantic World,* 308. For more on King's opinion of Newfoundland's entry into Confederation, see Raymond Blake, 'WLMK's Attitude towards Newfoundland's Entry into Confederation,' *Newfoundland Quarterly* 82, no. 4 (1987), 26–37.

11 Bridle, *Documents,* 575–6. Unfortunately, the Gallup polls do not break down Maritime opinion to the provincial level. It is therefore impossible to quantify support in the individual Maritime Provinces.

12 Peter Neary, *Newfoundland in the North Atlantic World,* 308.

13 *Saint John Telegraph-Journal,* 24 March 1949.

14 For an example of the link between region and political groupings, see William Cross, 'The Increasing Importance of Region to Canadian Election Campaigns,' in *Regionalism and Party Politics in Canada,* ed. Lisa Young and Keith Archer (Toronto: Oxford University Press, 2002), 116–28.

15 Margaret R. Conrad and James K. Hiller, *Atlantic Canada: A Region in the Making* (Toronto: Oxford University Press, 2001), 6.

16 Janine Brodie, *The Political Economy of Canadian Regionalism* (Toronto: Harcourt Brace Jovanovich, 1990).

17 Widdis made the claim with regard to the nation-state, but it is equally applicable to region. See Randy William Widdis, 'Globalization, Glocalization, and the Canadian West as Region: A Geographer's View,' *Acadiensis* 35, no. 2 (Spring 2006), 129. In a similar fashion, Wallace Clement had earlier contended that all Canadian regionalisms were geographically rooted expressions of national inequality. See Wallace Clement, 'A Political Economy of Regionalism in Canada,' in *Modernization and the Canadian State,* ed. Daniel Glenday, Hubert Guindon, and Allan Turowetz (Toronto: Macmillan, 1978), 89–110.

18 Colin Howell, 'Economism, Ideology, and the Teaching of Maritime History,' in *Teaching Maritime Studies,* ed. P.A. Buckner (Fredericton: Acadiensis Press, 1986), 19. For a detailed examination of the Maritime

Rights Movement, see E.R. Forbes, *The Maritime Rights Movement, 1919–1927* (Montreal and Kingston: McGill–Queen's University Press, 1979).

19 See, for example, Gerald Friesen, *Citizens and Nation: An Essay on History, Communication, and Canada* (Toronto: University of Toronto Press, 2000); and idem, 'The Evolving Meanings of Region in Canada,' *Canadian Historical Review* 82, no. 3 (September 2001), 530–45.

20 Benedict Anderson, *Imagined Communities: Reflections on the Origin and Spread of Nationalism* (London: Verso, 1983). Ian McKay has argued that the scholars of Atlantic Canada must move past viewing the region simply as a product of underdevelopment and examine the region as a cultural construction. See Ian McKay, 'A Note on Region in Writing the History of Atlantic Canada,' *Acadiensis* 29, no. 2 (Spring 2000), 89–101.

21 Andrew Nurse, 'Rethinking the Canadian Archipelago: Regionalism and Diversity in Canada,' report prepared for Department of Canadian Heritage, 2002, 7. http://www.mta.ca/faculty/arts/canadian_studies/anurse/regionalism.pdf. This is not entirely the case, as certain geographic areas – islands in particular – can be cogent and well-defined regions.

22 This study does not concern itself with the presence of other identities located within Atlantic Canada, such as Acadian, Mi'kmaq, or Africadian. This is not in order to minimize the importance of these forms of identification, but rather because these ethnically based identities do not necessarily conflict with a Maritime or Atlantic Canadian identity. As British historian Linda Colley has suggested: 'Identities are not like hats. Human beings can and do put on several at a time.' See Linda Colley, *Britons: Forging a Nation, 1707–1837* (New Haven: Yale University Press, 1992), 6.

23 Jeff A. Webb, *The Voice of Newfoundland: A Social History of the Broadcasting Corporation of Newfoundland, 1939–1949* (Toronto: University of Toronto Press, 2009), 199.

24 Blake, *Canadians at Last*, 179.

25 Though New Brunswick Premier John McNair was informing the Canadian press that the 'Atlantic Provinces are a vital part of our country' as early as 1951, a search of the *Globe and Mail*'s online archival database reveals that the terms 'Atlantic Canada' and 'Atlantic Provinces' did not come into widespread use until later in the 1950s. See Speech by J.B. McNair to the Canadian Press, 21 September 1951, RS 414, D5a1c, J.B. McNair Papers, PANB, and http://heritage.theglobeandmail.com/Default.asp.

26 The tendency of Maritime regionalism to rise and fall in waves also helps

explain the different opinions proffered by Mildred Schwartz and J. Murray Beck regarding the very existence of a Maritime regional consciousness. Schwartz, an American sociologist, contended in 1974 that the Maritimes constitute a region and display an 'in-group consciousness.' Less than a decade later, political scientist J. Murray Beck observed that 'unless the criteria of a region are taken simply as geographical propinquity, likeness in historical and population background, and similarity of economic problems, the Maritime provinces ... do not constitute a region in any meaningful way.' Though their opposing views on Maritime regionalism can in part be explained by their having adopted different approaches to the subject – Schwartz examined a 1965 national election survey, while Beck provided a historiographical analysis – the time period when each published their findings must also be considered. Schwartz published her study shortly after the 1970 publication of the Deutsch Commission's Report on Maritime Union, making it likely that a spirit of regionalism would be more pronounced in the early 1970s and in her work. By contrast, Beck published his study in 1981, after the union movement had fallen apart amidst sectional differences. See Mildred A. Schwartz, *Politics and Territory: The Sociology of Regional Persistence in Canada* (Montreal and Kingston: McGill–Queen's University Press, 1974), 104; and J. Murray Beck, 'An Atlantic Region Political Culture: A Chimera,' in *Eastern and Western Perspectives: Papers from the Joint Atlantic Canada / Western Canadian Studies Conference*, ed. David Jay Bercuson and Phillip A. Buckner (Toronto: University of Toronto Press, 1981), 148. See also J. Murray Beck, 'The Maritimes: A Region or Three Provinces?' Royal Society of Canada, *Transactions*, series 4, no. 15 (1977), 301–13. For a more recent examination of the lack of a homogeneous Maritime political culture, see Ian Stewart, *Roasting Chesnuts: The Mythology of Maritime Political Culture* (Vancouver: UBC Press, 1994).

27 For an excellent example of this trend, see *The Atlantic Provinces in Confederation*, which treats Newfoundland as a separate entity until its 1949 entry into Confederation. For a pointed critique of this approach, see Malcolm Macleod, 'Another Look at *The Atlantic Provinces in Confederation*,' *Acadiensis* 23, no. 2 (Spring 1994), 191–7. For a recent example of a regional synthesis, see Conrad and Hiller, *Atlantic Canada: A Concise History*. That this important work resulted from a collaboration between a Maritime historian and a Newfoundland historian speaks to the continued separateness of the two historiographies. An exception to this general trend can be found in the work of Newfoundland historian Malcolm MacLeod. the focus of his scholarship is

Canada–Newfoundland relations; while Maritime–Newfoundland connections occasionally appear in his work, they are never the primary
focus. See, for example, Malcolm Macleod, 'Subsidized Steamers to a
Foreign Country: Canada and Newfoundland, 1892–1949,' *Acadiensis* 14,
no. 2 (Spring 1985), 66–92; idem, 'Students Abroad: Pre-Confederation
Educational Links between Newfoundland and the Mainland of Canada,'
Historical Papers / Communications historiques (1985), 172–92; idem, 'Edging
into North America: Lives and Foreign Linkages in Pre-Confederation
Newfoundland,' *Acadiensis* 21, no. 2 (1992), 146–61; idem, *Kindred Countries: Canada and Newfoundland before Confederation* (Ottawa: Canadian
Historical Association, 1994); idem, 'Disaster Documents 1914: The Official Canadian Response to Newfoundland's Sealing Tragedies,' in *Connections: Newfoundland's Pre-Confederation Links with Canada and the World*,
ed. Malcolm MacLeod (St John's: Creative Publishers, 2003), 215–20;
idem, 'Searching the Wreckage for Signs of Region: Newfoundland and
the Halifax Explosion,' in *Connections: Newfoundland's Pre-Confederation
Links with Canada and the World*, ed. Malcolm MacLeod (St John's: Creative Publishers, 2003), 221–37; idem, 'Labrador for Sale – 27% Off,' *Newfoundland Quarterly* (Fall 1979), 13–14; idem, 'You Must Go Home Again:
A Newfoundland–Canada Quarrel over Deportations, 1932–1933,' *Newfoundland Quarterly* (Spring 1983), 23–5; and idem, 'Confederation, 1937,'
Newfoundland Studies 1, no. 2 (Fall 1985), 201–10.

28 An observation made by James Hiller. See Hiller, 'Robert Bond and the
Pink, White and Green,' 113. What is more, MacNutt's study, solicited for
W.L. Morton's Canadian Centenary Series, would only take the history of
the Atlantic colonies up until 1857, at which point Maritime history
would be incorporated into supposedly broader national studies of
Canada. See W.S. MacNutt, *The Atlantic Provinces: The Emergence of Colo-
nial Society, 1712–1857* (Toronto: McClelland and Stewart, 1965). See also
Lyle Dick, '"A Growing Necessity for Canada": W.L. Morton's Centenary
Series and the Forms of National History, 1955–80,' *Canadian Historical
Review* 82, no. 2 (June 2001), 223–52. It is also important to note that by
1965, when MacNutt wrote his book, the term 'Atlantic Canada' was a
more prominent part of public discourse.

29 It is important to note that Hiller qualified his claim by stating that the
Maritimes might be a 'historic' region, suggesting that though they may
share a common experience and history, they do not share a common
identity. James K. Hiller, 'Is Atlantic Canadian History Possible?' *Acadiensis* 30, no. 1 (Autumn 2000), 20. Archaeologist and historian Peter Pope
takes the argument one step further, suggesting in reference to the early

modern period that Atlantic Canada was 'an improbable creature: this was not a colony, nor even a region, in the sense that New England was. Atlantic Canada is, in a sense, a chimera given coherent identity only by the faint scent of cod.' See Peter Pope, 'Comparisons: Atlantic Canada,' in *A Companion to Colonial America*, ed. Daniel Vickers (Oxford: Blackwell, 2005), 503.

30 Hiller, 'Is Atlantic Canadian History Possible?' 21.

31 *Antigonish Casket*, 31 March 1949.

32 David Alexander, 'Economic Growth in the Atlantic Region, 1880–1940,' *Acadiensis* 8, no. 1 (Autumn 1978), 47.

33 McKay, 'A Note on Region,' 92.

34 Underdevelopment was a long-standing feature of the Newfoundland economy as well. See, for example, David Alexander, 'Development and Dependence in Newfoundland, 1880–1970,' in *Atlantic Canada and Confederation: Essays in Canadian Political Economy*, ed. David Alexander (Toronto: University of Toronto Press, 1983), 3–31.

35 Donald Savoie, *Visiting Grandchildren: Economic Development in the Maritimes* (Toronto: University of Toronto Press, 2006), 28; Alexander, 'Development and Dependence in Newfoundland,' 4.

36 For a detailed study of the effect of the National Policy on the Maritimes, see T.W. Acheson, 'The National Policy and the Industrialization of the Maritimes, 1880–1910,' *Acadiensis* 1, no. 2 (Spring 1972), 3–28.

37 Savoie, *Visiting Grandchildren*, 29.

38 E.R. Forbes, 'The Origins of the Maritime Rights Movement,' *Acadiensis* 5, no. 5 (Autumn 1975), 57.

39 In the 1921 election the Liberals won 25 of the region's 31 seats; in 1925 the Conservatives took 23 of 29 seats.

40 Forbes, *The Maritime Rights Movement*, vii. For more on the Maritime Freight Rates Act, see E.R. Forbes, 'Misguided Symmetry: The Destruction of Regional Transportation Policy for the Maritimes,' in *Canada and the Burden of Unity*, ed. David Bercuson (Toronto: Macmillan of Canada, 1977), 60–86.

41 In historian David Frank's opinion, 'the failure of the report and the weakness of subsequent action may simply have increased Maritime cynicism about the prospects for achieving significant changes through the political process.' David Frank, 'The 1920s: Class and Region, Resistance and Accommodation,' in *The Atlantic Provinces in Confederation*, ed. E.R. Forbes and D.A. Muise (Toronto and Fredericton: University of Toronto Press and Acadiensis Press, 1993), 261. See also Edward MacDonald, *If You're Stronghearted: Prince Edward Island in the Twentieth Century* (Char-

lottetown: Prince Edward Island Museum and Heritage Foundation, 2000), 147–9.

42 For example, in 1933 the Maritime per capita income was $185, which was on par with Prairie per capita income of $181 though well below the national average of $262. A 1935 survey of monthly relief payments in ten cities found that the average payment in the three Maritime cities surveyed was $3.77, much lower than the $9.47 average payment in the other seven cities. Similarly, the unemployment rate in the region was 19 per cent, which was higher than Ontario's 16.6 per cent rate and Quebec's 16.9 per cent rate. Only in the West were unemployment rates higher than in the Maritimes, ranging from 19.9 per cent in Saskatchewan to 24.7 per cent in British Columbia. See E.R. Forbes, 'Cutting the Pie into Smaller Pieces: Matching Grants and Relief in the Maritime Provinces during the 1930s,' *Acadiensis* 17, no. 1 (Autumn 1987), 36–7.

43 For a thorough discussion of the Maritime Provinces and the matching grant relief system, see Forbes, 'Cutting the Pie,' 34–55. The amount of each relief allocation depended on the decisions of the municipal governments. This meant that affluent jurisdictions could choose to make lower relief payments than poorer ones.

44 See James Struthers, *Unemployment and the Canadian Welfare State, 1914–1941* (Toronto: University of Toronto Press, 1983), 175–84.

45 *Proceedings of Dominion–Provincial Conference 1941* (Ottawa: King's Printer, 1941), 15–16. Ontario also had a vested interest in avoiding the implementation of the Rowell-Sirois recommendations, for – as John Saywell has argued – 'there was nothing for it in the report.' John Saywell, *'Just call me Mitch': The Life of Mitchell F. Hepburn* (Toronto: University of Toronto Press, 1991), 459. For an overview of the Rowell-Sirois Commission, see David Fransen, 'Unscrewing the Unscrutable: The Rowell-Sirois Commission, the Ottawa Bureaucracy, and Public Finance Reform, 1935–1941' (PhD diss., University of Toronto, 1984). For an analysis of the animosity between Ontario Premier Mitch Hepburn and Prime Minister King surrounding the commission, see Richard M.H. Alway, 'Hepburn, King, and the Rowell-Sirois Commission,' *Canadian Historical Review* 48, no. 2 (June 1967), 113–41. For a Maritime interpretation of the Rowell-Sirois Commission, see Corey Slumkoski, 'Prelude to Equalization: New Brunswick and the Tax Rental Agreements, 1941–1957' (MA thesis, University of New Brunswick, 1999), 19–75.

46 E.R. Forbes, 'Consolidating Disparity: The Maritimes and the Industrialization of Canada during the Second World War,' *Acadiensis* 15, no. 2 (Spring 1986), 3–27.

47 For example, when Ottawa allocated contracts for shipbuilding – an industry the Maritimes was historically and geographically well suited to – it nearly bypassed the region entirely. The Maritimes received only 6.2 per cent of the total wartime shipbuilding contracts issued, whereas British Columbia was granted 50 per cent, Quebec 28.6 per cent, and Ontario 15 per cent. Forbes, 'Consolidating Disparity,' 20.

48 As Forbes has observed, 'it is ironic that the region which received the least wartime investment would later be identified as the one which would have the greatest difficulty adjusting to a peacetime economy.' Forbes, 'Consolidating Disparity,' 4.

49 For an overview of New Brunswick's reconstruction policy, see R.A. Young, '"… and the people will sink into despair": Reconstruction in New Brunswick, 1942–1952,' *Canadian Historical Review* 69, no. 2 (June 1988), 127–66. See also *Report of the New Brunswick Committee on Reconstruction* (Fredericton: 1944); and J.R. Petrie, *The Regional Economy of New Brunswick* (Fredericton: 1944). For a critique of Young, see Ken Taylor, 'Reconstruction and Recovery in the Hinterlands: Resources, Industry, and Infrastructure in New Brunswick and Saskatchewan, 1945–1970' (PhD diss., University of New Brunswick, 2005). For more on Prince Edward Island's cultivation of export markets, see Corey Slumkoski, 'Let Them Eat Beef: The Prince Edward Island–Newfoundland Beef Cattle Trade, 1941–1946,' *Acadiensis* 35, no. 2 (Spring 2006), 106–26. For more on Nova Scotia and the modernization of the fishery, see Miriam Wright, 'Fishing in Modern Times: Stewart Bates and the Modernization of the Canadian Atlantic Fishery,' in *How Deep is the Ocean: Historical Essays on Canada's Atlantic Fishery*, ed. James E. Candow and Carol Corbin (Sydney: University College of Cape Breton Press, 1997), 195–206.

50 T. Stephen Henderson, '"A New Federal Vision": Nova Scotia and the Rowell-Sirois Report, 1938–1948,' in *Framing Canadian Federalism*, ed. Dimitry Anastakis and Penny Bryden (Toronto: University of Toronto Press, 2009), 64.

51 For more on the Tax Rental Agreements, see R.M. Burns, *The Acceptable Mean: The Tax Rental Agreements, 1941–1962* (Toronto: Canadian Tax Foundation, 1980).

52 Margaret Conrad, 'The 1950s: The Decade of Development,' in *The Atlantic Provinces in Confederation*, ed. E.R. Forbes and D.A. Muise (Toronto and Fredericton: University of Toronto Press and Acadiensis Press, 1993), 414.

53 Conrad and Hiller, *Atlantic Canada: A Region in the Making*, 6.

1: Newfoundland–Maritime Connections

1 *Gloucester Northern Light*, 31 March 1949.
2 Margaret R. Conrad and James K. Hiller, *Atlantic Canada: A Concise History* (Toronto: Oxford University Press, 2006), 56–9.
3 Peter Pope, 'Comparisons: Atlantic Canada,' in *A Companion to Colonial America*, ed. Daniel Vickers (Oxford: Blackwell, 2005), 495. In comparison, as early as 1742 over 16,382 people lived in the New England port city of Boston. See Lawrence W. Kennedy, *Planning the City upon the Hill: Boston since 1630* (Amherst: University of Massachusetts Press, 1992), 255.
4 Graeme Wynn, 'A Province Too Much Dependent on New England,' *Canadian Geographer* 31, no. 2 (1987), 100; George Rawlyk, *Nova Scotia's Massachusetts: A Study of Massachusetts–Nova Scotia Relations, 1630 to 1784* (Montreal and Kingston: McGill–Queen's University Press, 1973), 219–22. For more on the Planters, see the essays in Margaret Conrad, ed., *Making Adjustments: Change and Community in Planter Nova Scotia, 1759–1800* (Fredericton: Acadiensis Press, 1991).
5 J.M. Bumsted, '1763–1783: Resettlement and Rebellion,' in *The Atlantic Region to Confederation: A History*, ed. Philip A. Buckner and John G. Reid (Toronto and Fredericton: University of Toronto Press and Acadiensis Press, 1994), 168.
6 For more on the impact of New England religion in Nova Scotia, see George Rawlyk, *Ravished by the Spirit: Religious Revivals, Baptists, and Henry Alline* (Montreal and Kingston: McGill–Queen's University Press, 1984).
7 Stephen E. Patterson, '1744–1763: Colonial Wars and Aboriginal Peoples,' in *The Atlantic Region to Confederation: A History*, ed. Philip A. Buckner and John G. Reid (Toronto and Fredericton: University of Toronto Press and Acadiensis Press, 1994), 151.
8 Bumsted, '1763–1783: Resettlement and Rebellion,' 162.
9 For an analysis of the demographics of the Nova Scotian population on the eve of the American Revolution, see ibid., 167–8.
10 For a discussion of Nova Scotia's neutrality, see J.B. Brebner, *The Neutral Yankees of Nova Scotia: A Marginal Colony during the Revolutionary Years* (New York: Columbia University Press, 1937); and John G. Reid, 'Pax Britannica or Pax Indigena: Planter Nova Scotia (1760–1782) and Competing Strategies of Pacification,' *Canadian Historical Review* 85, no. 4 (December 2004), 669–92.
11 Ann Gorman Condon, '1783–1800: Loyalist Arrival, Acadian Return, Imperial Reform,' in *The Atlantic Region to Confederation: A History*, ed.

Philip A. Buckner and John G. Reid (Toronto and Fredericton: University of Toronto Press and Acadiensis Press, 1994), 195.

12 By 1783 approximately 12,000 people lived on Newfoundland year round. See Condon, '1783–1800,' 188.

13 For more on British settlement policy to Newfoundland, see W. Gordon Handcock, *Soe longe as there comes noe woman: Origins of English Settlement in Newfoundland* (St John's: Breakwater, 1989).

14 See Rev. W. Pilot, 'The Church of England in Newfoundland,' in *A History of Newfoundland*, ed. D.W. Prowse (London: Eyre and Spottiswoode, 1896), 584–7.

15 C. Grant Head, *Eighteenth-Century Newfoundland: A Geographer's Perspective* (Toronto: McClelland and Stewart, 1976), 209.

16 Patrick C.T. White, ed., *Lord Selkirk's Diary, 1803–1804: A Journal of His Travels in British North America and the Northeastern United States* (Toronto: Champlain Society, 1958), 25, 41.

17 *Prince Edward Island Gazette*, 15 March 1819. As cited in Nicolas J. De Jong and Marvin E. Moore, *Shipbuilding on Prince Edward Island: Enterprise in a Maritime Setting, 1787–1920* (Hull: Canadian Museum of Civilization, 1994), 29. Emphasis in De Jong and Moore. See also Keith Matthews, *Lectures on the History of Newfoundland* (St John's: Breakwater, 1988), 45; and Matthew G. Hatvany, '"Wedded to the Marshes": Salt Marshes and Socio-Economic Differentiation in Early Prince Edward Island,' *Acadiensis* 30, no. 2 (Spring 2001), 47.

18 In 1847, Middle River exported 300 cattle, 500 sheep, and 400 firkins of butter, most of which would have been destined for Newfoundland. See Rusty Bittermann, 'The Hierarchy of the Soil: Land and Labour in a Nineteenth-Century Cape Breton Community,' *Acadiensis* 18, no. 1 (Autumn 1988), 36.

19 Graeme Wynn, *Timber Colony: A Historical Geography of Early Nineteenth-Century New Brunswick* (Toronto: University of Toronto Press, 1981), 71.

20 This information appears in the appendices to the *Journal of the House of Assembly of Prince Edward Island* (Charlottetown: King's Printer) for the subsequent year. Unfortunately, Nova Scotia and New Brunswick did not keep itemized records on the Newfoundland trade, which suggests that Newfoundland trade was of less significance to them. When PEI entered Confederation in 1873, island trade to Newfoundland became Canadian foreign trade – a federal responsibility – and PEI stopped keeping detailed records for imports from and exports to Newfoundland.

21 That same year, Newfoundland shipped 3,865 barrels of wet fish while Nova Scotia exported 13,363 barrels. See Irving's Report on the American

Fisheries, A2, vol. 8, 89n216, MG 23, LAC, as cited in Neil MacKinnon, *This Unfriendly Soil: The Loyalist Experience in Nova Scotia, 1783–1791* (Montreal and Kingston: McGill–Queen's University Press, 1986), n216.

22 For more on Newfoundland's involvement in the international saltfish trade, see Peter E. Pope, *Fish into Wine: The Newfoundland Plantation in the Seventeenth Century* (Chapel Hill: University of North Carolina Press, 2004).

23 *Newfoundlander*, 16 September 1852, as cited in Patrick O'Flaherty, *Lost Community: The Rise and Fall of Newfoundland, 1843–1933* (St John's: Long Beach, 2005), 97.

24 Ibid.

25 Shannon Ryan, *Fish Out of Water: The Newfoundland Saltfish Trade, 1814–1914* (St John's: Breakwater, 1986), 235. Despite the conflict over the West Indies market, Newfoundland and Nova Scotia did not see each other as each industry's most serious threat. That title was reserved for the Americans. See Raymond B. Blake, *From Fishermen to Fish: The Evolution of Canadian Fishery Policy* (Toronto: Irwin, 2000), 12.

26 De Jong and Moore, *Shipbuilding on Prince Edward Island*, 24. Though their focus is on the shipbuilding industry, De Jong and Moore provide the most sustained analysis of colonial trade between PEI and Newfoundland.

27 Gillian T. Cell, *English Enterprise in Newfoundland, 1577–1660* (Toronto: University of Toronto Press, 1969), 64.

28 J. Derek Green, 'Miners' Unions on Bell Island' (BComm paper, Memorial University of Newfoundland, 1968), 6–7, as cited in Peter Neary, '"Traditional" and "Modern" Elements in the Social and Economic History of Bell Island and Conception Bay,' Canadian Historical Association, *Historical Papers* (1973), 122.

29 James Hiller, 'The Origins of the Pulp and Paper Industry in Newfoundland,' *Acadiensis* 11, no. 2 (Spring 1982), 43. See also James K. Hiller, 'The Politics of Newsprint: The Newfoundland Pulp and Paper Industry, 1915–1939,' *Acadiensis* 19, no. 2 (Spring 1990), 3–39.

30 Ibid., 49.

31 Ibid., 54–5.

32 Alan A. Brookes, 'Out-Migration from the Maritime Provinces, 1860–1900: Some Preliminary Considerations,' *Acadiensis* 5, no. 2 (Spring 1976), 28.

33 Ibid. For a study of the Nova Scotia apple industry, see Margaret Conrad, 'Apple Blossom Time in the Annapolis Valley, 1880–1957,' *Acadiensis* 11, no. 2 (Spring 1980), 14–39.

34 Brookes, 'Out-Migration from the Maritime Provinces,' 28.
35 Ibid., 33.
36 T.W. Acheson, 'A Study in the Historical Demography of a Loyalist County,' *Social History / Histoire sociale* 1 (April 1968), 64.
37 That both Maritimers and Newfoundlanders were emigrating in search of better jobs has led Malcolm MacLeod to conclude that 'Newfoundland's experience paralleled what was happening in the Maritime Provinces in those same years [and] it seems clear the same forces were at work across the whole of the area now called Canada's Atlantic region, ignoring the international boundary which ran through (but did not divide) it.' Malcolm MacLeod, *Kindred Countries: Canada and Newfoundland before Confederation* (Ottawa: Canadian Historical Association, 1994), 5. A much more nuanced study of out-migration can be found in Patricia Thornton, 'The Problem of Out-Migration from Atlantic Canada, 1871–1921: A New Look,' *Acadiensis* 11, no. 1 (Autumn 1985), 3–31. Thornton suggests that while on the surface out-migration from the Maritimes and Newfoundland may appear similar, different causative factors were at play.
38 David Alexander, 'Newfoundland's Traditional Economy and Development to 1934,' *Acadiensis* 5, no. 2 (Spring 1976), 62–3.
39 Ron Crawley, 'Off to Sydney: Newfoundlanders Emigrate to Industrial Cape Breton, 1890–1914,' *Acadiensis* 17, no. 2 (Spring 1988), 28.
40 Ibid., 43, 49.
41 O'Flaherty, *Lost Community*, 97.
42 Peter Neary, 'Canadian Immigration Policy and the Newfoundlanders, 1912–1939,' *Acadiensis* 11, no. 2 (Spring 1982), 71; Crawley, 'Off to Sydney,' 29.
43 This generous offering was supplemented by a $10,000 donation from the St John's Board of Trade, $30,000 from the St John's municipal council, and $30,000 donated to the 'Halifax Relief Fund' set up by the St John's Board of Trade. Malcolm MacLeod, 'Searching the Wreckage for Signs of Region: Newfoundland and the Halifax Explosion,' in *Connections: Newfoundland's Pre-Confederation Links with Canada and the World*, ed. Malcolm Macleod (St John's: Creative Publishers, 2003), 222–3.
44 Ibid., 225–9 passim.
45 It is also possible that Newfoundland was simply returning the favour of Canadian assistance following the St John's fire of 1892 and the sealing disaster of 1914. See Malcolm MacLeod, 'Disaster Documents 1914: The Official Canadian Response to Newfoundland's Sealing Tragedies,' in Malcolm MacLeod, ed., *Connections: Newfoundland's Pre-Confederation*

Links with Canada and the World (St John's: Creative Publishers, 2003), 215–20.

46 Malcolm MacLeod, 'Students Abroad: Pre-Confederation Educational Links between Newfoundland and the Mainland of Canada,' *Canadian Historical Association Historical Papers / Communications historiques* 20, no. 1 (1985), 175.

47 Ibid., 185.

48 After 1910, immigrants to Canada would have to satisfy a monetary test prior to entry. See Neary, 'Canadian Immigration Policy and the Newfoundlanders,' 70. Newfoundland's immigration policy, in contrast, focused on excluding such 'undesirables' as Asians and Eastern Europeans. See Gerhard P. Bassler, '"Deemed Undesirable": Newfoundland's Immigration Policy, 1900–49,' in James Hiller and Peter Neary, eds., *Newfoundland: Explorations* (St John's: Breakwater, 1994), 153–77.

49 Neary, 'Canadian Immigration Policy and the Newfoundlanders,' 71.

50 See ibid., 75–82. Similar curtailment of Newfoundland labour occurred with regard to the mining industry.

51 For a detailed discussion of Canada–Newfoundland relations regarding labour, see Peter Neary, 'Canada and the Newfoundland Labour Market, 1939–1949,' *Canadian Historical Review* 62, no. 4 (December 1981), 470–95.

52 Conrad and Hiller, *Atlantic Canada: A Concise History*, 178.

53 Ibid., 179. See also Norman Robertson to W.L.M. King, 15 July 1941, in John Edward FitzGerald, ed., *Newfoundland at the Crossroads: Documents on Confederation with Canada* (St John's: Terra Nova, 2002), 24–7.

54 For more on the establishment of the Canadian High Commission, see Katheryn Ellen Hayman, 'The Origins and Function of the Canadian High Commission in Newfoundland, 1941–1949' (MA thesis, University of Western Ontario, 1979).

55 Steven High, 'Working for Uncle Sam: The "Comings" and "Goings" of Newfoundland Base Construction Labour, 1940–1945,' *Acadiensis* 32, no. 2 (Spring 2003), 84. The Leased Bases Agreement was finalized by June 1941.

56 Conrad and Hiller, *Atlantic Canada: A Concise History*, 180.

57 High, 'Working for Uncle Sam,' 87.

58 Neary, 'Canada and the Newfoundland Labour Market,' 474–5.

59 These companies included the Par-Tex Foundation Company of Toronto, the Foundation Company of Canada, and the Aluminum Company at Arvida, Quebec. Maritime-based companies that recruited Newfoundland labour included New Brunswick's St John Drydock Company, Halifax's Brookfield Construction Company, the Nova Scotia Sanatorium

in Kentville, and the Dominion Steel and Coal Corporation. See Neary, 'Canada and the Newfoundland Labour Market,' 476–87.

60 Ibid., 490.

61 Macleod, *Kindred Countries*, 4.

62 Conrad and Hiller, *Atlantic Canada: A Concise History*, 120.

63 For a detailed examination of the 1869 election in Newfoundland, see James K. Hiller, 'Confederation Defeated: The Newfoundland Election of 1869,' in *Newfoundland in the Nineteenth and Twentieth Centuries: Essays in Interpretation*, ed. James K. Hiller and Peter Neary (Toronto: University of Toronto Press, 1980), 67–94. James Hiller has observed that 'the confederation debate seems to have solidified a deep suspicion of central Canada – not, it should be noted, of the Maritime Provinces, with which Newfoundland had many connections.' James K. Hiller, 'Robert Bond and the Pink, White, and Green: Newfoundland Nationalism in Perspective,' *Acadiensis* 36, no. 2 (Spring 2007), 120.

64 See S.J.R. Noel, *Politics in Newfoundland* (Toronto: University of Toronto Press, 1971), 36; and A.M. Fraser, 'Fisheries Negotiations with the United States, 1783–1910,' in *Newfoundland: Economic, Diplomatic, and Strategic Studies*, ed. R.A. MacKay (Toronto: Oxford University Press, 1946), 359–72.

65 Noel, *Politics in Newfoundland*, 37.

66 Ibid.

67 The other bank that closed was the Commercial Bank.

68 For more on Newfoundland's attempts to secure British financial assistance following the bank collapse of 1894, see A.M. Fraser, 'Relations with Canada,' in *Newfoundland: Economic, Diplomatic, and Strategic Studies*, ed. R.A. MacKay (Toronto: Oxford University Press, 1946), 450–1.

69 Noel, *Politics in Newfoundland*, 37.

70 MacLeod further claims that 'the sway of Canada's dollar in Newfoundland, for a full half-century prior to political union, is the clearest of all indications that Newfoundland was firmly within Canada's sphere of influence.' MacLeod, *Kindred Countries*, 13.

71 David Alexander, 'Development and Dependence in Newfoundland, 1880–1970,' in *Atlantic Canada and Confederation: Essays in Canadian Political Economy*, ed. David Alexander (Toronto: University of Toronto Press, 1983), 9.

72 The definitive study of the Commission of Government is Peter Neary, *Newfoundland in the North Atlantic World* (Montreal and Kingston: McGill–Queen's University Press, 1988). Neary has also written about Sir John Simpson, one of the first appointed commissioners. See Peter Neary,

White Tie and Decorations: Sir John and Lady Hope Simpson in Newfoundland, 1934–1936 (Toronto: University of Toronto Press, 1997).

2: Nova Scotia and Newfoundland's Entry into Confederation

1 *Antigonish Casket*, 7 April 1949.
2 Mount Saint Vincent College was a prime attraction for Newfoundland's female Roman Catholics desirous of higher education, and as early as 1922 a chapter of the Mount Saint Vincent College alumni association was active in St John's. See Theresa Corcoran, *Mount Saint Vincent University: A Vision Unfolding, 1873–1988* (Lanham: University Press of America, 1999), 54.
3 *Sydney Post-Record*, 12 November 1945.
4 *Sydney Post-Record*, 26 June 1946.
5 A 13 June 1946 article in the *Sydney Post-Record* anticipated that 'the acquisition of the new up-to-date steamer on the route between North Sydney and Port-aux-Basques with the two smaller ships on the Newfoundland coastal routes' would occasion 'a decided impetus to the passenger and freight business' between the two islands.
6 Said Duchemin, '[Confederation] has never been urged or even suggested by any Canadian Government, and every proposal of the kind that has ever been put forward by Newfoundland statesmen has proved unpopular with the people at large.' *Sydney Post-Record*, 17 September 1946.
7 Confederation with Canada finished well ahead of both continuing with the existing Commission of Government (1,600 votes) and responsible government (500 votes). *Sydney Post-Record*, 12 October 1946.
8 *Sydney Post-Record*, 12 October 1946.
9 *Sydney Post-Record*, 5 July 1947.
10 *Sydney Post-Record*, 1 August 1947.
11 *Halifax Herald*, 2 June 1948. The *Sydney Post-Record* concurred, describing the terms as 'lavish.' See *Sydney Post-Record*, 2 October 1947.
12 The population of Nova Scotia at the time was approximately 600,000, while Newfoundland's population was 300,000. Newfoundland was offered subsidies totalling $20,000,000; Nova Scotia received only $10,000,000 from Ottawa. See *Sydney Post-Record*, 2 October 1947.
13 *Sydney Post-Record*, 2 October 1947.
14 *Halifax Herald*, 2 June 1948.
15 As the editor wrote: 'We would welcome this union, if for no other reason, as a demonstration of British Commonwealth solidarity on this

side of the Atlantic in times that are witnessing so much disintegration of elements of the Empire.' *Halifax Herald*, 29 July 1948.

16 11,031 passengers passed through North Sydney on their way to Canada, while 9,709 left Canada for Newfoundland through the port. *Halifax Chronicle-Herald*, 23 February 1949.

17 *Halifax Chronicle-Herald*, 23 February 1949.

18 *Sydney Post-Record*, 29 April 1949. Unfortunately, the papers of the Sydney Board of Trade have been lost and the *Sydney Post-Record* contains no further reference to the Newfoundland Relations Committee or to its actions.

19 James Hiller, 'Newfoundland Confronts Canada, 1867–1949,' in *The Atlantic Provinces in Confederation*, ed. E.R. Forbes and D.A. Muise (Toronto and Fredericton: University of Toronto Press and Acadiensis Press, 1993), 379.

20 *Halifax Herald*, 22 July 1948. As Champion wrote in an earlier editorial, 'the letters from expatriates, alternately praising and deploring a Canadian link, confuse the average person ... He hears about the Baby Bonus and Old Age Pensions on the one hand, and on the other he is warned about taxes, and the "fate" of that "poor relation," Nova Scotia.' *Halifax Herald*, 21 July 1948.

21 An editorial in the *Halifax Herald* downplayed the extent of expatriate Newfoundlanders criticizing Confederation, acknowledging that while 'there are natives of Newfoundland, resident in Canada, who give such [anti-confederate] advice [they were] not many, it is true, but some.' *Halifax Herald*, 4 November 1948.

22 It is surprising that the Canso Causeway has received little academic scrutiny. Two commemorative studies of the causeway exist: L.J. Doucet's official history, which was given out at the causeway's opening ceremony, and a fifty-year retrospective celebrating the causeway's construction. See L.J. Doucet, *The Road to the Isle: The Canso Causeway – Deepest in the World* (Fredericton: UNB Press, 1955); and Elaine Ingalls Hogg, *When Canada Joined Cape Breton: Celebrating Fifty Years of the Canso Causeway* (Halifax: Nimbus, 2005). The only academic examinations of the Canso Causeway are Meaghan Beaton and Del Muise, 'The Canso Causeway: Tartan Tourism, Industrial Development, and the Promise of Progress for Cape Breton,' *Acadiensis* 37, no. 2 (Summer–Autumn 2008), 39–69; and Meaghan Beaton, 'The Canso Causeway: Regionalism, Reconstruction, Representations, and Results' (MA thesis, Saint Mary's University, 2001).

23 In 1937, Nova Scotia Attorney General Malcolm Patterson introduced a resolution in the provincial legislature urging the federal government to

construct a permanent crossing. Hogg, *When Canada Joined Cape Breton*, 30.

24 Doucet, *The Road to the Isle*, 10.

25 Rand H. Matheson, 'Memorandum in the matter of The Proposed Bridge or Causeway at the Strait of Canso,' 5 June 1946, MG 2/981 F1/3, Angus L. Macdonald Papers, Nova Scotia Archives and Records Management (NSARM).

26 Lionel Chevrier, the Minister of Transportation who oversaw the construction of the St Lawrence Seaway, wrote a history of the project. It makes no mention of Nova Scotia's lobbying for a crossing at Canso. See Lionel Chevrier, *The St Lawrence Seaway* (Toronto: Macmillan of Canada, 1959).

27 *Sydney Post-Record*, 15 February 1949.

28 As cited in the *Sydney Post-Record*, 21 May 1947.

29 Dominion of Canada, *Official Report of Debates, House of Commons*, 1949 (Ottawa: King's Printer, 1949), 1303.

30 House of Commons, *Debates*, 1949, 1303–4.

31 The delegation included Premier Angus L. Macdonald, chief engineer for Dominion Steel William Wilson, and Associated Board of Trade members J.E. McCurdy and M.R. Chappell. See Beaton, 'The Canso Causeway,' 69–70.

32 *Sydney Post-Record*, 21 January 1949.

33 The Canso Crossing Association, 'For a Permanent Crossing over the Strait of Canso,' undated, MG 2/981 F3/125, Angus L. Macdonald Papers, NSARM. The CCA also used the Trans-Canada Highway, another transportation program of national importance, as justification for the building of a crossing.

34 Ibid.

35 *Halifax Chronicle-Herald*, 25 February 1949. The *Halifax Herald* and the *Halifax Chronicle* merged in December 1949 to become the *Halifax Chronicle-Herald*.

36 *Halifax Chronicle-Herald*, 25 February 1949.

37 Ibid.

38 The CCA's national newspaper campaign is illustrated by a reprint of a *Winnipeg Tribune* editorial in the pages of the *Halifax Chronicle-Herald*. The *Tribune* editorial quoted almost verbatim from the CCA's memorandum on the Canso Crossing. A 29 January 1949 editorial in the *Halifax Chronicle-Herald* also used similar language. See *Halifax Chronicle-Herald*, 6 January 1949; Canso Crossing Association, 'For a Permanent Crossing'; and *Halifax Chronicle-Herald*, 29 January 1949.

39 The board consisted of D.S. Ellis, Dean of the Faculty of Applied Science of Queen's University, Arthur Surveyor, and P.I. Pratley, consulting engineers from Montreal.

40 *Sydney Post-Record*, 14 March 1949. The allocation of federal and provincial funding responsibility proved to be an ongoing problem. See, for example, Letter from Angus L. Macdonald to Lionel Chevrier, undated, MG2/981 F3/130, Angus L. Macdonald Papers, NSARM, in which Macdonald tries to whittle the provincial share of the cost of the project from one-third to one-quarter.

41 'Memo of Meeting: Strait of Canso Bridge,' MG2/981 F2/10, Angus L. Macdonald Papers, NSARM.

42 Doucet, *The Road to the Isle*, 25.

43 E.R. Forbes, 'Consolidating Disparity: The Maritimes and the Industrialization of Canada during the Second World War,' *Acadiensis* 15, no. 2 (Spring 1986), 6–7.

44 James P. Bickerton, *Nova Scotia, Ottawa, and the Politics of Regional Development* (Toronto: University of Toronto Press, 1990), 107.

45 *Sydney Post-Record*, 18 May 1948.

46 A similar plea was made to the provincial cabinet by the Nova Scotia Federation of Labour in March 1949. See *Halifax Chronicle-Herald*, 8 March 1949.

47 *Sydney Post-Record*, 26 June 1948. The UMW apparently had trouble with both distance and direction, as Labrador ore fields lie approximately 400 miles north of Sydney.

48 *Sydney Post-Record*, 26 June 1948.

49 *Halifax Herald*, 3 June 1948.

50 As cited in *Sydney Post-Record*, 23 January 1949.

51 *Sydney Post-Record*, 23 January 1949.

52 As cited in *Halifax Chronicle-Herald*, 25 January 1949.

53 *Halifax Chronicle-Herald*, 7 February 1949. See also the *Halifax Chronicle-Herald*, 29 January 1949, which states: 'For economic and military reasons … it would appear to be sound national policy for Canada to employ this [Labrador] ore in her own steel-making, rather than to sell it outside the country to steel-makers who would sell their product back to us.'

54 As the *Halifax Chronicle-Herald* stated, 'no part of Canada's steel industry is better situated to employ this Northern ore than the tide-water steel industry in Nova Scotia, which lies hard by our coal fields and which can bring the ore by water from the Bay of Seven Islands where the railway serving the new ore fields will have its terminus.' See *Halifax Chronicle-Herald*, 7 February 1949.

55 *Halifax Chronicle-Herald*, 7 February 1949.

56 House of Commons, *Debates*, 1948, 5019–20.

57 For a biographical treatment of Nowlan, see Margaret Conrad, *George Nowlan: Maritime Conservative in National Politics* (Toronto: University of Toronto Press, 1986).

58 House of Commons, *Debates*, 1949, 608. See also *Halifax Chronicle-Herald*, 17 February 1949.

59 *Halifax Chronicle-Herald*, 17 February 1949.

60 House of Commons, *Debates*, 1949, 608.

61 House of Commons, *Debates*, 1949, 609. See also *Halifax Chronicle-Herald*, 17 February 1949.

62 House of Commons, *Debates*, 1949, 609. See also *Halifax Chronicle-Herald*, 17 February 1949.

63 House of Commons, *Debates*, 1949, 609. See also *Halifax Chronicle-Herald*, 17 February 1949. In a later debate about the applicability of the MFRA to Halifax-based shippers, Isnor stated that 'in Halifax we have four or five large shipping companies which have been doing a good business between the mainland of Nova Scotia and Newfoundland. Naturally we don't want those firms to be put out of business because of a monopoly in transportation.' See House of Commons, *Debates*, 1949, 622.

64 House of Commons, *Debates*, 1949, 610. See also *Halifax Chronicle-Herald*, 17 February 1949.

65 Dickey went so far as to state that 'the port of Halifax not only will not be discriminated against but will get its full share of advantage from the increase in traffic which will come about after the union of Canada and Newfoundland.' See House of Commons, *Debates*, 1949, 611.

66 House of Commons, *Debates*, 1949, 612. See also *Halifax Chronicle-Herald*, 17 February 1949.

67 *Halifax Chronicle-Herald*, 19 February 1949.

68 *Halifax Chronicle-Herald*, 21 February 1949.

69 *Halifax Chronicle-Herald*, 23 March 1949.

70 *Sydney Post-Record*, 19 February 1949.

71 Ibid. Diamond Junction is near Lévis, Quebec.

72 *Sydney Post-Record*, 28 March 1946.

73 Gene Barrett, 'Mercantile and Industrial Development to 1945,' in *Emptying Their Nets: Small Capital and Rural Industrialization in the Nova Scotia Fishing Industry*, ed. Richard Apostle and Gene Barrett (Toronto: University of Toronto Press, 1992), 39–60.

74 Some Phases of the Nova Scotia Fishing Industry, 7 August 1940, GN 38, Box-S-2-1-3, File 5, Commission of Government Papers, PANL.

75 David Alexander, *The Decay of Trade: The Economic History of the Newfound-land Saltfish Trade, 1935–1965* (St John's: Institute of Social and Economic Research, 1977), 4.

76 Address by J. Howard MacKichan, President of the Canadian Atlantic Salt Fish Exporters Association, 23–4 July 1947, MG 3, vol. 754, no. 3, National Sea Products Fonds, NSARM.

77 David MacKenzie, *Inside the Atlantic Triangle: Canada and the Entrance of Newfoundland into Confederation, 1939–1949* (Toronto: University of Toronto Press, 1986), 16.

78 Ibid.

79 As Raymond Gushue, Chairman of the Newfoundland Fisheries Board, wrote in 1940, 'there is no country which has been more dependent on its fisheries than Newfoundland, and no country in which, up to the present, the salt codfishery has so completely dwarfed all others.' See Raymond Gushue, 'Newfoundland and Its Fisheries,' *Public Affairs: A Maritime Quarterly for Discussion of Public Affairs* (March 1940), 109.

80 T. Stephen Henderson, *Angus L. Macdonald: A Provincial Liberal* (Toronto: University of Toronto Press, 2007), 83.

81 Ibid., 85.

82 See Stewart Bates, 'The Report on the Canadian Atlantic Sea-Fishery,' in *Nova Scotia Royal Commission on Reconstruction and Rehabilitation* (Halifax: 1944). For a detailed study of this report and of Stewart Bates's role in the modernization of the Canadian fishery, see Miriam Wright, 'Fishing in Modern Times: Stewart Bates and the Modernization of the Canadian Atlantic Fishery,' in *How Deep Is the Ocean? Historical Essays on Canada's Atlantic Fishery*, ed. James E. Candow and Carol Corbin (Sydney: University College of Cape Breton Press, 1997), 195–206.

83 For a detailed examination of Nova Scotia's postwar fishery policy, see Gene Barrett, 'Post-War Development,' in *Emptying Their Nets: Small Capital and Rural Industrialization in the Nova Scotia Fishing Industry*, ed. Richard Apostle and Gene Barrett (Toronto: University of Toronto Press, 1992), 61–84.

84 S.A. Beatty, 'Problems of Nova Scotia Fisheries,' *Public Affairs: A Maritime Quarterly for Discussion of Public Affairs* (June 1946), 166.

85 Alexander, *The Decay of Trade*, 140.

86 Miriam Wright, *A Fishery for Modern Times: The State and the Industrialization of the Newfoundland Fishery, 1934–1968* (Toronto: Oxford University Press, 2001), 22.

87 Alexander, *The Decay of Trade*, 140.

88 R.D. Howland and D.M. Fraser, 'The Maritimes and Foreign Trade,'

Public Affairs: A Maritime Quarterly for the Discussion of Public Affairs (Spring 1950), 27.

89 Beatty, 'Problems of Nova Scotia Fisheries,' 166.

90 Howland and Fraser, 'The Maritimes and Foreign Trade,' 27.

91 See Department of External Affairs, 'Advantages of Incorporating Newfoundland into the Dominion,' MG 30, series E159, vol. 4, 13 June 1947, LAC.

92 Keld Christensen, 'An Economic Review of Nova Scotia for 1946,' *Public Affairs: A Maritime Quarterly for Discussion of Public Affairs* (March 1947), 82. The Nova Scotia government would put up $300,000 for a cold storage plant, Ottawa would pay $210,000 for a wharf, and two American firms would ante up $250,000 each for processing plants. See Henderson, *Angus L. Macdonald*, 190.

93 Howland and Fraser, 'The Maritimes and Foreign Trade,' 27.

94 *Antigonish Casket*, 28 October 1948.

95 Newfoundland's entry factored into arguments for conservation of fisheries. As the *Halifax Chronicle-Herald* pointed out, 'wasteful fishing and especially the destruction of immature fish is a threat to the food supply of many lands ... Most of the important fishing grounds of the Northwest Atlantic lie off our shores, especially with the prospective entry of Newfoundland into the Canadian Confederation. Canada, more than any other land, should be concerned with the conservation of these fisheries.' See *Halifax Chronicle-Herald*, 19 January 1949.

96 *Antigonish Casket*, 28 October 1948.

97 Ibid.

98 Miriam Wright has examined in great detail the conflict between the traditional shore-based fishery and the modern fresh-frozen industry in Newfoundland. See Wright, *A Fishery for Modern Times*.

99 Beatty, 'Problems of Nova Scotia Fisheries,' 166–7.

100 'Port and other figures for the month of October 1948 compared with 1947 and for the ten months of both years,' November 1948, MG 20, vol. 652, reel 12395, Halifax Board of Trade Fonds, NSARM.

101 See O.F. MacKenzie to Angus L. Macdonald, 27 April 1953, MG 2/974 F16-1/one, Angus L. Macdonald Papers, NSARM; Angus L. Macdonald to S.R. Balcom, 10 December 1953, MG 2/974 F16-1/11, Angus L. Macdonald Papers, NSARM; and S.R. Balcom to Angus L. Macdonald, 14 December 1953, MG 2/974 F16-1/12, Angus L. Macdonald Papers, NSARM.

102 J.M. McKee, 'Address of the Secretary,' Canadian Atlantic Saltfish Exporters Association Annual Meeting, 29 May 1946, MG 3, vol. 754, no. 2, National Sea Products Fonds, NSARM.

103 The events of the three-day meeting are spelled out in detail in 'Minutes of Meeting Between Representatives of the Canadian and Newfoundland Salt Fish Trade Held at the Newfoundland Hotel,' 4–6 December 1946, MG 3, vol. 754, no. 2, National Sea Products Fonds, NSARM.

104 For a detailed iteration of the functioning of the Newfoundland marketing scheme, see 'Minutes of Meeting Between Representatives of the Canadian and Newfoundland Salt Fish Trade.'

105 Special General Meeting of the Canadian Atlantic Saltfish Exporters Association, 14–15 January 1947, MG 3, vol. 754, no. 2, National Sea Products Fonds, NSARM.

106 Igor Gouzenko, a Soviet cypher clerk based in Ottawa, defected and revealed the presence of a Russian spy ring operating in the Canadian capital. For more information on the Gouzenko Affair, see *Defection of Igor Gouzenko: Report of the Canadian Royal Commission* (Walnut Creek: Aegean Park, 1984). For more on the strike at National Sea Products, see E. Jean Nisbet, 'Free Enterprise at Its Best: National Sea and the Defeat of the Nova Scotia Fishermen, 1946–1947,' in *Workers and the State in Twentieth Century Nova Scotia*, ed. Michael Earle (Fredericton: Acadiensis Press, 1989), 170–90.

107 Special General Meeting of the Canadian Atlantic Saltfish Exporters Association, 14–15 January 1947.

108 MacKenzie and Macdonald were close friends, as the Halifax fish baron had invited the premier to spend time at his lodge in Cape Breton. See O.F. MacKenzie to Angus L. Macdonald, 15 November 1949, MG2/945 F31-1/280, Angus L. Macdonald Papers, NSARM.

109 O.F. MacKenzie to Angus L. Macdonald, 20 January 1947, MG 2/914, F16-3/2, Angus L. Macdonald Papers, NSARM. MacKenzie put things even more forcefully in a speech he gave sometime in late 1947.

110 Speech by O.F. MacKenzie, undated, MG 2/934 F31-1/404, Angus L. Macdonald Papers, NSARM.

111 This is not to say that Macdonald was convinced of the necessity, or the desirability, of large-scale state intervention in the economy. As T. Stephen Henderson points out, 'Macdonald's rejection of substantial state intervention almost surely contributed to Nova Scotia's relative decline after 1945.' See Henderson, *Angus L. Macdonald*, 213.

112 For a detailed analysis of Macdonald's liberalism, see ibid.

113 In a 14 January 1944 letter to Canadian High Commissioner to Newfoundland C.J. Burchell, Macdonald confessed that he 'often marvelled at the character and brilliance of students who came to the institution

[Dalhousie University] from Newfoundland.' Angus L. Macdonald to C.J. Burchell, 14 January 1944, MG 2, vol. 1520, 876/58, Angus L. Macdonald Papers, NSARM.

114 Henderson, *Angus L. Macdonald*, 150. Macdonald had been a law professor at Dalhousie University.

115 For more on this conference, see Marc J. Gotlieb, 'George Drew and the Dominion-Provincial Conference on Reconstruction of 1945–1946,' *Canadian Historical Review* 66, no. 1 (1985), 27–47, and Alvin Finkel, 'Paradise Postponed: A Re-examination of the Green Book Proposals of 1945,' *Journal of the Canadian Historical Association*, new series, vol. 4 (1993), 120–42.

116 Henderson, *Angus L. Macdonald*, 158.

117 *Halifax Chronicle*, 10 September 1945. As quoted in J. Murray Beck, *Politics in Nova Scotia*, vol. 2 (Tantallon: Four East, 1985), 205.

118 Letter from Angus L. Macdonald to W.A. MacDonald, 25 February 1947, MG 2/920 F31-2/79, Angus L. Macdonald Papers, NSARM.

119 Angus L. Macdonald, Speech in Legislature on Dominion-Provincial Agreement, 26 August 1947, MG 2, vol. 150, 487/8, Angus L. Macdonald Papers, NSARM. See also *Montreal Gazette*, 27 August 1947.

120 *Sydney Post-Record*, 11 October 1947.

121 Ibid.

122 Letter from Angus L. Macdonald to Charles G. Power, 15 September 1947, MG2/920 F31-2/105, Angus L. Macdonald Papers, NSARM.

123 *Sydney Post-Record*, 11 October 1947.

124 'Report of the Legal Sub-Committee on the constitutional position with respect to possible consultation with the existing provinces in the matter of the admission of Newfoundland,' 28 March 1947, RG 2, series 18, vol. 89, File N-18, LAC.

125 *Sydney Post-Record*, 11 October 1947.

126 Letter from Charles G. Power to Angus L. Macdonald, 2 October 1947, MG2/920 F31-2/113, Angus L. Macdonald Papers, NSARM.

127 *Sydney Post-Record*, 15 February 1949.

128 The bill, now with sub-amendment, was defeated 179 to 12, with only a handful of opposition Quebec MPs and some Alberta members of the Social Credit Party supporting it. *Sydney Post-Record*, 16 February 1949, and *Sydney Post-Record*, 17 February 1949. See also Raymond Blake, *Canadians at Last: Canada Integrates Newfoundland as a Province* (Toronto: University of Toronto Press, 1994), 38.

129 *Halifax Chronicle-Herald*, 1 April 1949.

3: Prince Edward Island and Newfoundland's Entry into Confederation

1 *Summerside Journal*, 4 April 1949.
2 According to Agnew, the only Island export commodity that did not fare as well in 1949 as in 1948 was potatoes. This claim is incorrect, as Island shipments of swine, cattle, horses, fruit, cheese, milk, hay, and oysters to Newfoundland all declined marginally, while the amount of feed and flour shipped across the Cabot Strait dropped precipitously. See Annual Report of the Department of Industry and Natural Resources, *Journal of the Legislative Assembly of Prince Edward Island* (Charlottetown: King's Printer, 1951).
3 *Charlottetown Patriot*, 7 May 1947.
4 As Agnew related, 'the benefits of Family Allowances, Unemployment Insurance, Old Age and Widows' Pensions ... means a great deal to Newfoundland and they are benefits which they could never hope to enjoy were they not part of Canada.' The combination of declining prices and increased purchasing power of Newfoundlanders resulted in increased exports of other products, 'thus our over-all trade showed substantial increase over 1948.' In Agnew's opinion, 'considering the keen competition from all over the world for markets, Prince Edward Island got her fair share of business.' See Annual Report of the Department of Industry and Natural Resources, *Journal of the Legislative Assembly of Prince Edward Island*, 1951.
5 Ibid.
6 See William Janssen, 'Agriculture in Transition,' in *The Garden Transformed: Prince Edward Island, 1945–1980*, ed. Verner Smitheram, David Milne, and Satadal Dasgupta (Charlottetown: Ragweed, 1982), 115–30.
7 Wayne E. MacKinnon, 'The Farmer Premier: J. Walter Jones and His Vision of Prince Edward Island,' *The Island Magazine* 35 (Spring–Summer 1994), 7. See also idem, *The Life of the Party: A History of the Liberal Party in Prince Edward Island* (Summerside: Williams and Crue, 1973).
8 David A. Milne, 'Politics in a Beleaguered Garden,' in *The Garden Transformed: Prince Edward Island, 1945–1980*, ed. Verner Smitheram, David Milne, and Satadal Dasgupta (Charlottetown: Ragweed, 1982), 42. It was even suggested by the *Summerside Journal* that this decline could be remedied after Newfoundland entered Confederation, as Newfoundlanders might be willing to relocate to PEI to take up vacant farm positions. *Summerside Journal*, 25 March 1949.

9 Annual Report of the Department of Agriculture, *Journal of the Legislative Assembly of Prince Edward Island* (Charlottetown: 1945).
10 See *Summerside Journal*, 25 March 1946 and 25 November 1946. In 1945 the US Army also used Prince Edward Island produce to feed the 1,500 hungry American troops stationed at Harmon Air Base their Thanksgiving dinner, sending a transport plane to Charlottetown for turkeys, potatoes, fresh milk, and 'other staples and delicacies.' *Summerside Journal*, 22 November 1945. Throughout the 1940s, PEI supplied American air bases in Newfoundland with potatoes and vegetables shipped across the Cabot Strait in American military ships. Annual Report of the Department of Industry and Natural Resources, *Journal of the Legislative Assembly of Prince Edward Island*, 1951. By 1948, the Island was the primary supplier of feed for the US Army's Newfoundland dairy herd, a development that 'means that all sections of the Province will share in its [US Army purchases] advantages.' *Charlottetown Guardian*, 22 September 1948.
11 Even the US Army initially had trouble securing the required permits for its milk shipments from Ideal Dairy. See *Summerside Journal*, 25 March 1946.
12 Prince Edward Island Brief to Members Prince Edward Island Legislature, 12 April 1945, RG 25, series 33, subseries 3, file 1b, J. Walter Jones Papers, Prince Edward Island Public Archives and Records Office (PEIPARO). See also F.S. Grisdale to J. Ralph Kirk, 16 June 1944, RG 25, series 33, subseries 2, file 10, J. Walter Jones Papers, PEIPARO. PEI's struggle to secure the Newfoundland export market in the 1940s is examined more fully in Corey Slumkoski, 'Let Them Eat Beef: The Prince Edward Island–Newfoundland Beef Cattle Trade, 1941–1946,' *Acadiensis* 35, no. 2 (Spring 2006), 114–15.
13 *Journal of the Legislative Assembly of Prince Edward Island*, 1945, 12. In opening the 1945 session of the PEI Legislature, Lieutenant-Governor Joseph Bernard blamed 'war-time controls' and 'the lack of shipping' for this drop. Bernard reiterated this view in the 1946 Speech from the Throne, when he expressed his hope that the 'removal of some of the war-time controls will induce more trading' with Newfoundland. *Journal of the Legislative Assembly of Prince Edward Island*, 1946, 12.
14 MacKinnon, *The Life of the Party*, 109–10. See also idem, 'The Farmer Premier,' 3–9; and Edward MacDonald, *If You're Stronghearted: Prince Edward Island in the Twentieth Century* (Charlottetown: Prince Edward Island Museum and Heritage Foundation, 2000), 218.
15 For more on the relationship between Jones and Island farmers, see Milne, 'Politics in a Beleaguered Garden,' 42–3.

16 *Summerside Journal*, 6 September 1943. Trade with Newfoundland also factored into the 1947 PEI election with 'extension of trade, to Newfoundland' being part of that campaign's Liberal platform. *Charlottetown Patriot*, 2 December 1947. Moreover, during the 1947 campaign Walter Jones trumpeted that 'the increase in the Newfoundland trade is entirely due to the unceasing efforts of this Government to promote it.' *Summerside Journal*, 13 November 1947.

17 The genesis of Prince Edward Island's focus on Newfoundland in its reconstruction plans can be found in a 1945 brief by the province's Federation of Agriculture, which states 'the development of export markets is vital to this province in which an exportable surplus of practically every farm product is available. In this connection the development of Newfoundland trade is particularly important.' See Prince Edward Island Federation of Agriculture Brief to Members Prince Edward Island Legislature, 12 April 1945. The Federation of Agriculture's concerns were addressed in Prince Edward Island's official plan for postwar reconstruction, *Interim Report of the PEI Advisory Reconstruction Committee* (Charlottetown: King's Printer, 1945), 255; and in Dominion-Provincial Conference (1945), *Dominion and Provincial Submissions and Plenary Conference Discussions* (Ottawa: King's Printer, 1946).

18 *Summerside Journal*, 1 October 1945. In the 1946 Speech from the Throne, PEI Lieutenant-Governor Joseph Bernard noted the 'assurance of a diesel-powered service to Newfoundland outports from our own smaller harbours' given by the Jones government. *Journal of the Legislative Assembly of Prince Edward Island*, 1946, 12.

19 *Journal of the Legislative Assembly of Prince Edward Island*, 1945, 24–5.

20 As political scientist David Milne has argued, 'both Newfoundland and Prince Edward Island have developed essentially as peripheral resource-based economies, principally within the confines of the British Empire and subsequently within the Canadian federation. Both supplied staples – principally fish and agricultural products – to satisfy metropolitan markets, and purchased many of their required manufactured goods from the outside. This legacy of extensive exporting–importing activity, built up within a larger imperial or national economy, certainly equipped both islands for learning the lessons of survival through trade and success in export markets.' David Milne, 'The Federal Model: Newfoundland and Prince Edward Island,' in *Lessons from the Political Economy of Small Islands: The Resourcefulness of Jurisdiction*, ed. Godfrey Baldacchino and David Milne (New York: St Martin's, 2000), 79.

21 The earliest reference to Agnew's mission to Newfoundland is a letter

Agnew wrote to Jones on 25 May 1944 from North Sydney, Nova Scotia, while on route to Newfoundland. See W.E. Agnew to J. Walter Jones, 25 May 1944, RG 25, series 33, subseries 3, file 25, J. Walter Jones Papers, PEIPARO; and J. Walter Jones to Unknown, 22 January 1945, RG 25, series 33, subseries 1, File 1A, J. Walter Jones Papers, PEIPARO.

22 W.E. Agnew to J. Walter Jones, 9 June 1944, RG 25, series 33, subseries 3, file 25, J. Walter Jones Papers, PEIPARO.

23 W.E. Agnew to J. Walter Jones, 22 June 1944, RG 25, series 33, subseries 3, file 25, J. Walter Jones Papers, PEIPARO.

24 As Jones said in reference to his trade agent: 'With the acquaintance we have now with the local officials [in Newfoundland] we can steer … trade through our trade agent here. This agent now has a full time job and more looking after Newfoundland and other trade.' *Charlottetown Guardian*, 17 March 1945.

25 Prince Edward Island Brief to Members Prince Edward Island Legislature, 12 April 1945, RG 25, series 33, subseries 3, file 1b, J. Walter Jones Papers, PEIPARO.

26 Arthur Day to J. Walter Jones, 31 July 1944, RG 25, series 33, subseries 1, file 6c:C, J. Walter Jones Papers, PEIPARO.

27 J. Walter Jones to E.E. Kirchner, 2 September 1944, RG 25, series 33, subseries 3, file 24, J. Walter Jones Papers, PEIPARO. In addition, the company overcharged the Prince Edward Island government. They had agreed that the cost of shipping from Charlottetown to St John's would be the same 70 cents per 100 pounds rate as was charged on shipments from Halifax to the Newfoundland capital. That was not the case, however; Prince Edward Islanders were being charged 5 1/4 cents more than were Nova Scotians, a discrepancy quickly acknowledged and remedied by the shipping company. See E.E. Kirchner to J. Walter Jones, 11 August 1944, RG 25, series 33, subseries 3, file 24, J. Walter Jones Papers, PEIPARO; J. Walter Jones to E.E. Kirchner, 2 October 1944, RG 25, series 33, subseries 3, file 24, J. Walter Jones Papers, PEIPARO; and E.E. Kirchner to J. Walter Jones, 6 October 1944, RG 25, series 33, subseries 3, file 24, J. Walter Jones Papers, PEIPARO.

28 J. Walter Jones to C.D. Howe, 12 November 1945, RG 25, series 33, subseries 2, file 11, J. Walter Jones Papers, PEIPARO.

29 P.A. Belanger to J. Walter Jones, 17 December 1945, RG 25, series 33, subseries 3, file 25, J. Walter Jones Papers, PEIPARO.

30 That the contract offered the Clarke Steamship Company was to run for four years is significant. As Director of Trade Routes and Steamship Subsidies F.E. Bawden made clear in a letter to MacKinnon endorsing Clarke,

any contract that was to run for five years or longer would require the parliamentary endorsement of an Order-in-Council. To receive such an endorsement could take a while. This would be especially true were Maritime parliamentarians to take exception to the granting of a non-tendered contract to a Central Canadian firm without any allowance for bids from shippers situated within their constituencies. F.E. Bawden to J.A. MacKinnon, 31 January 1946, RG 46, vol. 1314, file T53, Canadian Maritime Commission Papers, LAC.

31 The *Surewater* set sail on 29 April, and the *Keybar* left Charlottetown on 16 May. See Inter Island Steamship Co., Limited Date of Sailings from Charlottetown to St John's, RG 46, vol. 1314, file T53, Canadian Maritime Commission Papers, LAC.

32 Heenan was Bawden's replacement as Director of Trade Routes and Steamship Subsidies.

33 J.A. Heenan to J. Walter Jones, 3 May 1947, RG 46, vol. 1314, file T53, Canadian Maritime Commission Papers, LAC.

34 *Summerside Journal*, 18 December 1947. This boded well for PEI agriculture, which would, according to provincial Deputy Minister of Agriculture W.R. Shaw, see a 'substantial increase' in farm production in 1948. *Charlottetown Guardian*, 11 September 1948.

35 *Summerside Journal*, 5 January 1948.

36 *Summerside Journal*, 28 March 1948.

37 The substantial increases in butter and cheese exports from PEI to Newfoundland were facilitated by a 286,000 pound, or 38 per cent increase in the federal quota on cheese to Newfoundland and by a 275,000 pound increase in the butter quota. See *Charlottetown Patriot*, 26 February 1948; and 'Annual Report of the Department of Agriculture, year ended March 31, 1947,' *Journal of the Legislative Assembly of Prince Edward Island*, 1948, 23.

38 In addition, the number of live poultry shipped to Newfoundland decreased slightly from 1947's record high of 29,500 to 27,092, while the number of turnips fell from 23,877 to 20,873 bushels. Despite the downturn in livestock shipments from 1947 to 1948, these numbers compared favourably to 1943 exports. That year PEI shipped 1,977 head of cattle (97 dairy cattle and 1,880 beef cattle), 6,835 swine, and 61 horses to Newfoundland. In addition, 430,700 pounds of meat, 37,000 gallons of milk, 881 tons of hay, 10,593 cases of eggs, 89 barrels of oysters, 138 barrels of apples, and 7,877 cases of canned goods were shipped from PEI to Newfoundland in 1948. All export statistics from *Summerside Journal*, 1 April 1949; and *Journal of the Legislative Assembly of Prince Edward Island*, 1945, 16.

39 *Charlottetown Patriot*, 7 May 1947. A later issue of the *Patriot* made the point even plainer: 'Doubtless we shall profit from the additional market in the new Province.' *Charlottetown Patriot*, 6 October 1948.

40 PEI agriculture accounted for approximately 5.45 per cent of Canada's total exports of $55,000,000 to Newfoundland. *Charlottetown Guardian*, 5 June 1948 and 8 June 1948. See also Charlottetown Board of Trade, Minutes of the March Monthly Meeting, 23 March 1948, RG 3147, vol. 8-1, Greater Charlottetown Chamber of Commerce Fonds, PEIPARO.

41 *Charlottetown Patriot*, 8 September 1948.

42 *Summerside Journal*, 25 February 1949. The *Charlottetown Patriot* was certainly convinced by Jones's argument, stating that 'the new tenth province will give a larger Canadian market for Prince Edward Island farm products.' *Charlottetown Patriot*, 13 October 1948.

43 See *Charlottetown Guardian*, 26 March 1949.

44 *Summerside Journal*, 25 February 1949.

45 See the letter from S.H. Burhoe, President of the PEI Fisheries Federation, printed in the *Charlottetown Patriot*, 2 March 1948, for details on the impact of the European tariff on Island fishermen. In his letter Burhoe does not mention any detrimental effects that Newfoundland's Confederation would have on the PEI fishing industry. Moreover, this tariff would have applied not only to PEI but to other Maritime Provinces and Newfoundland as well.

46 For example, in 1952 cod accounted for 66 per cent of both the total Newfoundland landed catch and its value. Government of Newfoundland and Labrador, *Historical Statistics of Newfoundland and Labrador* (St John's: Queen's Printer, 1970), 176–7.

47 In 1948, for example, the $1,416,006 generated by the lobster fishery accounted for 67 per cent of all PEI fisheries revenue. In contrast, the landed value of the PEI cod fishery was only $151,721, or a little more than 7 per cent of all fisheries revenue. Report of the Director of Fisheries and Fish and Game, *Journal of the Legislative Assembly of Prince Edward Island*, 1951.

48 For example, New Brunswickers caught $4,627,203 worth of lobster in 1946. Lewis Dean Brown, 'Fisheries of New Brunswick (Canada),' American Consulate Report No. 12, Saint John, NB, 15 March 1949, 10, University of New Brunswick Archives and Special Collections.

49 *Sydney Post-Record*, 15 February 1949.

50 *Charlottetown Guardian*, 26 March 1949.

51 For more on the legalization of margarine in Canada, see W.H. Heick, *A Propensity to Protect: Butter, Margarine and the Rise of Urban Culture in*

Canada (Waterloo, ON: Wilfrid Laurier University Press, 1991). See also W.H. Heick, 'Margarine in Newfoundland History,' *Newfoundland and Labrador Studies* 2, no. 2 (1986), 29–37; and Ruth Dupre, '"If It's Yellow, It Must Be Butter": Margarine Regulation in North America since 1886,' *Journal of Economic History* 59, no. 2 (June 1999), 353–71.

52 In 1947 the butter shortage prompted the federal government to import 2,000,000 pounds of butter from New Zealand in order to meet public demand, while 1948 saw the importation of 9,000,000 pounds from Denmark and New Zealand. *Charlottetown Guardian*, 11 January 1947 and 16 September 1948.

53 *Charlottetown Patriot*, 7 May 1947. This concern was later repeated by the *Summerside Journal*, which suggested that by the time Newfoundland joined the Dominion, Canadian factories would be churning out 'butterine,' or margarine. *Summerside Journal*, 27 December 1948.

54 *Charlottetown Patriot*, 14 December 1948.

55 *Summerside Journal*, 17 January 1949. The sale and production of margarine in Prince Edward Island had actually been banned in 1937, with that year's Provincial Dairy Industry Act. Though that act had been passed in 1937, it was not actually proclaimed until 13 January 1949.

56 Even though the production and sale of margarine was banned in PEI, there was nothing to prevent Islanders from purchasing margarine in a province where its sale was legal and bringing it to the Island.

57 *Summerside Journal*, 16 March 1949. A 10 July 1948 editorial in the *Charlottetown Guardian* also notes the increase in PEI's butter production: 'Butter production in Prince Edward Island has already exceeded the peak of last year's volume, despite the fact that the number of dairy cattle in production this season is below that of a year ago.' *Charlottetown Guardian*, 10 July 1948.

58 *Summerside Journal*, 1 April 1949; and Annual Report of the Department of Industry and Natural Resources, *Journal of the Legislative Assembly of Prince Edward Island*, 1951.

59 *Charlottetown Guardian*, 6 October 1947. See also *Charlottetown Guardian*, 10 November 1947.

60 *Charlottetown Guardian*, 2 August 1948.

61 *Charlottetown Guardian*, 13 October 1948.

62 *Charlottetown Guardian*, 13 March 1947.

63 Their efforts would eventually lead to the appointment of the Turgeon Commission. For more on the Maritime Provinces' reaction to the freight rate hike of 1948 and the resulting Royal Commission, see T. Stephen Henderson, 'A Defensive Alliance: The Maritime Provinces and the

Turgeon Commission on Transportation, 1948–1951,' *Acadiensis* 35, no. 2 (Spring 2006), 46–63.

64 *Charlottetown Patriot*, 23 October 1948.
65 *Charlottetown Guardian*, 15 July 1947. This view was later endorsed by the PEI Federation of Agriculture, which suggested that 'in view of the threat of increasing freight rates every avenue of water transportation for our produce should be thoroughly investigated.' *Charlottetown Patriot*, 8 March 1949.
66 *Charlottetown Patriot*, 20 October 1948. The idea of a Georgetown–Newfoundland ferry arose a number of times in the *Charlottetown Patriot*. See, for example, *Charlottetown Patriot*, 23 November and 13 December 1948. The *Charlottetown Guardian* also endorsed the idea of more thoroughly utilizing Georgetown: 'The suggestion … that the S.S. Prince Edward Island should be utilized in service between Georgetown and Pictou should be followed up by all interested in maintaining and developing our trade with the mainland. Why should we be shut off from Nova Scotia and Newfoundland trade from December to May when we have an ice-breaker like the Prince Edward at our disposal? Now is the time for both Government and Opposition to push for and demand something worth while and easily obtainable instead of sighing for political means.' *Charlottetown Guardian*, 18 November 1947.
67 Annual Report of the Department of Industry and Natural Resources, *Journal of the Legislative Assembly of Prince Edward Island*, 1951.
68 Ibid.
69 In May 1948 the Charlottetown Board of Trade unanimously passed a resolution in favour of securing a vessel for the Newfoundland trade. Charlottetown Board of Trade, Minutes of the May Monthly Meeting, 18 May 1948, RG 3147, vol. 8-1, Greater Charlottetown Chamber of Commerce Fonds, PEIPARO. For Agnew's lobbying for a dedicated PEI vessel for the Newfoundland route, see 'P.E. Island Sells Newfoundland,' *Maritime Farmer and Cooperative Dairyman*, 5 April 1949; and *Summerside Journal*, 23 May 1949.
70 *Summerside Journal*, 23 May 1949.
71 *Summerside Journal*, 11 July 1949. See also Charlottetown Board of Trade, Minutes of the September Monthly Meeting, 23 September 1949, RG 3147, vol. 8-1, Greater Charlottetown Chamber of Commerce Fonds, PEIPARO.
72 Annual Report of the Department of Industry and Natural Resources, *Journal of the Legislative Assembly of Prince Edward Island*, 1951.
73 Charlottetown Board of Trade, Minutes of the Regular May Monthly

Meeting, 10 May 1950, RG 3147, vol. 8-1, Greater Charlottetown Chamber of Commerce Fonds, PEIPARO.

74 Annual Report of the Department of Industry and Natural Resources, *Journal of the Legislative Assembly of Prince Edward Island*, 1951.

75 Ibid.

76 As quoted in the *Charlottetown Patriot*, 31 December 1948. As Agnew had informed the *Patriot* in May 1947, 'the population of Newfoundland is not great and is spread over 1,500 settlements, most of which are distributed around a 3,000-mile coastline. The present road and railway communications contact only a fraction of these communities. Of the remainder, a fair proportion is reached by ship at varying intervals. This makes it essential for Canadian exporters to have individual sales organizations in Newfoundland. That is, he must sell through a local representative or make direct sales arrangements with Newfoundland import or wholesale houses.' *Charlottetown Patriot*, 10 May 1947.

4: New Brunswick and Newfoundland's Entry into Confederation

1 *North Shore Leader*, 1 April 1949. It is unknown whether the new radio station mentioned Newfoundland's Confederation in its broadcast.

2 See *Report of the New Brunswick Committee on Reconstruction* (Fredericton: 1944); and J.R. Petrie, *The Regional Economy of New Brunswick* (Fredericton: 1944). For an examination of postwar reconstruction in New Brunswick, see R.A. Young, '"... and the people will sink into despair": Reconstruction in New Brunswick, 1942–1952,' *Canadian Historical Review* 69, no. 2 (June 1988), 127–66; and Ken Taylor, 'Reconstruction and Recovery in the Hinterlands: Resources, Industry, and Infrastructure in New Brunswick and Saskatchewan, 1945–1970' (PhD diss., University of New Brunswick, 2005).

3 See E.R. Forbes, 'Consolidating Disparity: The Maritimes and the Industrialization of Canada during the Second World War,' *Acadiensis* 15, no. 2 (Spring 1986), 3–27.

4 J.A. Guthrie, 'Post-War Prospects for Canadian Newsprint,' *Public Affairs: A Maritime Quarterly for Discussion of Public Affairs* (Autumn 1942), 16.

5 C.D. Howe to Joey Smallwood, 22 December 1950, Collection 285, 2.19.002, J.R. Smallwood Papers, Centre for Newfoundland Studies Archives, Queen Elizabeth II Library, Memorial University of Newfoundland.

6 *Gloucester Northern Light*, 24 March 1949.
7 Harold Horwood, *Corner Brook: A Social History of a Paper Town* (St John's: Breakwater, 1986), 92.
8 J.W. Pickersgill and D.F. Forster, eds., *The Mackenzie King Record: Volume 4, 1947–1948* (Toronto: University of Toronto Press, 1970), 76.
9 Corey Slumkoski, 'Prelude to Equalization: New Brunswick and the Tax Rental Agreements, 1941–1957' (MA thesis, University of New Brunswick, 1999), 102–5.
10 Calculations regarding statutory subsidies, undated, unsigned, RS 414, C7, J.B. McNair Papers, Provincial Archives of New Brunswick (PANB).
11 J.B. McNair to W.L.M. King, 17 September 1947, RS 414, B5A, J.B. McNair Papers, PANB.
12 As cited in Ned Bossé to R.A. Tweedie, 28 August 1947, RS 414, C1C2, J.B. McNair Papers, PANB. Despite Pickersgill's conviction, there is no evidence that New Brunswick was 'dead against' Newfoundland's Confederation.
13 Lewis Dean Brown, 'Fisheries of New Brunswick (Canada),' American Consulate Report No. 12, Saint John, NB, 15 March 1949, 9, University of New Brunswick Archives and Special Collections (UNBASC).
14 Ibid., 9.
15 The canned lobster industry was not restricted to one county, but was instead spread throughout the province. Despite accounting for roughly 25 per cent of Canada's canned lobster production during the 1940s, New Brunswick's canned lobster industry was seen as in decline by 1949. See Brown, 'Fisheries of New Brunswick (Canada),' 10–12.
16 The market value of New Brunswick cod for 1947 was $1,488,187. Brown, 'Fisheries in New Brunswick (Canada),' 15.
17 Ibid.
18 As chapter 2 illustrates, there was cooperation between Newfoundland and Maritime saltcod fishers.
19 Caraquet was home to twelve draggers used for the New Brunswick cod fishery. Brown, 'Fisheries in New Brunswick (Canada),' 17.
20 *L'Evangeline*, 31 March 1949.
21 Brown, 'Fisheries in New Brunswick (Canada),' 10.
22 *Canadian Fisheries Manual* (1945), 45.
23 Ibid., 64.
24 *The Fundy Fisherman*, 12 September 1945.
25 *The Fundy Fisherman*, 7 November 1945.
26 *The Fundy Fisherman*, 2 July 1947. See also Debates of the Senate of the Dominion of Canada, *Official Report*, 1947 (Ottawa: King's Printer, 1947),

448–9. Similar views by McLean can be found in a 16 February 1949 Senate speech reprinted in a later issue of the paper. See Debates of the Senate of the Dominion of Canada, *Official Report*, 1949, 86–7; and *The Fundy Fisherman*, 23 February 1949.

27 A.N. McLean, *Letters from a Business Man to a Student of Economics* (undated). Copy in the possession of H.A. Fredericks, Fredericton.

28 Newfoundland National Convention, Fisheries Committee, Appendix 'H,' 5, Collection 285 8.01.001, J.R. Smallwood Papers, QEII, MUN.

29 Newfoundland National Convention, Fisheries Committee, Appendix 'H,' 35, Collection 285 8.01.001, J.R. Smallwood Papers, QEII, MUN.

30 A.N. McLean to W.L.M. King, 26 March 1947, in Paul Bridle, ed., *Documents on Relations between Canada and Newfoundland*, vol. 2, pt I (Ottawa: 1984), 425.

31 L.R. Brookes to Secretary for Natural Resources, 29 January 1946, GN 31/2, box 87, file 422, Commission of Government Papers, PANL.

32 Ibid. Brookes even contended that the road was originally a private one, but the failure of the property's former owners to erect a gate had led to it becoming a public access route.

33 Assistant Secretary for Natural Resources to Secretary for Public Works, 12 February 1946, GN 31/2, box 87, file 422, Commission of Government Papers, PANL.

34 T.J. Wade to Unknown, 28 March 1946, GN 31/2, box 87, file 422, Commission of Government Papers, PANL. The case referred to is *His Majesty's Attorney General at the relation of George Allen v. John A. Petries and William T Petries*, no. 408, Supreme Court of Newfoundland, 1938.

35 J.G. to Secretary, 8 April 1946, GN 31/2, box 87, file 422, Commission of Government Papers, PANL.

36 W. Verge to Department of Public Works, 5 July 1946, GN 31/2, box 87, file 422, Commission of Government Papers, PANL.

37 T.J. Wade to unknown, 28 March 1946, GN 31/2, box 87, file 422, Commission of Government Papers, PANL.

38 W. Verge to Department of Public Works, 5 July 1946.

39 See L.R. Brookes to Secretary for Natural Resources, 21 March 1947; and Secretary for Natural Resources to Trade Commissioner for Newfoundland in the United Kingdom, 28 March 1947, GN 31/2, box 87, file 422, Commission of Government Papers, PANL.

40 S.R. Raffan to unknown, 8 May 1947, GN 31/2, box 87, file 422, Commission of Government Papers, PANL.

41 M. Lally to unknown, 9 June 1947, GN 31/2, box 87, file 422, Commission of Government Papers, PANL.

42 E.L. Stratton to K.J. Carter, 3 May 1946, GN 31/2, box 87, file 422, Commission of Government Papers, PANL.
43 See Concessions to Connors Brothers, Blacks Harbour, N.B., Regarding Proposed Fish Canning Plant in Bay of Islands, undated, GN 31/2, box 87, file 4/10, Commission of Government Papers, PANL; and Commissioner for Finance to Commissioner for Natural Resources, 11 July 1946, GN 31/2, box 1, file 4/10, Commission of Government Papers, PANL.
44 Commissioner for Finance to Commissioner for Natural Resources, 11 July 1946, GN 31/2, box 1, file 4/10, Commission of Government Papers, PANL.
45 Commissioner for Natural Resources to Commissioner for Finance, 2 August 1946, GN 31/2, box 1, file 4/10, Commission of Government Papers, PANL.
46 A point McLean himself makes clear in a 1940 article. See A.N. McLean, 'The New Brunswick Sardine Fisheries,' *Public Affairs: A Maritime Quarterly for the Discussion of Public Affairs* (March 1940), 113.
47 Emphasis added. J.R. Smallwood to Neil McLean, 18 April 1948, Collection 285 8.03.004, J.R. Smallwood Papers, QEII, MUN.
48 David Mackenzie, *Inside the Atlantic Triangle: Canada and the Entrance of Newfoundland into Confederation, 1939–1949* (Toronto: University of Toronto Press, 1986), 198.
49 Ray Petten to J.R. Smallwood, 3 November 1949, Collection 285 3.10.048, J.R. Smallwood Papers, QEII, MUN.
50 *Sackville Tribune-Post*, 31 December 1948.
51 As cited in *Sackville Tribune-Post*, 26 June 1947.
52 Similar surveys were conducted in 1825 and 1826. See *Sackville Tribune-Post*, 26 June 1947; and Dominion of Canada, *Official Report of Debates House of Commons*, 1949 (Ottawa: King's Printer, 1949), 2135.
53 *Sackville Tribune-Post*, 26 June 1947. For a more detailed summary of the history of the idea of a canal across the Isthmus of Chignecto, see *Report of the Chignecto Canal Commission* (Ottawa: King's Printer, 1939), 13–20; and Donald E. Armstrong and D. Harvey, *The Chignecto Canal* (Montreal: Economic Research Corporation, 1960), 6–7.
54 The proposed plan to ferry ships across the isthmus via a railway has received some scholarly attention. See C.R. McKay, 'Investors, Government, and the CMTR: A Study of Entrepreneurial Failure,' *Acadiensis* 9, no. 1 (Autumn 1979), 71–94; and David Stephens, 'The Chignecto Ship Railway,' *Nova Scotia Historical Quarterly* 8 (June 1978), 135–45.
55 The commissioners further recommended that the canal project 'stand in abeyance until it can be further examined in the light of future develop-

ments in Canada's economic situation.' *Report of the Chignecto Canal Commission*, 11.

56 *Sackville Tribune-Post*, 30 June 1947. The project was supported by the Saint John Board of Trade, the Sackville Board of Trade, the Amherst Board of Trade, the Charlottetown Board of Trade, and the Maritime Board of Trade. The members of the Chignecto Canal Committee were Mayor N.S. Sanford, G. Fuller, and A.R. Lusby of Amherst, and Mayor H.A. Beale and E.R. Richard of Sackville. *Sackville Tribune-Post*, 2 November 1948.

57 Saint John Mayor J.D. McKenna urged: 'Build the canal, no matter the cost, Saint John is behind Sackville and Amherst in this movement.' *Sackville Tribune-Post*, 30 June 1947. Likewise, New Brunswick's Gloucester MP C.T. Richard implored Ottawa to support the project. *Gloucester Northern Light*, 10 March 1949.

58 As early as 1933 the Chignecto Canal Commission was reporting that 'the people of the Maritime Provinces, while justly proud of Canada's inland waterways, are inclined to consider that the development of the Great Lakes–St. Lawrence waterway has to a certain extent involved the neglect of similar possibilities of importance to Maritime interests.' *Report of the Chignecto Canal Commission*, 22.

59 C.C. Avard, Editorial, *Maritime Advocate and Busy East* 36, no. 9 (April 1946), 24.

60 Avard suggested that 'even if the canal was useless ... we would be getting back some of the money that we have contributed towards the building of canals in Ontario.' C.C. Avard, 'Editorial,' *Maritime Advocate and Busy East* 35, no. 9 (April 1945), 26. For the views of MPs Brooks and Black, see House of Commons, *Debates*, 1948, 4012–15, 4968–9.

61 Brooks continued that 'the rest of Canada, particularly Ontario, owes the maritime provinces a great debt, so far as canals are concerned.' House of Commons, *Debates*, 1948, 4969.

62 House of Commons, *Debates*, 1949, 2136.

63 *Report of the New Brunswick Committee on Reconstruction*. See also Petrie, *The Regional Economy of New Brunswick*; and B.S. Keirstead, *The Economic Effects of the War on the Maritime Provinces of Canada* (Halifax: Dalhousie Institute of Public Affairs, 1943).

64 *Sackville Tribune-Post*, 2 November 1948.

65 Ibid.

66 Ibid.

67 Both the Sackville Board of Trade and the Amherst Board of Trade endorsed this line of argument. See, for example, *Sackville Tribune-Post*, 26 June 1947.

68 *Sackville Tribune-Post*, 18 April 1949. For a detailed study of the Annapolis
    Valley apple industry, see Margaret Conrad, 'Apple Blossom Time in the
    Annapolis Valley, 1880–1957,' *Acadiensis* 9, no. 2 (Spring 1980), 14–39.
69 *Sackville Tribune-Post*, 30 June 1947. For more on the dispute surrounding
    Maritime freight rates during the late 1940s, see T. Stephen Henderson,
    'A Defensive Alliance: The Maritime Provinces and the Turgeon Commis-
    sion on Transportation, 1948–1951,' *Acadiensis* 35, no. 2 (Spring 2006),
    46–63.
70 Members of the Saint John Board of Trade included G.H. Nichol, P.W.
    Oland, P.H. Hamon, J.T. Gifford, George M. Flood, J.K. Kennedy, E.D.
    Angevine, R.H. Fales, C.S. Christie, Gordon W. Berry, H. Dwight Magee,
    R.L Grannan, H.G. Black, J. Packard Campbell, F. Gordon Spencer, K.C.
    Irving, A.F. Blake, and F.C. Mortimer. See Minutes of the Nominating
    Committee, Saint John Board of Trade, 5 November 1947, S230, F215,
    Saint John Board of Trade Fonds, New Brunswick Museum (NBM).
71 Council Minutes, Saint John Board of Trade, 13 February 1947, S230,
    F213, Saint John Board of Trade Fonds, NBM. See also Meeting of the
    Council, Saint John Board of Trade, 19 December 1946, S230, F213, Saint
    John Board of Trade Fonds, NBM; and Quarterly Report, Saint John
    Board of Trade, 17 February 1947, S230, F213, Saint John Board of Trade
    Fonds, NBM.
72 A direct steamship service between Saint John and St John's run by New-
    foundland's Blue Peter Steamship Company was in place by the time
    Confederation was completed. See *Synoptic Report of the Proceedings of the
    Legislative Assembly of the Province of New Brunswick* (Fredericton: King's
    Printer, 1949), 121; and Council Minutes, Saint John Board of Trade, 27
    April 1949, S230, F218, Saint John Board of Trade Fonds, NBM.
73 By early 1949 some on the Saint John Board of Trade believed that there
    was 'the possibility of industry moving to Saint John if the Canal was
    built.' This influx of industry occasioned some 'who are in a position to
    know [to] claim that the population of Saint John would double in ten
    years if this project is proceeded with.' See Council Minutes, Saint John
    Board of Trade, 12 January 1949, S230, F218, Saint John Board of Trade
    Fonds, NBM.
74 *The Fundy Fisherman*, 15 January 1947.
75 *Sackville Tribune-Post*, 29 September 1947.
76 See 1947 President's Report, Saint John Board of Trade, 2 December 1947,
    S230, F216, Saint John Board of Trade Fonds, NBM; and President's
    Report, Saint John Board of Trade, 7 December 1948, S230, F217, Saint
    John Board of Trade Fonds, NBM.

77 New Brunswick, *Synoptic Report*, 1948, 48.

78 For Morse's support of the Chignecto Canal, see New Brunswick, *Synoptic Report*, 1948, 89. For McInerney's support, see New Brunswick, *Synoptic Report*, 1948, 138.

79 New Brunswick, *Synoptic Report*, 1949, 85.

80 Ibid., 120. MLAs Robert H. Carlin and James W. Brittain also believed that Newfoundland's entry into Confederation justified the construction of the Chignecto Canal. See ibid., 123, 241–2.

81 *The Fundy Fisherman*, 12 January 1949.

82 Ibid.

83 John H. Bradbury, 'The Rise and Fall of the "Fourth Empire of the St Lawrence": The Québec-Labrador Iron Ore Mining Region,' *Cahiers de Géographie du Québec* 29, no. 78 (décembre 1985), 357–8.

84 House of Commons, *Debates*, 1949, 2136. New Brunswick MP D.A. Riley agreed. Speaking on 9 November 1949, Riley stated that 'with the advent of the grand province of Newfoundland into Confederation, and the exploitation of the iron ore deposits in Labrador a distinct probability, it is easy to envision that part of this ore will be shipped to eastern United States ports.' House of Commons, *Debates*, 1949, 1589. This same line of argument was advanced in the New Brunswick legislature by Saint John MLA E. Roy Kelly. See New Brunswick, *Synoptic Report*, 1949, 118.

85 *Gloucester Northern Light*, 24 March 1949.

86 For details of this trip, see James Gallagher, 'First U.S. Ore Carrier Trip into the Seaway,' *Inland Seas* 41, no. 2 (1985), 89–99.

87 As Moncton MLA E.R. Fryers stated in the provincial legislature, 'the Chignecto Canal meant as much to the Maritimes as did the St Lawrence Seaway to the Central Provinces.' New Brunswick, *Synoptic Report*, 1949, 85.

88 House of Commons, *Debates*, 1951, Second Session, 1644.

89 So enthused with the seaway project was Chevrier that after it was completed he wrote a book about it. See Lionel Chevrier, *The St Lawrence Seaway* (Toronto: Macmillan of Canada, 1959).

90 As New Brunswick Premier McNair stated in a 1949 radio address on the project, 'for my part I am glad to see interest in it revived. I feel every New Brunswicker could support such development. But it must have the support of the entire Maritimes. If Nova Scotia will also support it … we may have some success.' Radio Address by J.B. McNair, 21 June 1949, RS 414, D5a1b, J.B. McNair Papers, PANB.

91 C.H. Blakeny to Angus L. Macdonald, 14 June 1950, MG 2, 951 F196/2, Angus L. Macdonald Papers, NSARM.

92 Martin J. Kaufman to Angus L. Macdonald, 16 June 1950, MG 2, 951, F19-
6/5, Angus L. Macdonald Papers, NSARM.
93 See Report to Council, Saint John Board of Trade, 23 October 1947, S230,
F215, Saint John Board of Trade Fonds, NBM; and Council Minutes, Saint
John Board of Trade, 27 April 1949, S230, F218, Saint John Board of Trade
Fonds, NBM.
94 A view also held by F.C. Mortimer of the Saint John Board of Trade, who
stated in June 1949 that 'Saint John would benefit more than any section
of the Maritimes when the Canal is built.' See Council Minutes, Saint
John Board of Trade, 23 June 1949, S230, F218, Saint John Board of Trade
Fonds, NBM.
95 Angus L. Macdonald to Martin J. Kaufman, 17 June 1950, MG 2, 951, F19-
6/4, Angus L. Macdonald Papers, NSARM.
96 *Report of the Royal Commission on Transportation* (Ottawa: King's Printer,
1951), 171. Of the three projects, only the Prince Edward Island Causeway, reworked into a bridge, ever saw completion. The Confederation
Bridge, connecting PEI to New Brunswick, saw its first traffic in 1997.
97 House of Commons, *Debates*, 1951, 2296.

5: Regional Union and Newfoundland in the 1940s

1 *Halifax Chronicle-Herald*, 18 November 1995.
2 Among the background papers to the Deutsch Report is a brief history of
the idea of Maritime union written J. Murray Beck, *The History of Maritime Union: A Study in Frustration* (Fredericton: Queen's Printer, 1969).
3 Maritime Union Study, *The Report on Maritime Union Commissioned by the
Governments of Nova Scotia, New Brunswick, and Prince Edward Island* (Fredericton: Queen's Printer, 1970), 70.
4 W.L.M. King Diary, 21 September 1943, MG 26, LAC. King likely
endorsed the idea of Atlantic union in order to offset the power wielded
by Ontario and Quebec in dominion–provincial relations. The union of
Canada and the West Indies has received some attention from scholars.
See, for example, Alice R. Stewart, 'Canadian-West Indian Union,
1884–1885,' and Brinsley Samaroo, 'The Politics of Disharmony: The
Debate on the Political Union of the British West Indies and Canada,
1884–1921,' in *Canada and the Commonwealth Caribbean*, ed. Brian Douglas Tennyson (Boston: University Press of America, 1988), 161–90 and
191–214.
5 It should not be overlooked that *The Fundy Fisherman* was owned by A.
Neil McLean, a Liberal Senator appointed by King.

6 *The Fundy Fisherman*, 12 September 1945.
7 For a brief discussion of Newfoundlanders' expectations regarding their entry into Canadian Confederation, see Peter Neary, *Newfoundland in the North Atlantic World, 1929–1949* (Montreal and Kingston: McGill–Queen's University Press, 1988), 358–9.
8 *The Fundy Fisherman*, 5 June 1946. What is more, the editor suggested that Newfoundland would 'see no reason under present circumstances for thinking they could expect any better treatment [than the Maritime Provinces]' if they were to become simply another Atlantic province.
9 *The Fundy Fisherman*, 5 June 1946.
10 In addition to being a journalist, Merkel was a noted poet as one of the Song Fishermen. For more on Merkel's poetry, see Gwendolyn Davies, 'The Song Fishermen: A Regional Poetry Celebration,' in *People and Place: Studies of Small Town Life in the Maritimes*, ed. Larry McCann (Fredericton: Acadiensis Press, 1987), 137–52.
11 Andrew Merkel to C.R. Blackburn, 7 February 1946, and C.R. Blackburn to Andrew Merkel, 25 February 1946, MS2, 326, H2 A and B, Andrew Merkel Papers, Dalhousie University Archives.
12 Fisher had recently won the Beaver Award for distinguished service to Canadian radio; he had also claimed the La Fleche Trophy for the most important contribution to Canadian radio as a commentator for the previous two years running. He was taken with the idea of political unification, an idea that was running wild in the postwar period. In his convocation address, Fisher noted that 'Mr Churchill wants a United States of Europe. Others talk of Hemispheric solidarity. Canadians cry for greater unity and some speak in global terms.' *Sackville Tribune-Post*, 18 August 1947.
13 Ibid.
14 Ibid.
15 Despite the pessimistic reactions of the New Brunswick and Prince Edward Island premiers to the idea of union, J.H. Parthing, secretary to the Moncton Board of Trade, generously volunteered his city to be the mega-province's capital. *Charlottetown Guardian*, 7 April 1947. The *Sydney Post-Record* stated that the 'name of the nation-builder responsible for this crack-pot proposal is not given.' *Sydney Post-Record*, 7 April 1947. It seems likely that the parliamentarian in question was Neil McLean, whose paper, *The Fundy Fisherman*, had also advocated for union, and who had extensive ties to the Newfoundland herring fishery. Just over two months after the story ran, on 17 June 1947, McLean rose in the Senate and suggested that 'it is not beyond a possibility ... that some day,

in the not too distant future, we may have one large maritime province consisting of the three present Maritime Provinces and Newfoundland.' Dominion of Canada, *Debates of the Senate of the Dominion of Canada, Official Report* (Ottawa: King's Printer, 1947), 449.

16 For Gordon Bradley's comments on the issue, see *Sydney Post-Record*, 23 June 1947.

17 *Sydney Post-Record*, 3 June 1948.

18 Letter from J. Walter Jones to Andrew Merkel, 24 August 1948, MG 2/934 F31-1/450, Angus L. Macdonald Papers, Nova Scotia Archives and Records Management (NSARM).

19 Letter from J. Walter Jones to Andrew Merkel, 24 August 1948, MG 2/934 F31-1/450, Angus L. Macdonald Papers, NSARM.

20 *Synoptic Report of the Proceedings of the Legislative Assembly of the Province of New Brunswick* (Fredericton: King's Printer, 1947), 96.

21 Ibid.

22 Ibid. Flemming's speech to the legislature in which he endorsed the idea of union contains no mention of Newfoundland.

23 *Sydney Post-Record*, 18 March 1947.

24 *Sydney Post-Record*, 7 April 1947.

25 *Sydney Post-Record*, 12 January 1949.

26 New Brunswick, *Synoptic Report*, 1947, 269. It is also likely that Flemming tempered his view on union amid concerns that the Acadian population of New Brunswick would be opposed to such a merger. A survey of the French-language Acadian newspaper, *L'Evangeline*, reveals little engagement with the topic of union throughout 1947 and 1948. It was not until after Newfoundland's Confederation had been consolidated, and after the drive for union had subsided, that the paper addressed the subject. In July 1949 *L'Evangeline* reprinted an editorial from Montreal's *Le Droit* critical of both Atlantic Union and Ottawa's handling of Acadian concerns. Titled 'Injustice aux Acadiens,' the editorial suggested that the Acadians, as a small minority within an amalgamated province that encompassed New Brunswick, Nova Scotia, Prince Edward Island, and Newfoundland, would have difficulty getting their specific concerns heard by the newly formed provincial government, though the new body might still prove more receptive than had Ottawa: 'Croit-on que les Acadiens n'auraient pas autant de difficultés à obtenir justice de leur gouvernement provincial unificateur qu'ils en éprouvent actuellement vis-à-vis du gouvernement fédéral?' *L'Evangeline*, 16 July 1949.

27 New Brunswick, *Synoptic Report*, 1947, 269.

28 Ibid., 269–70. It is in this impassioned speech to the New Brunswick Leg-

islature that one can see the genesis of the Atlantic Revolution movement that came to prominence under Flemming's government in the next decade. See New Brunswick, *Synoptic Report*, 268–71. For more on the Atlantic Revolution, see Margaret Conrad, 'The Atlantic Revolution of the 1950s,' in *Beyond Anger and Longing: Community and Development in Atlantic Canada*, ed. Berkeley Fleming (Fredericton: Acadiensis Press, 1988), 55–98. For more on Flemming's role in the Atlantic Revolution, see James Kenny, 'Politics and Persistance: New Brunswick's Hugh John Flemming and the Atlantic Revolution, 1952–1960' (MA thesis, University of New Brunswick, 1988).

29 *Hartland Observer*, 17 April 1947.
30 *The Fundy Fisherman*, 15 December 1948.
31 C.C. Avard, Editorial, *Maritime Advocate and Busy East* 34, no. 10 (May 1944), 29–30.
32 C.C. Avard, Editorial, *Maritime Advocate and Busy East* 37, no. 11 (June 1947), 3.
33 Nowhere was Maritime Liberal MPs' subservience to the whip more prominently displayed than when they agreed to the 1948 freight rate hikes. Conrad, 'The Atlantic Revolution of the 1950s,' 65.
34 The identity of 'Grant Evans' is unknown. As Avard wrote, Evans 'lives in Nova Scotia, but is familiar with all sections of the Maritimes. He is particularly well-informed and is a man of unusual ability. For reasons best known to himself he does not want his real name to appear above the article.' See C.C. Avard, Editorial, *Maritime Advocate and Busy East* 39, no. 6 (January 1949), 8. In years to follow, Evans would continue to contribute the occasional article on regional or national affairs to the *Maritime Advocate and Busy East*.
35 Grant Evans, 'What's the Matter with the Maritimes?' *Maritime Advocate and Busy East* 39, no. 6 (January 1949), 8.
36 Ibid.
37 C.C. Avard, Editorial, *Maritime Advocate and Busy East* 39, no. 11 (June 1949), 3.
38 Ibid.
39 C.C. Avard, 'Newfoundland Will Become Canada's Tenth Province,' *Maritime Advocate and Busy East* 29, no. 2 (September 1948), 4.
40 *Charlottetown Patriot*, 1 August 1948.
41 *The Fundy Fisherman*, 3 November 1948.
42 *Sydney Post-Record*, 12 January 1949.
43 Dalton Camp, *Gentlemen, Players, and Politicians* (Toronto: McClelland and Stewart, 1970), 5. For a discussion of Macdonald's non-candidacy for the

Liberal leadership in 1948, see T. Stephen Henderson, *Angus L. Macdonald: A Provincial Liberal* (Toronto: University of Toronto Press), 176–9.

44 *Charlottetown Patriot*, 7 August 1948.
45 Despite the breakdown of the regional front, Maritime politicians were able to get their concerns articulated in the Liberal platform adopted at the convention. These concerns included continued recognition of the 'principles underlying' the Maritime Freight Rates Act, encouragement of the decentralization of industry and the development of cheap hydro-electricity in the Maritimes, the negotiation of trade treaties favourable to the Maritime fishing, farming, lumbering, and mining industries, and the improvement of the region's airports and ports. See *Resolutions: The National Liberal Convention, 1948* (Ottawa: Le Droit, 1948), 14.
46 *Halifax Herald*, 18 March 1949.
47 *Charlottetown Guardian*, 19 March 1949.
48 Ibid.
49 *Sydney Post-Record*, 3 June 1948.
50 Angus L. Macdonald to Andrew Merkel, 2 September 1948, MG 2/934 F31-1/451, Angus L. Macdonald Papers, NSARM.
51 Andrew Merkel to Angus L. Macdonald, 5 September 1948, MG 2/934 F31-1/449, Angus L. Macdonald Papers, NSARM.
52 Ibid.
53 Ibid.

Epilogue

1 *Proceedings of the Conference of Federal and Provincial Governments, 1950* (Ottawa: Queen's Printer, 1950), 43.
2 Ibid., 41.
3 Ibid., 56. It should not be overlooked that this was precisely the level to which Term 29 of the Newfoundland Act promised to raise Newfoundland.
4 Margaret Conrad, 'The 1950s: The Decade of Development,' in *The Atlantic Provinces in Confederation*, ed. E.R. Forbes and D.A. Muise (Toronto and Fredericton: University of Toronto and Acadiensis Press, 1993), 401.
5 Margaret Conrad, 'The Atlantic Revolution of the 1950s,' in *Beyond Anger and Longing: Community and Development in Atlantic Canada*, ed. Berkeley Fleming (Fredericton: Acadiensis Press, 1988), 60.
6 Ibid., 70.
7 Conrad, 'The 1950s: The Decade of Development,' 414.

 8 Ibid., 401.
 9 T. Stephen Henderson has examined the Maritime response to the freight
    rate increases. Notably, he does not detail the Newfoundland stance. As
    Henderson states, 'the transportation concerns of Canada's newest
    province differed substantially from those of the Maritime provinces.' T.
    Stephen Henderson, 'A Defensive Alliance: The Maritime Provinces and
    the Turgeon Commission on Transportation, 1948–1951,' *Acadiensis* 35, no.
    2 (Spring 2006), 47ff.
10 Joey Smallwood, *I Chose Canada. The Memoirs of the Honourable Joseph R.
    'Joey' Smallwood*, vol. II, *The Premiership* (Toronto: Signet, 1973), 26.
11 *Ottawa Journal*, 21 June 1955.
12 Canada, 'Term 29,' *An Act to confirm and give effect to Terms of Union agreed
    between Canada and Newfoundland*, assented to 23 March 1949.
13 Smallwood, *I Chose Canada*, vol. II, 100.
14 Ibid., 100.
15 Smallwood was waiting to meet Jack Pickersgill when the plane landed
    with Diefenbaker aboard. Other small favours that Smallwood details
    having performed for Diefenbaker include ensuring Diefenbaker received
    a standing ovation after a speech, releasing a doctor from a contract in
    Newfoundland at the prime minister's behest, and introducing Diefen-
    baker at a Dominion–Provincial Conference. See ibid., 96–7.
16 Margaret Conrad, 'The Atlantic Revolution of the 1950s,' 82.
17 In the 1957 election the Progressive Conservatives won twenty-one seats
    in Atlantic Canada, which was sixteen more than they tallied in 1953. In
    the 1958 election the number of PC seats in Atlantic Canada increased to
    twenty-five.
18 *Atlantic Advocate*, October 1959, 28.
19 Della Stanley, *Louis Robichaud: A Decade of Power* (Halifax: Nimbus, 1984),
    116–17.
20 *Atlantic Advocate*, November 1964, 14–15.
21 For more on the demise of the Atlantic Revolution, see Conrad, 'The
    Atlantic Revolution of the 1950s,' 88–96.
22 Moreover, the Royal Commission mandated by Term 29 helped sunder
    the tenuous regional bonds that were forming during the 1950s when the
    disappointing recommendations of the McNair Commission were
    released in July 1958.
23 Christopher Harvie, *The Rise of Regional Europe* (New York: Routledge,
    1994), x.

Bibliography

Manuscript Sources

Ottawa
Canadian Maritime Commission Papers. RG 46, LAC.
Department of Trade and Commerce Papers. RG 20, LAC.
Wartime Prices and Trade Board Papers. RG 64, LAC.
W.L.M. King Papers. MG 26, LAC.

New Brunswick
Brown, Lewis Dean. 'Fisheries of New Brunswick (Canada).' American Consulate Report No. 12, Saint John, 15 March 1949. University of New Brunswick Archives.
J.B. McNair Papers. RS 414, PANB.
Saint John Board of Trade Papers. S230, New Brunswick Museum.

Newfoundland and Labrador
Commission of Government Papers. GN Series, PANL.
J.R. Smallwood Papers. Centre for Newfoundland Studies Archives, Queen Elizabeth II Library, Memorial University of Newfoundland.

Nova Scotia
Andrew Merkel Papers. MS 2, Dalhousie University Archives.
Angus L. Macdonald Papers. MG 2, NSARM.
Halifax Board of Trade Papers. MG 20, vol. 652, reel 12395, NSARM.

Prince Edward Island
Greater Charlottetown Chamber of Commerce Fonds. RG 3147, PEIPARO.
J. Walter Jones Papers. RG 25, PEIPARO.

Government Documents

Bates, Stewart. 'The Report on the Canadian Atlantic Sea-Fishery,' in *Nova Scotia Royal Commission on Reconstruction and Rehabilitation*. Halifax: 1944.

Bridle, Paul, ed. *Documents on Relations between Canada and Newfoundland*. Ottawa: Ministry of Supply and Services, 1984.

Canada. Dominion Bureau of Statistics. *The Maritime Provinces Since Confederation*. Ottawa: King's Printer, 1927.

Dominion of Canada. *Debates of the Senate of the Dominion of Canada, Official Report*. Ottawa: King's Printer, 1945–50.

Dominion of Canada. *Official Report of Debates, House of Commons*. Ottawa: King's Printer, 1945–50.

Dominion Provincial Conference (1945). *Dominion and Provincial Submissions and Plenary Conference Discussions*. Ottawa: King's Printer, 1946.

Government of Newfoundland and Labrador. *Historical Statistics of Newfoundland and Labrador*. St John's: Queen's Printer, 1970.

Interim Report of the PEI Advisory Reconstruction Committee. Charlottetown: King's Printer, 1945.

Journal of the House of Assembly of Prince Edward Island. Charlottetown: King's Printer, 1858–71.

Journal of the Legislative Assembly of Prince Edward Island. Charlottetown: King's Printer, 1945–51.

Leacy, F.H., ed. *Historical Statistics of Canada* (electronic edition).

Maritime Union Study. *The Report on Maritime Union Commissioned by the Governments of Nova Scotia, New Brunswick, and Prince Edward Island*. Fredericton: 1970.

Newfoundland Act. 1949.

Proceedings of Dominion–Provincial Conference, 1941. Ottawa: King's Printer, 1941.

Proceedings of the Conference of Federal and Provincial Governments, 1950. Ottawa: Queen's Printer, 1953.

Report of the Chignecto Canal Commission. Ottawa: King's Printer, 1939.

Report of the New Brunswick Committee on Reconstruction. Fredericton: 1944.

Report of the Royal Commission on Provincial Development and Rehabilitation. Halifax: King's Printer, 1944.

Report of the Royal Commission on Transportation. Ottawa: King's Printer, 1951.

Synoptic Report of the Proceedings of the Legislative Assembly of the Province of New Brunswick. Fredericton: King's Printer, 1946–50.

Newspapers and Periodicals

Antigonish Casket
Atlantic Advocate
Charlottetown Guardian
Charlottetown Patriot
L'Evangeline (Moncton, NB)
Fredericton Daily Gleaner
The Fundy Fisherman (Blacks Harbour, NB)
The Globe and Mail (Toronto)
Gloucester Northern Light
Halifax Chronicle
Halifax Chronicle Herald
Halifax Herald
Hartland Observer
The Maritime Farmer and Cooperative Dairyman (Sussex, NB)
Newfoundlander (St John's, NF)
The North Shore Leader (Newcastle, NB)
Ottawa Journal
The Prince Edward Island Agriculturalist (Summerside, PEI)
Sackville Tribune-Post
Saint John Telegraph-Journal
St John's Evening Telegram
Summerside Journal
Summerside Pioneer
Sydney Post-Record

Secondary Sources

Acheson, T.W. 'A Study in the Historical Demography of a Loyalist County.' *Social History* 1 (April 1968): 53–65.
– 'The National Policy and the Industrialization of the Maritimes, 1880–1910.' *Acadiensis* 1, no. 1 (Spring 1972): 3–28.
Alexander, David. *The Decay of Trade: The Economic History of the Newfoundland Saltfish Trade, 1935–1965.* St John's: Institute of Social and Economic Research, 1977.
– 'Development and Dependence in Newfoundland, 1880–1970,' in *Atlantic Canada and Confederation: Essays in Canadian Political Economy*, ed. David Alexander. Toronto: University of Toronto Press, 1983. 3–31.

- 'Economic Growth in the Atlantic Region, 1880–1940.' *Acadiensis* 8, no. 1 (Autumn 1978): 47–76.
- 'Newfoundland's Traditional Economy and Development to 1934.' *Acadiensis* 5, no. 2 (Spring 1976): 56–78.
Alway, Richard M.H. 'Hepburn, King, and the Rowell-Sirois Commission.' *Canadian Historical Review* 48, no. 2 (June 1967): 113–41.
Anderson, Benedict. *Imagined Communities: Reflections on the Origin and Spread of Nationalism.* London: Verso, 1983.
Armstrong, Donald E., and D. Harvey. *The Chignecto Canal.* Montreal: Economic Research Corporation, 1960.
Avard, C.C. Editorial. *Maritime Advocate and Busy East* 34, no. 10 (May 1944): 29–30.
- Editorial. *Maritime Advocate and Busy East* 35, no. 9 (April 1945): 26.
- Editorial. *Maritime Advocate and Busy East* 36, no. 9 (April 1946): 24.
- Editorial. *Maritime Advocate and Busy East* 37, no. 11 (June 1947): 3.
- Editorial. *Maritime Advocate and Busy East* 39, no. 6 (January 1949): 3.
- Editorial. *Maritime Advocate and Busy East* 39, no. 11 (June 1949): 3.
- 'Newfoundland Will Become Canada's Tenth Province.' *Maritime Advocate and Busy East* 29, no. 2 (September 1948): 4.
Barrett, Gene. 'Mercantile and Industrial Development to 1945,' in *Emptying Their Nets: Small Capital and Rural Industrialization in the Nova Scotia Fishing Industry,* ed. Richard Apostle and Gene Barrett. Toronto: University of Toronto Press, 1992. 39–60.
- 'Post-War Development,' in *Emptying Their Nets: Small Capital and Rural Industrialization in the Nova Scotia Fishing Industry,* ed. Richard Apostle and Gene Barrett. Toronto: University of Toronto Press, 1992. 61–84.
Bassler, Gerhard P. '"Deemed Undesirable": Newfoundland's Immigration Policy, 1900–49,' in *Twentieth-Century Newfoundland: Explorations,* ed. James Hiller and Peter Neary. St John's: Breakwater, 1994. 153–77.
Beaton, Meaghan. 'The Canso Causeway: Regionalism, Reconstruction, Representations, and Results.' MA thesis, Saint Mary's University, 2001.
Beaton, Meaghan and Del Muise. 'The Canso Causeway: Tartan Tourism, Industrial Development, and the Promise of Progress for Cape Breton.' *Acadiensis* 37, no. 2 (Summer–Autumn 2008): 39–69.
Beatty, S.A. 'Problems of Nova Scotia Fisheries.' *Public Affairs: A Maritime Quarterly for Discussion of Public Affairs* (June 1946): 161–8.
Beck, J. Murray. 'An Atlantic Region Political Culture: A Chimera,' in *Eastern and Western Perspectives: Papers from the Joint Atlantic Canada / Western Canadian Studies Conference,* ed. David Jay Bercuson and Phillip A. Buckner. Toronto: University of Toronto Press, 1981. 147–68.

– *The History of Maritime Union: A Study in Frustration.* Fredericton: Maritime Union Study, 1969.
– 'The Maritimes: A Region or Three Provinces?' *Proceedings and Transactions of the Royal Society of Canada*, series IV, no. 15 (1977). 301–13.
– *Politics in Nova Scotia*, vol. 2. Tantallon: Four East, 1985.
Bickerton, James P. *Nova Scotia, Ottawa, and the Politics of Regional Development.* Toronto: University of Toronto Press, 1990.
Bittermann, Rusty. 'The Hierarchy of the Soil: Land and Labour in a Nineteenth-Century Cape Breton Community.' *Acadiensis* 18, no. 1 (Autumn 1988): 33–55.
Blake, Raymond. 'WLMK's Attitude towards Newfoundland's Entry into Confederation.' *Newfoundland Quarterly* 82, no. 4 (1987): 26–37.
Blake, Raymond B. *Canadians at Last: Canada Integrates Newfoundland as a Province.* Toronto: University of Toronto Press, 1994.
– *From Fishermen to Fish: The Evolution of Canadian Fishery Policy.* Toronto: Irwin, 2000.
Bradbury, John H. 'The Rise and Fall of the "Fourth Empire of the St Lawrence": The Québec–Labrador Iron Ore Mining Region.' *Cahiers de Géographie du Québec* 29, no. 78 (décembre 1985): 351–64.
Brebner, J.B. *The Neutral Yankees of Nova Scotia: A Marginal Colony during the Revolutionary Years.* New York: Columbia University Press, 1937.
Brodie, Janine. *The Political Economy of Canadian Regionalism.* Toronto: Harcourt Brace Jovanovich, 1990.
Brookes, Alan A. 'Out-Migration from the Maritime Provinces, 1860–1900: Some Preliminary Considerations.' *Acadiensis* 5, no. 2 (Spring 1976): 26–55.
Bumsted, J.M. '1763–1783: Resettlement and Rebellion,' in *The Atlantic Region to Confederation: A History*, ed. Philip A. Buckner and John G. Reid. Toronto and Fredericton: University of Toronto Press and Acadiensis Press, 1994. 156–83.
Burns, R.M. *The Acceptable Mean: The Tax Rental Agreements, 1941–1962.* Ottawa: Canadian Tax Foundation, 1980.
Camp, Dalton. *Gentlemen, Players, and Politicians.* Toronto: McClelland and Stewart, 1970.
Canadian Fisheries Manual. 1945.
Cell, Gillian T. *English Enterprise in Newfoundland, 1577–1660.* Toronto: University of Toronto Press, 1969.
Chevrier, Lionel. *The St Lawrence Seaway.* Toronto: Macmillan of Canada, 1959.
Christensen, Keld. 'An Economic Review of Nova Scotia for 1946.' *Public Affairs: A Maritime Quarterly for Discussion of Public Affairs* (March 1947): 79–83.

Clement, Wallace. 'A Political Economy of Regionalism in Canada,' in *Modernization and the Canadian State*, ed. Daniel Glenday, Hubert Guindon, and Allan Turowetz. Toronto: Macmillan, 1978. 89–110.

Colley, Linda. *Britons: Forging a Nation, 1707–1837*. New Haven: Yale University Press, 1992.

Condon, Ann Gorman. '1783–1800: Loyalist Arrival, Acadian Return, Imperial Reform,' in *The Atlantic Region to Confederation: A History*, ed. Philip A. Buckner and John G. Reid. Toronto and Fredericton: University of Toronto Press and Acadiensis Press, 1994. 184–209.

Conrad, Margaret. 'Apple Blossom Time in the Annapolis Valley, 1880–1957.' *Acadiensis* 9, no. 2 (Spring 1980): 14–39.

– 'The "Atlantic Revolution" of the 1950s,' in *Beyond Anger and Longing: Community and Development in Atlantic Canada*, ed. Berkeley Fleming. Fredericton: Acadiensis Press, 1988. 55–98.

– 'The 1950s: The Decade of Development,' in *The Atlantic Provinces in Confederation*, ed. E.R. Forbes and D.A. Muise. Toronto and Fredericton: University of Toronto Press and Acadiensis Press, 1993. 382–420.

– *George Nowlan: Maritime Conservative in National Politics*. Toronto: University of Toronto Press, 1986.

– ed. *Intimate Relations: Family and Community in Planter Nova Scotia, 1759-1800*. Fredericton: Acadiensis Press, 1995.

– ed. *Making Adjustments: Change and Community in Planter Nova Scotia, 1759–1800*. Fredericton: Acadiensis Press, 1991.

Conrad, Margaret, and James K. Hiller. *Atlantic Canada: A Concise History*. Toronto: Oxford University Press, 2006.

– *Atlantic Canada: A History*. Toronto: Oxford University Press, 2010.

– *Atlantic Canada: A Region in the Making*. Don Mills: Oxford University Press, 2001.

Corcoran, Theresa. *Mount Saint Vincent University: A Vision Unfolding, 1873–1988*. Lanham: University Press of America, 1999.

Crawley, Ron. 'Off to Sydney: Newfoundlanders Emigrate to Industrial Cape Breton, 1890–1914.' *Acadiensis* 17, no. 2 (Spring 1988): 27–51.

Cross, William. 'The Increasing Importance of Region to Canadian Election Campaigns,' in *Regionalism and Party Politics in Canada*, ed. Lisa Young and Keith Archer. Toronto: Oxford University Press, 2002. 116–28.

Davies, Gwendolyn. 'The Song Fishermen: A Regional Poetry Celebration,' in *People and Place: Studies of Small Town Life in the Maritimes*, ed. Larry McCann. Fredericton: Acadiensis Press, 1987. 137–52.

Defection of Igor Gouzenko: Report of the Canadian Royal Commission. Walnut Creek: Aegean Park, 1984.

De Jong, Nicolas J., and Marvin E. Moore. *Shipbuilding on Prince Edward Island: Enterprise in a Maritime Setting, 1787–1920.* Hull: Canadian Museum of Civilization, 1994.

Dick, Lyle. '"A Growing Necessity for Canada": W.L. Morton's Centenary Series and the Forms of National History, 1955–80.' *Canadian Historical Review* 82, no. 2 (June 2001): 223–52.

Doucet, L.J. *The Road to the Isle: The Canso Causeway – Deepest in the World.* Fredericton: UNB Press, 1955.

Dupre, Ruth. '"If It's Yellow, It Must Be Butter": Margarine Regulation in North America since 1886.' *Journal of Economic History* 59, no. 2 (June 1999): 353–71.

Evans, Grant. 'What's the Matter with the Maritimes?' *Maritime Advocate and Busy East* 39, no. 6 (January 1949): 8.

Finkel, Alvin. 'Paradise Postponed: A Re-examination of the Green Book Proposals of 1945.' *Journal of the Canadian Historical Association*, new series, vol. 4 (1993): 120–42.

FitzGerald, John E. 'The Confederation of Newfoundland with Canada, 1946–1949.' MA thesis, Memorial University, 1992.

– ed. *Newfoundland at the Crossroads: Documents on Confederation with Canada.* St John's: Terra Nova, 2002.

Forbes, E.R. 'Consolidating Disparity: The Maritimes and the Industrialization of Canada during the Second World War.' *Acadiensis* 15, no. 2 (Spring 1986): 3–27.

– 'Cutting the Pie into Smaller Pieces: Matching Grants and Relief in the Maritime Provinces in the 1930s.' *Acadiensis* 26, no. 1 (Autumn 1987): 34–55.

– *The Maritime Rights Movement, 1919–1927: A Study in Canadian Regionalism.* Montreal and Kingston: McGill–Queen's University Press, 1979.

– 'Misguided Symmetry: The Destruction of Regional Transportation Policy for the Maritimes,' in *Canada and the Burden of Unity,* ed. David Bercuson. Toronto: Macmillan of Canada, 1977. 60–86.

– 'The Origins of the Maritime Rights Movement.' *Acadiensis* 5, no. 5 (Autumn 1975): 54–66.

Forbes, E.R., and D.A. Muise, eds. *The Atlantic Provinces in Confederation.* Toronto and Fredericton: University of Toronto Press and Acadiensis Press, 1993.

Frank, David. 'The 1920s: Class and Region, Resistance and Accommodation,' in *The Atlantic Provinces in Confederation,* ed. E.R. Forbes and D.A. Muise. Toronto and Fredericton: University of Toronto Press and Acadiensis Press, 1993. 233–71.

Fransen, David. 'Unscrewing the Unscrutable: The Rowell-Sirois Commission, the Ottawa Bureaucracy, and Public Finance Reform, 1935–1941.' PhD diss., University of Toronto, 1984.

Fraser, A.M. 'Fisheries Negotiations with the United States, 1783–1910,' in *Newfoundland: Economic, Diplomatic, and Strategic Studies*, ed. R.A. MacKay. Toronto: Oxford University Press, 1946. 333–410.

– 'Relations with Canada,' in *Newfoundland: Economic, Diplomatic, and Strategic Studies*, ed. R.A. MacKay. Toronto: Oxford University Press, 1946. 411–74.

Friesen, Gerald. *Citizens and Nation: An Essay on History, Communication, and Canada*. Toronto: University of Toronto Press, 2000.

– 'The Evolving Meanings of Region in Canada.' *Canadian Historical Review* 82, no. 3 (September 2001): 530–45.

Gallagher, James. 'First U.S. Ore Carrier Trip into the Seaway.' *Inland Seas* 41, no. 2 (1985): 89–99.

Gotlieb, Marc J. 'George Drew and the Dominion-Provincial Conference on Reconstruction of 1945–1946.' *Canadian Historical Review* 66, no. 1 (1985): 27–47.

Gushue, Raymond. 'Newfoundland and Its Fisheries.' *Public Affairs: A Maritime Quarterly for Discussion of Public Affairs* (March 1940): 109–111.

Guthrie, J.A. 'Post-War Prospects for Canadian Newsprint.' *Public Affairs: A Maritime Quarterly for Discussion of Public Affairs* (Autumn 1942): 13–16.

Handcock, W. Gordon. *Soe longe as there comes noe woman: Origins of English Settlement in Newfoundland*. St John's: Breakwater, 1989.

Harvie, Christopher. *The Rise of Regional Europe*. New York: Routledge, 1994.

Hatvany, Matthew G. '"Wedded to the Marshes": Salt Marshes and Socio-Economic Differentiation in Early Prince Edward Island.' *Acadiensis* 30, no. 2 (Spring 2001): 40–55.

Hayman, Katheryn Ellen. 'The Origins and Function of the Canadian High Commission in Newfoundland, 1941–1949.' MA thesis, University of Western Ontario, 1979.

Head, C. Grant. *Eighteenth-Century Newfoundland: A Geographer's Perspective*. Toronto: McClelland and Stewart, 1976.

Heick, W.H. 'Margarine in Newfoundland History.' *Newfoundland and Labrador Studies* 2, no. 2 (1986): 29–37

Henderson, T. Stephen. *Angus L. Macdonald: A Provincial Liberal*. Toronto: University of Toronto Press, 2007.

– 'A Defensive Alliance: The Maritime Provinces and the Turgeon Commission on Transportation, 1948–1951.' *Acadiensis* 35, no. 2 (Spring 2006): 46–63.

– '"A New Federal Vision": Nova Scotia and the Rowell-Sirois Report,

1938–1948,' in *Framing Canadian Federalism*, ed. Dimitry Anastakis and Penny Bryden. Toronto: University of Toronto Press, 2009. 51–74.

High, Steven. 'Working for Uncle Sam: The "Comings" and "Goings" of Newfoundland Base Construction Labour, 1940–1945.' *Acadiensis* 32, no. 2 (Spring 2003): 84–107.

Hiller, James K. 'Confederation Defeated: The Newfoundland Election of 1869,' in *Newfoundland in the Nineteenth and Twentieth Centuries: Essays in Interpretation*, ed. James K. Hiller and Peter Neary. Toronto: University of Toronto Press, 1980. 67–94.

– 'Is Atlantic Canadian History Possible?' *Acadiensis* 30, no. 1 (Autumn 2000): 16–22.

– 'Newfoundland Confronts Canada, 1867–1949,' in *The Atlantic Provinces in Confederation*, ed. E.R. Forbes and D.A. Muise. Toronto and Fredericton: University of Toronto Press and Acadiensis Press, 1993. 349–81.

– 'The Origins of the Pulp and Paper Industry in Newfoundland.' *Acadiensis* 11, no. 2 (Spring 1982): 42–68.

– 'The Politics of Newsprint: The Newfoundland Pulp and Paper Industry, 1915–1939.' *Acadiensis* 19, no. 2 (Spring 1990): 3–39.

– 'Robert Bond and the Pink, White, and Green: Newfoundland Nationalism in Perspective.' *Acadiensis* 36, no. 2 (Spring 2007): 113–33.

Hogg, Elaine Ingalls. *When Canada Joined Cape Breton: Celebrating Fifty Years of the Canso Causeway*. Halifax: Nimbus, 2005.

Horwood, Harold. *Corner Brook: A Social History of a Paper Town*. St John's: Breakwater, 1986.

Howell, Colin. 'Economism, Ideology, and the Teaching of Maritime History,' in *Teaching Maritime Studies*, ed. P.A. Buckner. Fredericton: Acadiensis, 1986. 17–23.

Howland, R.D., and D.M. Fraser. 'The Maritimes and Foreign Trade.' *Public Affairs: A Maritime Quarterly for the Discussion of Public Affairs* (Spring 1950): 23–31.

Janssen, William. 'Agriculture in Transition,' in *The Garden Transformed: Prince Edward Island, 1945–1980*, ed. Verner Smitheram, David Milne, and Satadal Dasgupta. Charlottetown: Ragweed, 1982. 115–30.

Keirstead, B.S. *The Economic Effects of the War on the Maritime Provinces of Canada*. Halifax: Dalhousie Institute of Public Affairs, 1943.

Kennedy, Lawrence W. *Planning the City upon the Hill: Boston since 1630*. Amherst: University of Massachusetts Press, 1992.

Kenny, James. 'Politics and Persistence: New Brunswick's Hugh John Flemming and the Atlantic Revolution, 1952–1960.' MA thesis, University of New Brunswick, 1988.

MacDonald, Edward. *If You're Stronghearted: Prince Edward Island in the Twentieth Century.* Charlottetown: Prince Edward Island Museum and Heritage Foundation, 2000.

Mackenzie, David. *Inside the Atlantic Triangle: Canada and the Entrance of Newfoundland into Confederation, 1939–1949.* Toronto: University of Toronto Press, 1986.

MacKinnon, Neil. *This Unfriendly Soil: The Loyalist Experience in Nova Scotia, 1783–1791.* Montreal and Kingston: McGill–Queen's University Press, 1986.

MacKinnon, Wayne E. 'The Farmer Premier: J. Walter Jones and His Vision of Prince Edward Island.' *The Island Magazine* 35 (Spring–Summer 1994): 3–9.

– *The Life of the Party: A History of the Liberal Party in Prince Edward Island.* Summerside: Williams and Crue, 1973.

MacLeod, Malcolm. 'Another Look at *The Atlantic Provinces in Confederation.*' *Acadiensis* 23, no. 2 (Spring 1994): 191–7.

– 'Confederation, 1937.' *Newfoundland Studies* 1, no. 2 (Fall 1985): 201–10.

– 'Disaster Documents 1914: The Official Canadian Response to Newfoundland's Sealing Tragedies,' in *Connections: Newfoundland's Pre-Confederation Links with Canada and the World,* ed. Malcolm Macleod. St John's: Creative Publishers, 2003. 215–20.

– 'Edging into North America: Lives and Foreign Linkages in Pre-Confederation Newfoundland.' *Acadiensis* 21, no. 2 (Spring 1992): 146–61.

– *Kindred Countries: Canada and Newfoundland before Confederation.* Ottawa: Canadian Historical Association, 1994.

– 'Labrador for Sale – 27% Off.' *Newfoundland Quarterly* (Fall 1979): 13–14.

– 'Searching the Wreckage for Signs of Region: Newfoundland and the Halifax Explosion,' in *Connections: Newfoundland's Pre-Confederation Links with Canada and the World,* ed. Malcolm Macleod. St John's: Creative Publishers, 2003. 221–37.

– 'Students Abroad: Pre-Confederation Educational Links between Newfoundland and the Mainland of Canada.' *Historical Papers / Communications historiques* (1985): 172–92.

– 'Subsidized Steamers to a Foreign Country: Canada and Newfoundland, 1892–1949.' *Acadiensis* 14, no. 2 (Spring 1985): 66–92.

– 'You Must Go Home Again: A Newfoundland–Canada Quarrel over Deportations, 1932–1933.' *Newfoundland Quarterly* (Spring 1983): 23–5.

MacNutt, W.S. *The Atlantic Provinces: The Emergence of Colonial Society, 1712–1857.* Toronto: McClelland and Stewart, 1965.

Matthews, Keith. *Lectures on the History of Newfoundland.* St John's: Breakwater, 1988.

Mayo, H.B. 'Newfoundland and Canada: The Case for Union Examined.' DPhil thesis, Oxford University, 1948.

– 'Newfoundland's Entry into the Dominion.' *Canadian Journal of Economics and Political Science* 15, no. 4 (November 1949): 505–22.

McKay, C.R. 'Investors, Government, and the CMTR: A Study of Entrepreneurial Failure.' *Acadiensis* 9, no. 1 (Autumn 1979): 71–94.

McKay, Ian. 'A Note on Region in Writing the History of Atlantic Canada.' *Acadiensis* 29, no. 2 (Spring 2000): 89–101.

McLean, A.N. *Letters from a Business Man to a Student of Economics.* Undated.

– 'The New Brunswick Sardine Fisheries.' *Public Affairs: A Maritime Quarterly for Discussion of Public Affairs* (March 1940): 112–14.

Milne, David. 'The Federal Model: Newfoundland and Prince Edward Island,' in *Lessons from the Political Economy of Small Islands: The Resourcefulness of Jurisdiction*, ed. Godfrey Baldacchino and David Milne. New York: St Martin's, 2000. 75–90.

– 'Politics in a Beleaguered Garden,' in *The Garden Transformed: Prince Edward Island, 1945–1980*, ed. Verner Smitheram, David Milne, and Satadal Dasgupta. Charlottetown: Ragweed, 1982. 39–72.

Neary, Peter. 'Canada and the Newfoundland Labour Market, 1939–1949.' *Canadian Historical Review* 62, no. 4 (December 1981): 470–95.

– 'Canadian Immigration Policy and the Newfoundlanders, 1912–1939.' *Acadiensis* 11, no. 2 (Spring 1982): 69–83.

– *Newfoundland in the North Atlantic World, 1929–1949.* Montreal and Kingston: McGill–Queen's University Press, 1988.

– 'Newfoundland's Union with Canada, 1949: Conspiracy or Choice?' *Acadiensis* 12, no. 2 (Spring 1983): 110–19.

– '"Traditional" and "Modern" Elements in the Social and Economic History of Bell Island and Conception Bay.' Canadian Historical Association, *Historical Papers, 1973.* 105–36.

– *White Tie and Decorations: Sir John and Lady Hope Simpson in Newfoundland, 1934–1936.* Toronto: University of Toronto Press, 1997.

Nisbet, E. Jean. 'Free Enterprise at Its Best: The State, National Sea, and the Defeat of the Nova Scotia Fishermen, 1946–1947,' in *Workers and the State in Twentieth Century Nova Scotia*, ed. Michael Earle. Fredericton: Acadiensis Press, 1989. 170–90.

Noel, S.J.R. *Politics in Newfoundland.* Toronto: University of Toronto Press, 1971.

Nurse, Andrew. 'Rethinking the Canadian Archipelago: Regionalism and Diversity in Canada.' Report prepared for Department of Canadian Heritage, 2002. http://www.mta.ca/faculty/arts/canadian_studies/anurse/regionalism.pdf.

O'Flaherty, Patrick. *Lost Community: The Rise and Fall of Newfoundland, 1843–1933.* St John's: Long Beach, 2005.

Patterson, Stephen E. '1744–1763: Colonial Wars and Aboriginal Peoples,' in

The Atlantic Region to Confederation: A History, ed. Philip A. Buckner and John G. Reid. Toronto and Fredericton: University of Toronto Press and Acadiensis Press, 1994. 125–55.

Petrie, J.R. *The Regional Economy of New Brunswick.* Fredericton: New Brunswick Committee on Reconstruction, 1944.

Pickersgill, J.W., and D.F. Forster, eds. *The Mackenzie King Record: Volume 4, 1947–1948.* Toronto: University of Toronto Press, 1970.

Pope, Peter. 'Comparisons: Atlantic Canada,' in *A Companion to Colonial America,* ed. Daniel Vickers. Oxford: Blackwell, 2005. 489–507.

– *Fish into Wine: The Newfoundland Plantation in the Seventeenth Century.* Chapel Hill: University of North Carolina Press, 2004.

Prowse, D.W. *A History of Newfoundland.* London: Eyre and Spottiswoode, 1896.

Rawlyk, George. *Nova Scotia's Massachusetts: A Study of Massachusetts–Nova Scotia Relations, 1630 to 1784.* Montreal and Kingston: McGill–Queen's University Press, 1973.

– *Ravished by the Spirit: Religious Revivals, Baptists, and Henry Alline.* Montreal and Kingston: McGill–Queen's University Press, 1984.

Reid, John G. '*Pax Britannica* or *Pax Indigena*: Planter Nova Scotia (1760–1782) and Competing Strategies of Pacification.' *Canadian Historical Review* 85, no. 4 (December 2004): 669–92.

Resolutions: The National Liberal Convention, 1948. Ottawa: Le Droit, 1948.

Ryan, Shannon. *Fish Out of Water: The Newfoundland Saltfish Trade, 1814–1914.* St John's: Breakwater, 1986.

Samaroo, Brinsley. 'The Politics of Disharmony: The Debate on the Political Union of the British West Indies and Canada, 1884–1921,' in *Canada and the Commonwealth Caribbean,* ed. Brian Douglas Tennyson. Boston: University Press of America, 1988. 191–214.

Savoie, Donald. *Visiting Grandchildren: Economic Development in the Maritimes.* Toronto: University of Toronto Press, 2006.

Saywell, John. *'Just call me Mitch': The Life of Mitchell F. Hepburn.* Toronto: University of Toronto Press, 1991.

Schwartz, Mildred A. *Politics and Territory: The Sociology of Regional Persistence in Canada.* Montreal and Kingston: McGill–Queen's University Press, 1974.

Slumkoski, Corey. 'Let Them Eat Beef: The Prince Edward Island–Newfoundland Beef Cattle Trade, 1941–1946.' *Acadiensis* 35, no. 2 (Spring 2006): 106–26.

– 'Prelude to Equalization: New Brunswick and the Tax Rental Agreements, 1941–1957.' MA thesis, University of New Brunswick, 1999.

Smallwood, Joey. *I Chose Canada: The Memoirs of the Honourable Joseph R. 'Joey' Smallwood,* vol. 2: *The Premiership.* Scarborough: Signet, 1973.

Stanley, Della. *Louis Robichaud: A Decade of Power*. Halifax: Nimbus, 1984.

Stephens, David. 'The Chignecto Ship Railway.' *Nova Scotia Historical Quarterly* 8 (June 1978): 135–45.

Stewart, Alice R. 'Canadian–West Indian Union, 1884–1885,' in *Canada and the Commonwealth Caribbean*, ed. Brian Douglas Tennyson. Boston: University Press of America, 1988. 161–90.

Stewart, Ian. *Roasting Chesnuts: The Mythology of Maritime Political Culture*. Vancouver: UBC Press, 1994.

Struthers, James. *No Fault of Their Own. Unemployment and the Canadian Welfare State, 1914–1941*. Toronto: University of Toronto Press, 1983.

Taylor, Ken. 'Reconstruction and Recovery in the Hinterlands: Resources, Industry, and Infrastructure in New Brunswick and Saskatchewan, 1945–1970.' PhD diss., University of New Brunswick, 2005.

Thornton, Patricia. 'The Problem of Out-Migration from Atlantic Canada, 1871–1921: A New Look.' *Acadiensis* 11, no. 1 (Autumn 1985): 3–31.

Widdis, Randy William. 'Globalization, Glocalization, and the Canadian West as Region: A Geographers View.' *Acadiensis* 35, no. 2 (Spring 2006): 129–37.

Webb, Jeff A. 'Newfoundland's National Convention, 1946–48.' MA thesis, Memorial University, 1987.

Webb, Jeff. *The Voice of Newfoundland: A Social History of the Broadcasting Corporation of Newfoundland, 1939–1949*. Toronto: University of Toronto Press, 2008.

White, Patrick C.T., ed. *Lord Selkirk's Diary, 1803–1804: A Journal of His Travels in British North America and the Northeastern United States*. Toronto: Champlain Society, 1958.

Wright, Miriam. *A Fishery for Modern Times: The State and the Industrialization of the Newfoundland Fishery, 1934–1968*. Toronto: Oxford University Press, 2001.

– 'Fishing in Modern Times: Stewart Bates and the Modernization of the Canadian Atlantic Fishery,' in *How Deep is the Ocean? Historical Essays on Canada's Atlantic Fishery*, ed. James E. Candow and Carol Corbin. Sydney: University College of Cape Breton Press, 1997. 195–206.

Wynn, Graeme. 'A Province Too Much Dependent on New England.' *Canadian Geographer* 31, no. 2 (1987): 98–113.

– *Timber Colony: A Historical Geography of Early Nineteenth-Century New Brunswick*. Toronto: University of Toronto Press, 1981.

Young, R.A. '"… and the people will sink into despair": Reconstruction in New Brunswick, 1942–1952.' *Canadian Historical Review* 69, no. 2 (June 1988): 127–66.

Index